# Voices of
# CAMPTOWN

Untold Stories From a
Freedom Colony Cemetery

Published by Stoney Creek Publishing Group
StoneyCreekPublishing.com

Copyright © 2025 by Charles Swenson

ISBN: 978-1-965766-11-8
ISBN (ebook): 978-1-965766-13-2

Library of Congress Control Number: 2025905952

No part of this book may be reproduced in any form or by any electronic or mechanical means, including information storage and retrieval systems, without written permission from the author, except for the use of brief quotations in a book review.

Cover and interior design by Kimberly James
Printed in the United States

# Voices of
# CAMPTOWN

## Untold Stories From a Freedom Colony Cemetery

By Charles Swenson
with Tina B. Henderson, Ph.D.
and Robert R. Bubb, Ph.D.

*This book is dedicated to Eddie E. Harrison and his unending devotion to uncovering the stories behind Washington County's hidden tales. The Texas Ten Historical Explorers, Inc. is a non-profit organization whose mission is to recognize the forgotten history of African Americans during the development of early Washington County. The Texas Ten Historical Explorers were established by the late historian and former Washington County Genealogical Society member Harrison, whose vision was for history to be more inclusive of these previously neglected voices from the past.*

*Photo Credit: Cecil Webster*

# CONTENTS

| | |
|---|---|
| Introduction | 9 |
| 1. The History of Camptown Cemetery | 21 |
| 2. Wiley Hubert: Building the Camptown Community | 39 |
| 3. Sam Love: A "Self-Made" Man | 63 |
| 4. Robert S. Sloan: "Texas Is Full of Opportunity" | 73 |
| 5. The Long, Strange Journey of Hiram Williams | 105 |
| 6. From Jamaica to Camptown: George P. Isaacs | 123 |
| 7. Australia Guy Comes Home to Stay | 135 |
| 8. A Hanging in Camptown | 145 |
| 9. "You Are Good for Twenty Years Yet!" Asa Rippetoe | 163 |
| 10. Alexander Thomas: The Two Ends of Slavery for a Black Lawyer | 168 |
| 11. "If It Were All Known and Could Be Written:" Mary Marks and "Unique Story" | 174 |
| 12. The Long Reach of the Civil War | 186 |
| 13. Black Lawmen in Post-Emancipation Brenham and Washington County | 205 |

14. "The Plows Are Still in the Fields…" An Introduction to
Brenham's Emancipation Celebrations: 1878-1923      240

15. Brenham's Forgotten Fire Department: The Protective Hook
and Ladder Company No. 2
                                                     255
16. "The Colored People's Park"                      266

17. Ed Henderson's Park                              272


Acknowledgements                                     281
Endnotes                                             287
Notes                                                288
About the Author                                     335

# INTRODUCTION

The sign as drivers enter Washington County calls it "The Birthplace of Texas," the place where Texas declared its freedom from Mexico in 1836. However, thirty years after that declaration, half the Texas population was not independent—or even free. They were enslaved.

In 1860, the United States Census found that the population of Washington County, located in the cotton-growing belt of Texas, considered 7,941 Black people to be the property of someone else. The population designated as white, which included many of those claiming the enslaved population as property, was nearly 10 percent less, only 7,280. Yet that same census, as inclusive as it sought to be, could only give the names of three members of the Black population, listed as in that census as "Free Colored." They were Jack and Sallie, aged sixty-five and sixty respectively, as well as Henry, who was living in the same household in Brenham. Jack and Sallie were farm laborers born in Virginia with a "personal estate" valued at $300, while Henry was a waggoneer born in Tennessee with an estate of $600. Oddly enough, a column checked for all three of them notes that they were unable to read or write—a designation not noted for most other county residents. The enslaved population, though enumerated in the "Slave Schedule," did not even have full names listed for them, only their gender and age.

By the time of the 1870 Federal Census, the Black and mulatto populations had increased to 12,241, still outnumbering the whites population of 10,863. But now this formerly enslaved majority was identified not only by their names, but also by marital status, familial relationships, occupation, the value of the property they held, educational status, and a wealth of other information to give shape, rough as it might be, to their existence as individuals. Little more than this smattering of information about their lives has been available even after this official recognition of their humanity. Histories of Brenham and Washington County barely mention their vast numbers during the nineteenth century except for references to the Union troops that were posted there as the rebellious Confederacy was winding down and the efforts during Reconstruction to ensure their citizenship. But that same camp of soldiers also gave rise to another far less recognized but no less important part of Brenham's history, that of Camptown.

This gathering of emancipated Blacks into an independent, self-cohesive community has come to be known as a "freedom colony." A number of such settlement groups arose throughout Washington County, mostly in rural settings and primarily based on agriculture, a way of life with which most of the members were already familiar. They were often located nearby the very plantations where they had previously labored or were working on a contract basis for wages or a portion of the crops.

The elimination of slavery in a state whose economy had depended on it so much that Texas was willing to separate from the Union, join the Confederacy, and fight a war, created a tenuous situation for the formerly enslaved. The federal government established the Bureau of Refugees, Freedmen and Abandoned Lands for the newly displaced, with the primary goals of not only protecting the freedmen, but also of enforcing labor contracts and establishing schools. In Texas, the bureau operated from late 1865 to early 1870, with a suboffice for Washington County operating in Brenham under the protection of an encampment of Union soldiers posted a mile east of town. Although the same General Order No. 3 that General Gordon Granger had issued in Galveston to announce Emancipation also stipulated that freedmen "will not be allowed at military posts and they will not be supported in idleness either there or elsewhere," a freedom colony sprang up in the immediate area and quickly became known as Camptown. Over the coming years, other Black settlements were established in Brenham as well, including Watrousville, Hog Branch, Post Oak, Baptist Hill, Tappan Lake, Silver Hill, and Wilkins Addition. But Camptown was one of the first.

Key elements in defining freedom colonies include the presence of a church, a school, a cemetery, and associated business enterprises, all of which quickly followed Camptown's establishment. Due to its non-rural location to the nearby town center, Camptown's economy avoided being predominantly agricultural, with several cotton mills, a major railroad, and numerous local business enterprises hiring its inhabitants. This allowed for a flow of cash through the community that enabled real estate transactions, leading to a significant amount of Black ownership and an accumulation of capital for the growing settlement.

One of these early property deals in February 1869 was the purchase for $400 "in coin" of a tract of land by a group of six prominent Black citizens acting as trustees. This acquisition was specified in the deed as "expressly understood" as being "for the said educational interests of the colored people of Brenham except that the same may be used by the said colored people as a house of worship with the consent of the trustees," and "when used by a house of worship no preference will be given to any particular denomination." This was the first of a number of other churches that opened in Camptown, and the old building that was being used as a school, a church, and a public hall was repaired and furnished under a contract from the Freedmen's Bureau. It continued to be used until it was later replaced by East End School.

Although a cemetery already had existed in the area for the enslaved populace to use before the Union camp's existence—as noted on a map of the Post of Brenham—it was formally purchased by a group of trustees of the Mount Rose Cemetery Association. Many of them had previously been involved in the transaction involving the school and church building. The availability of cash played a role; the property was bought from its previous owner for "100 gold dollars" at a time when paper money was considered a less reliable form of currency.

Another distinction that helped set apart Camptown and other Washington County freedom colonies from so many others was the degree of real political power. Possessing a lion's share of the populace and allied with the large number of German immigrants, the Republican Party held sway in local elections until the People's Party began to split them over the issue of corruption. That coincided with violence occurring at polling places in the elections of 1884 and 1886. Donald Nieman explored this in his 1989 article, "Black Political Power and Criminal Justice: Washington County, Texas, 1868-1884:"

During fifteen years of Republican control, Washington County Blacks possessed significant political power. Freedmen did not win a share of county offices equal to their percentage of the population, and no Black man received the party nomination for the powerful positions of sheriff, district judge, or county judge. Nevertheless, they were not excluded from the spoils," including "most of the Republican nominations for state legislature during the 1870s and 1880s."

Although Black political power slipped in the following years, the severity of animosity between the races afterward didn't slip back to the levels found even in surrounding counties. This was pointed out by Annie Mae Hunt in her memoir as she reminisced on her family's move in the early 1920s to Grimes County, just across the Navasota River: "...Washington County was a free country, and Grimes County was slavery—well, that's what they say. Well, it was like slavery times, it was."

I had no idea about this in 2012 when I first became involved in the work that resulted in this book. I'd been working with Bob Wishoff, a close friend pursuing his master's degree in archaeology for over a decade on various archeological projects, including his inventory of artifacts at the Panhandle-Plains Historical Museum in Canyon, Texas. The artifacts hadn't been looked at by researchers in almost half a century, nor had any mapping taken place at the pits where they had been mined at the Alibates Flint Quarries National Monument on the frigid windblown banks of the Canadian River. As he was completing his master's degree, Bob had been invited to use his newly minted skills by Doug Price, executive director of the Brenham Museum, to investigate local historic sites, and I was doing what I could to assist him. After several sites had been investigated, it became clear we needed to look more deeply at the location of the former federal Post of Brenham, which had housed the occupying Union troops in the tumultuous years following the Civil War but had also been sorely overlooked by researchers for decades.

One of the most famous events in Brenham's history was known as the Burning of Brenham, when much of the town's center caught fire after an altercation between some of the Union soldiers based there. This conflagration became an ongoing source of antagonism. Much of the population saw an occupying military force after the defeat of the Confederacy, but the exact location of the soldiers' base was unclear. Much of the negative feelings about them clearly remained, as well as the ill-informed but persistent impression that Black troops were involved despite none being stationed there. During a conversation at the museum about the location of the Union post at Brenham, Bob and I first met Eddie Harrison, a man who would prove to be instrumental to us in writing this book.

Eddie was a man of many impressive accomplishments, but his humility kept him from wearing his achievements on his sleeve. He was eighty-two years old when I met him, a graduate of Prairie View A&M University with a bachelor's degree in agricultural education. He entered the Army as a second lieutenant and eventually rose to the rank of a full colonel. After retiring he returned to Brenham, attending Texas A&M University for a Master of Agriculture degree in rural sociology, using both as the first Black county agent in Washington County. He later served as a small farm specialist for Prairie View A&M and Texas A&M, as well as lending his expertise with the U.S. Department of Agriculture, the U.S. Agency for International Development, and the U.S. State Department in Somalia, Kenya, and the Republic of the Upper Volta. Locally, his work with the Boy Scouts of America, the Brenham Chamber of Commerce, the 4-H, the American Legion, a sixteen-year stint as a municipal court judge, and numerous other community contributions earned him the Washington County Man of the Year Award in 1996.

One afternoon Bob, Doug, and I were talking about the old Union camp and its possible location. Eddie, a long-standing member of the museum's board of trustees, mentioned that he knew just where it had been, on the other side of Camptown Cemetery. The very name "Camptown" had been affixed to the freedom colony after the war because so many of those who had been set free from bondage sought security around the camp of soldiers who had fought against the former government that tried to keep them as chattel. This bit of knowledge was sure to be helpful, even though at that time we hadn't heard about the cemetery nor had most people living in Brenham. Eddie said it was several blocks east of the original location of Blue Bell Ice Cream and adjacent to Mount Rose Missionary Baptist Church, where he served as a deacon and trustee. Offering to lead us out there, we followed behind him out to the eastern dead end of Mangrum Street where I first saw the site, although it wasn't immediately clear that it was even a cemetery.

The location was next to a large open lot that had once served as a playing field for Pickard High School, a much-respected Rosenwald school building that served the Black community before closing due to desegregation. Just east of this was a vast expanse of trees and dense undergrowth, giving no clear indication what was within it. Many locals were not even aware it was a graveyard, much less one of such historic significance.

To say it was overgrown is an understatement. Only the first set of graves near the edge of the street, the Hubert plot, was even visible. Being assured that there were more ahead, we made our way into this dense thicket of weeds, bushes, shrubs, vines, and massive pecan trees, some upright, some lying on the ground. The canopy of trees overhead created a dark and eerie quietness that increased with every step.

Pushing and at times hacking our way through the brush, we suddenly came across a headstone, and then another, as well as an occasional waist-high wrought-iron fence surrounding a plot. The soil felt soft as we walked over depressions that were unmarked graves, giving us the unsettled sensation that the ground might give way beneath our feet. Walking in one direction, we'd suddenly be redirected by an impenetrable mass of vegetation. Unable to follow a straight line, we had an eerie feeling of not knowing where we were, how we got there, and how to find our way back. Overriding all this, though, was a fascination at not only the number of graves there, but also the dates. Many of them indicated that these were the final resting places of individuals who had been born into slavery and lived past Emancipation into an uncertain future. Perhaps they found their final freedom here.

This was one of the oldest cemeteries for African Americans in Washington County. Not only were their bodies buried here, but also their vital contributions to Brenham's history. Cemeteries are hardy places, however. They are designed as a place of memory, a place to remember those who lay beneath the markers commemorating a past life. Despite the innumerable divots in the soil where unknown graves lay long forgotten, stone markers carried names to us as we wandered among the dense vegetation, heralding the time these individuals entered their world and lamenting the time they left it.

Eddie knew this ground well. He had tried to clear the cemetery before, prompted in part by complaints from the city about the site's condition. His enthusiasm helped Bob realize that this was the project that he had been looking for. Help was sought from the museum, Mount Rose church, and local volunteers. The first step was the tedious clearing of overgrowth to reveal the cemetery's condition. Newspapers ran articles that helped to bring in additional volunteers, including its longest-serving caretaker, Ray Mildren, who later nearly died after suffering a heart attack on the site and still returned to the work once he'd recovered. Cutting and hauling away so much brush would take more time and hard work than anticipated. Fortunately, Bob had a gift for marshalling additional help, and he contacted Rolling Thunder TX2, a motorcycle club of dozens of retired veterans with a passion for maintaining the graves of veterans, a number of whom had been buried in Camptown Cemetery. Soon the Combat Veteran Motorcycle Association and the Houston branch of the Buffalo Soldiers Motorcycle Club joined the effort.

With the names of cemetery occupants at last known, traces of their lives began to emerge. By looking deeper, the stories of Camptown began to unfold in a time spanning from the Freedmen's Bureau through the period known as Jim Crow. Buried no longer, the stories finally could be told.

A starting point for compiling such a history begins with a census of the names of those known to be buried in the cemetery. Such a list can be gathered not only from marked grave sites, but also from death certificates and obituaries that list where a person is buried. Those names can be associated with available census data with relative ease thanks to the growing number of online genealogical research sites. A basic census of the known names in the cemeteries had been put together earlier with the help of the Washington County Genealogical Society. As the work in the cemetery revealed more markers, I compiled a more complete census of persons buried there. From the names and dates of births and deaths, more information could be gleaned from decennial federal census data.

Another important source of information comes from the increased availability of online newspaper archives. In 2011, the University of North Texas began adding digital newspapers to its Portal to Texas History website, including a sizeable collection of Brenham newspapers from the mid-1870s forward. Fortunately, many of the Brenham newspapers from this period are available and can be readily searched for names or keywords, though there are certain caveats. Using the ability to search these and other sources there, I was slowly able to piece together a greater understanding of the Camptown community from this period, as well as specific information about many of the individuals whose graves we were clearing.

But content of a broader nature also appeared in Brenham's and Washington County's newspapers. Although these stories tended to focus on crimes, court cases, and politics, enough information emerges to gain a broader picture of life and lives in this freedom colony, including stories the importance of Black law enforcement officials. One concern in depending too much on criminal offenses, minor or otherwise, is that the most frequently reported stories about them tend to offer a stilted view of the Black communities, Another is that as Camptown became a part of the greater Brenham community, deep-seated prejudices often appeared in the reporting. This can also have useful aspects, since almost every time a Black man was mentioned, he was identified as "colored," but all too often seriously derogatory terms such as "nigger," "negro," "darkey" or even more disturbingly terms are used in these newspaper articles. It should be noted that when they are preserved in this context of articles it is simply for historical and scholarly reasons.

With that being said, newspapers also often contained valuable information about subjects such as politics, with frequent reporting on the Republican opposition from a paper that strongly supported the Democratic party. In the Brenham papers the most frequent stories in which prominent Black citizens were mentioned involved Republican party activities. Civic government stories offer considerable insights, such as the makeup of grand and petit juries, as well as detailed lists of city and county payments for work done, often by Black citizens. Real estate transactions by individuals were reported regularly and often involved considerable sums of money and gave some indication of where property was owned. Education-related information abounds, at least in the Brenham papers, including the number and location of enrolled Black and white students, articles about graduation ceremonies, and names of students and teachers and the leadership of ongoing county-wide "Colored Teachers Institutes." Church events also found frequent mention, including the church most associated with Camptown Cemetery, Mount Rose Baptist Church.

Over time a deeper understanding came from information gleaned from other documents found in the Portal to Texas History, as well as court cases and property records in the Washington County Court House. Although less readily accessible, county courthouse records can also be useful, not only for further insight into criminal cases and civil lawsuits, but also for property transactions. These often contain detailed information that cannot be found elsewhere. Information in courtroom documents can often clarify and expand a story that is only hinted at in newspaper accounts. But even these must be approached with a wary eye.

In the process of researching one story from Camptown Cemetery, several court documents came to light regarding a married couple. One was an affidavit substantiating a property claim made long after their death, testifying that the couple had lived together as man and wife until the wife's death, contrary to divorce proceedings that showed that a messy legal separation had occurred well before her death. Another legal document also came to light regarding their story in the form of a patent grant applied for by her father and signed by the husband.

The FamilySearch website maintained by the Church of Jesus Christ of Latter-Day Saints was an invaluable resource for free access to census data, marriage certificates, and birth and death records. Especially useful were digitized contents of previously microfilmed Freedmen's Bureau records, while the Fold3 website provided records from a wide variety of military records for veterans buried in the cemetery. Not to be overlooked was assistance from living family members and current 'Brenhamites' who understood the importance of the work we were doing, both BIBs (Born in Brenham) and BOBs (Born outside of Brenham).

Eddie Harrison was certainly one of those individuals—even though a BOB—who understood the importance of the work we were doing. He had been hearing unrecorded stories about Washington County history since his early days as a county extension agent. Once again, he used his uncanny skills at marshalling interest into action with the founding of the Texas Ten History Explorers, a nonprofit organization dedicated to collecting and preserving these untold stories. I began to collect as many of these tales as I could, which ultimately led to this book. The Texas Ten, which refers to the counties previously encompassed by Washington County before it was finally pared down, remains an important force to make sure these untold stories find an outlet. Its effort was hampered by the 2020 COVID-19 pandemic as well as the loss that November of Eddie as a guiding light and invaluable source of the stories he'd collected about local history. Fortunately he had already chosen Dr. Tina B. Henderson to lead the Texas Ten, an excellent choice which continues to prove fruitful. The journey of retrieving history continues here with the story of Camptown Cemetery, and of how what was once lost can be found again. These stories are not just a simple presentation of names and dates, but an opportunity to see how history interacts with people as well as how people interact with history.

Chapter 1

# THE HISTORY OF CAMPTOWN CEMETERY

*Photo courtesy of Amy the Spirit Seeker*

The origins of Camptown Cemetery date to the early nineteenth century. The land was initially part of the Arabella Harrington league, a portion of a Spanish land grant given to the Harrington family as part of Stephen F. Austin's settlement program. Arabella's son, William Dever, had originally come to Washington County investigate the land's possibilities, and with him he brought Rueben, a young Black slave. Together they constructed a house on the banks of the Brazos River, the first example of the role Black people played in building Washington

VOICES OF CAMPTOWN | 21

County. More Harringtons arrived soon afterward, bringing even more slaves to help establish their plantation with additional houses, barns, and livestock.

Descendants of the Harrington family said the location that would later become Camptown Cemetery was used as a burial site for local Black people as long ago as the early 1850s. Oral traditions also cite that the land was in an area used by both freed and runaway slaves. The slave population of Washington County exceeded the White population in 1850 and 1860, with a mortality rate that likely exceeded the white population's as well, death was a fact of life. While it is fair to assume most of the burials took place on local plantations scattered throughout the county, an estimated three hundred slaves lived in Brenham by 1860, and all of them eventually would need a final resting place.[1]

Following the end of Civil War, the Post of Brenham was established by occupying federal troops just east of the cemetery's location. A military map of the post from the period located a "graveyard" where Camptown Cemetery currently is situated, indicating the cemetery's earlier presence. While the post existed between 1865 and 1870, three enlisted men and a captain died, possibly of yellow fever, and were buried in Brenham, possibly at that same graveyard. Their bodies later were exhumed and buried at the Alexandria National Cemetery in Pineville, Louisiana.[2]

After Emancipation, several Black communities began to emerge on Brenham's outskirts. To the west rose Watrousville, named after Benjamin O. Watrous, a leader and politically active Black leader. On the east was Camptown, named after the Union camp that had served as safe haven for many Blacks who suddenly found themselves able to choose where they lived. Churches were pivotal in these new communities. Mount Rose Missionary Baptist Church, established in 1868, used Camptown Cemetery less than three hundred yards away as its primary burial grounds. Although the church had been directly involved with the cemetery for over 150 years, no clear legal document could be located until 2016, when Robert Bubb of Auburn University found an early deed associated with it. J. M. Parker, Wiley Hubert, Daniel Allgood, Anderson Hallwen, Henry Milton, and S. L. Love, deacons of the Mount Rose Cemetery Association, paid "100 gold dollars" for around two acres of land from J. H. Hutchinson and became its first trustees.[3]

Although the cemetery had long been in use in 1878, the captain and secretary of the Brenham Greys, a local independent militia, petitioned the city council for the "privilege to practice 'Target Shooting' in city limits, near R.R. bridge in Camptown." Their request was referred to the street committee, whose members were to visit the site and report back. At the next meeting, the committee told the mayor "that the grounds in Camptown, assigned [to] the Brenham Greys for target practice, belonged to an association of colored people and was used by them as a graveyard. They object to its being used for a target ground. The report was adopted, and the mayor requested to notify the company to cease using the ground."[4]

The cemetery's location became a matter of controversy again in October 1891. That Halloween, Lee Hughes was scheduled to hang for the brutal murder of his wife. No local property owners were willing to have the execution take place on their property, so the gallows was erected on the city's powder magazines. Since this location was directly across the railroad on the cemetery's southern side, Camptown citizens threatened to seek an injunction to prevent it from taking place there. The reason, according to one contemporary press account, was that the "citizens living nearby are mostly negroes and they have a great deal of superstition and say they don't want Lee's 'hant' running about their neighborhood every night."[5] Unfortunately, the hanging went forward as planned, witnessed by an estimated eight thousand spectators, including passengers on a train stopped on the tracks for the morbid purpose of watching the first legal hanging of a Black man in Brenham in over a decade.

It is easy to forget just how quickly an unattended cemetery becomes overgrown. Articles from the local paper complained about people who were setting their livestock loose in graveyards to graze. In 1893, the Zion Baptist Church in Camptown hosted a meeting of "the Colored Cemetery Association," at which a "large number of colored people were present and manifested considerable interest in the meeting."[6] Oral histories by members of the Browne family, which has many family members buried at the cemetery, recount memories of Josie Browne Williams visiting and cleaning the burial site of Caroline Seward (1802-1903), her great- grandmother and a former maid at the Seward Plantation during the 1920s and 1930s. Reggie Browne also remembers spending much time in the cemetery during summers in his youth during the 1950s, when he would visit with his grandmother in Brenham. To keep him busy, he was tasked with cleaning the Browne family plot. Jean Jefferson, who attended Pickard High School in the 1940s, remembered knowing that the cemetery was there and already becoming overgrown with "rattan" reeds in the drainage ditch north of the tracks, which were used for switches for unruly students. Eddie would relate stories about balls kicked by Pickard students playing in the adjacent field, and the only one who would retrieve the ball was the son of the local funeral home proprietor. This hesitation to enter the cemetery was also exacerbated by whispered rumors that voodoo practitioners from Louisiana frequented it.

Although another Black graveyard, Walker Cemetery, was opened farther east of Brenham as Camptown Cemetery filled, Camptown Cemetery continued to be used as the primary location for burials by Mount Rose Baptist Church until mid-1930. It was used actively until the 1950s, when burials began to fall off dramatically, with one of the last known burials there in 1997. This was Alice Hubert, whose ancestor Wiley Hubert had been instrumental in founding the cemetery over a century earlier. Ray Hubert, great-grandson of Wiley Hubert, and his wife, Listene Graves Hubert, have since been interred in the Wiley plot, she in 2020 and he in 2022, and they will be the last who will find their final rest there.

The cemetery soon became overgrown again—and often overlooked. One young man who lived in the neighborhood during these years recalled wandering into it late at night looking for a lost calf and being suddenly surprised when he realized he was in the middle of a cemetery. Cynthia Eben, who attended nearby Alton Elementary School built across the street after Pickard was torn down, recalled being unaware of a cemetery so close by and knowing only that the location was an overgrown "forest."[7]

In response to complaints about the cemetery's condition, in 2001 a meeting of city staff members and the Neighborhood Response Team was called together "to discuss the cleaning and rehabilitating of the old African-American cemetery" to "resolve a long-standing problem of upkeep on this parcel, which the city has only been able to do in a most irregular and cursory manner." The idea was to do an "initial rough clean up, and assist with the fine clean up," after which the church planned to "take charge of the cemetery and...put it back into commission as an active cemetery." The church would then be assigned a "historical survey and possibly a historical designation."

As a result of such meetings, the city, the Neighborhood Response Team, the Washington County Genealogical Society, the Washington County Historical Society, and others agreed to cooperate on the restoration and maintenance of Camptown

Cemetery, with Eddie Harrison heading up a Camptown Cemetery Task Force. Thirteen local Black churches were then contacted to work toward this goal.

A group known as the Camptown Cemetery Project was established after the city had "declared the cemetery abandoned" and asked for "an organization to be responsible for the cemetery." Eight people attended a meeting on July 11, 2002, chaired by Harrison. After a brief discussion of the cemetery's historical significance, they considered options such as a memorial to be placed on the grounds, selling plots in the cemetery, and constructing a brush arbor and a permanent building to exhibit artifacts on the cemetery grounds. They decided to involve organizing citizens to sponsor the cemetery, hold fundraisers, focus on recruitment, conduct research on the land for the Texas Historical Society, and schedule further meetings and a preliminary clean-up of the site.

Reggie Browne, whose relatives had been buried in the cemetery for over a century and who has played a pivotal role in obtaining historical markers for other sites throughout Texas, became involved in the effort to recognize the cemetery. An open meeting of the Camptown Cemetery Association was held at Mount Rose Baptist Church in November 2007 with Anne Shelton of the Texas Historical Commission present. The purpose of the meeting included discussions on rescuing a neglected cemetery, conducting a survey and census of the cemetery, and continuing the work involved in designating it as a historic cemetery.

Many men and women, including Drs. Wilfred and Bobbie Dietrich of the Washington County Historical Commission, worked together to gather their research and present it, along with the required paper requesting designation as a historic Texas cemetery. Thanks to their efforts "the Texas Historical Commission...duly considered the evidence and historic use of said cemetery and... listed said cemetery and has listed said cemetery as a Historic Texas Cemetery, worthy of preservation" in a "Declaration of Dedication for Cemetery Purposes for the Camptown Cemetery" notarized by Terry Colley, deputy executive director, on July 9, 2009.

Work soon began on acquiring an official Texas Historic Marker from the Texas Historical Commission for the cemetery. More than sixteen thousand such markers commemorate various important aspects of Texas history, and they are a ubiquitous sight along highways throughout the state's 254 counties. Their design is easily recognizable and surprisingly durable; however, they are not cheap. A twenty-seven-inch by forty-two-inch marker (the size used at Camptown Cemetery), with post, costs $1,800 (2018 price), with an additional application fee of $100. Fortunately, the application fee, which began in 2006, goes into an account "intended to address historical gaps, promote diversity of topics, and proactively document underrepresented subjects or untold stories." One of those underrepresented topics that qualifies is "African American topics," a category into which the cemetery readily fits. Reggie Browne already had experience in applying for this class of marker, and soon managed to qualify for one in 2013. Its text reads as follows:

> This burial ground is the oldest predominantly African American cemetery in Brenham. It dates from the 1860s and historically has been associated with the nearby Mount Rose Missionary Baptist Church. After the Civil War former Washington County slaves, many of whom also organized Mount Rose and St. John A. M. E. Churches, relocated to the wooded area of what became known as the Camptown addition. The name is derived from the federal troops who camped here from

1865-68 to keep peace between emancipated blacks [sic] and landowners. A surveyed map of the post dated July 1868 shows the cemetery already in use, just north of the Washington County Railroad near Hog Branch. The 17th infantry troops maintained a sense of community with the residents of Camptown, offering their dining hall to host worship on Sundays. Among the estimated 400 burials here may be soldiers who were victims of yellow fever outbreaks in 1866-67. At least 40 former slaves are known to be buried in Camptown cemetery, including several from the Seward Plantation. Caroline Seward (1811-1902) is also buried here, as is Waltman Bynum (1873-81), whose headstone has the oldest marked date. The cemetery is still in use, but activity declined over the years as additional burial options for African Americans (Walker Cemetery, 1895; Home Improvement Community Cemetery, 1900; Willow Grove Cemetery, 1915) became available. In recent years, after the site had become overgrown and neglected, Mount Rose Missionary Baptist Church has taken a more active role in the cemetery's restoration and maintenance. Camptown Cemetery remains hallowed ground and a precious record of the early history of the community.

When we arrived there next to the "Dead End" sign at the eastern end of Mangrum Street, it wasn't immediately clear to Bob and me that this was a cemetery. The entire location was massively overgrown, despite previous attempts to clear the ever-growing wall of dense vegetation that kept it from view. The only indication was a marker Eddie pointed out to us in the Hubert plot a few dozen feet away from the street. Eddie then started telling us more about the cemetery and its historic significance.

Then Bob realized this was the site we were meant to be working on, and they began collaborating on a plan to bring its historic significance to light.

This was somewhat of a godsend for Eddie; although his past efforts were important in making clear the cemetery's historic importance, there was still work to be done. One essential though seemingly herculean step was clearing the cemetery of an overwhelming jungle of dense shrubs, vines, and downed trees, a daunting task. Fortunately, Bob is a wizard when it comes to getting attention to his projects, so he began to work his magic.

A key part of this was getting other people involved. Eddie was already working on his end, and his previous role as a justice of the peace in Brenham, deacon of the Mount Rose Baptist Church, and much beloved leader in numerous local organizations gave him many connections with the local community. Doug Price, the executive director of the Brenham Heritage Museum, also contributed significantly to the effort over the coming year, especially in getting support from local businesses. The city, already aware of the need to clear the brush, assisted in picking up the dead vegetation as it was brought to the street and then hauling it off to the dump.

Thanks to Bob's efforts, local and regional newspapers were soon contacted about the project to clear the cemetery and publicize its story. One of the first articles appeared in the *Houston Chronicle* on February 1, 2013, titled "Brenham hopes to uncover history with cemetery." It featured photographs of an overturned headstone and included pictures and interviews with Eddie and Doug. Eddie offered a brief history of the cemetery's significance as a slave burial site during the prewar period, when over half of Washington County's 15,000 residents were slaves: "During slavery," Harrison said, "the cemetery was just a place to get rid of waste. The slave masters didn't normally allow funeral services.

They had burials, and someone would be appointed to go out there with a wagon and shovel and maybe a few immediate family members, but they didn't want the Black slaves to congregate unsupervised."

Doug offered comments on his impression when he first saw the cemetery during our early visits to it with Eddie:

> "We had heard there was a Camp Town [sic] cemetery," Price said, "but we didn't know it was in such bad condition. It was so overgrown that we barely could get in. There were feral roses, gravestones overturned—the first was dated 1840. We knew we had to do something about this immediately." Plans call for the use of satellite images of the cemetery to discern the location of unmarked graves, some of which could lie beneath nearby streets or houses. "It could tell us where the people are," Price said, "but it won't tell us who they are… If we find there are folks interred in someone's backyard, we suspect they'd like to know these things. Some might want these burials reinterred rather than being on their property. We're not sure how that will pan out…This site is important…as far as Texas and the history of Brenham are concerned," Price said. "There are many stories to tell here, and we can."

The article also pointed out that work was to begin that Saturday on clearing the cemetery as "garden-gloved volunteers descend on the site with clippers and saws. Several such sessions will be required." This story in the *Houston Chronicle* highlighted one of the cemetery's most important volunteers, Ray Mildren, who not only helped with the early clearing, but also continued for over a decade to keep the cemetery maintained and prevent nature from taking it back over again. Ray later described how he came to be involved at the cemetery:

> "I started working on the Camptown Cemetery restoration after seeing an article in the *Houston Chronicle* in late January 2013. It told of Eddie Harrison Jr.'s interest in restoring the cemetery and he had scheduled a meeting at the Brenham Heritage Museum to explain the project and their goals. He had made several attempts since 2001, all with limited success but never a long-term comment or success. The article mentioned the cemetery dates back to the Civil War and Reconstruction period in U.S. History. Since I was interested that time period of U.S. history, I decided to attend the meeting to see what it was all about and since I am retired, I was looking for something to work on.
>
> The meeting was attended by about eight people with Eddie Harrison Jr., Doug Price, Charlie Swenson and Bob Wishoff being the ones talking about their goals and plans for restoring the Cemetery. All of us then went to the cemetery to see first-hand the scope of the project.
>
> What a mess!! The only way you knew it was a cemetery was the fact a couple of head stones could be seen if you stood on the side of Mangrum Road. You could not see 25 feet into the cemetery due the thick brush that had grown up. We came back two days later to start the clearing process and to explore the area we wanted to clear.... about three acres.
>
> As we explored the area, we found more and more markers. We decided to advertise for work day open to

any volunteers who wanted to participate. Eddie and Doug lined up businesses to provide breakfast and the Mount Rose Missionary Baptist Church provided lunch. Doug & Bob lined up donations from Home Depot for tools and equipment used to do the clearing. We had approximately 30 people show up to work and with this help we actually cleared enough area so you could see several plots and grave stones."

Other articles appeared in the *Brenham Banner*, with local churches also spreading the word about the work to be done. The Brenham Heritage Museum contributed portable toilets for the site, a necessity for the large number of volunteers who showed up. The work often required much more than just garden gloves to deal with the thorny vines that had overgrown the site and dangled from the trees, requiring clippers, saws, and chainsaws. Progress was slow, moving yard by yard into the dense overgrowth, and at times seemed as though it would be overwhelming. Working each Saturday with up to fifteen volunteers, eventually a core group of workers began to coalesce. As the bulk of saplings, cleared branches, and cut-up downed trees was dragged to the edge of the cul-de-sac and stacked there, the City of Brenham began to supply trucks to help haul the brush to the city dump. By early March a large area had opened up leading back from the street and along the western fence.

Several other projects were in the works along with the removal of years of neglect from the cemetery. Collecting names for a cemetery census was underway, with new names being added from several sources. A partial census already had been collected by the Washington County Historical Society, and it was added to by Washington County Genealogical Society and Browne family records. Additional gravestones continued to be discovered in the cemetery, supplying more names. A search of death certificates supplied a number of other names, likely accounting for at least some of the graves that were nothing more than sunken divots of ground lacking any headstones or other markings. The online newspaper database of Brenham newspapers found at the Portal of Texas History website was an additional source for obituaries, which often not only confirmed a burial at the Camptown Cemetery but also provided valuable background material.

An early example of this was the story of Waltman Bynum, who turned out to be a prominent citizen of Brenham. His gravesite bore a beautiful stone obelisk, one of the earliest markers found in the cemetery, commemorating his death on June 28, 1881. But by searching for him in the database, much more information became available not only about his life, but also his death. His obituary in the June 29, 1881, issue of the *Brenham Daily Banner* and titled "Death of Alderman Bynum," is quite revealing. For one thing, his name was possibly not Waltman, but Waterman, an odd discrepancy that has never been clarified. The article provides further information about his life and role in the Camptown community, including that he had come to Brenham "some eight years ago and for the past year or two had been successfully carrying on a store in Camptown. The article also noted that he was said to have "unlimited credit in Galveston, i.e., he could buy all the goods he wanted on time," was "quiet, orderly, and unassuming," had accumulate quite a handsome property," and "was highly respected by all the white people who knew him and had hosts of friends among his own color." Also, he had been elected the previous year as an alderman for the Third Ward, which included Camptown, and his funeral, which had taken place at four in the afternoon after dying at three in the morning, was "attended by the mayor and city council as well as by an immense concourse of colored people."

Additional information from newspaper articles and census data also showed that his daughter had been nominated as a "Goddess of Liberty" at the previous Emancipation Celebration (later to be known as Juneteenth), and his wife married after his death and carried on with the family store.

It was becoming clear that a great deal of information could be gleaned about many of the cemetery's residents. In turn the cemetery could be a focal point for better understanding the history of Camptown, of which little had remained except for a reference to it as a primarily Black community. Time has revealed this method of working back from the name of Black citizens, engraved in stone because they were not meant to be forgotten, is a valuable tool in reviving much of their life story and the world in which they lived. Using this method with other individuals buried in Camptown Cemetery has been a helpful tool in unearthing many stories that had previously been buried. The cemetery is no longer simply a place where dead people are buried, but also a place where people who once lived can still tell their story.

Although many clearly marked graves occupied the cemetery, many depressions, which were clearly unmarked graves, presented a potential danger since many had soft spots and even holes that could cause tripping or even the possibility of stumbling into a collapsing grave. The number of unmarked graves posed a problem in accounting for the potential number of burials as well.

As an archaeologist, Bob clearly understood the importance of such information. He contacted Dr. Mark Everett, a Texas A&M University professor in the Department of Geology and Geophysics specializing in near-surface applied geophysics. On visiting the cemetery for the first time and understanding the work that was underway, Dr. Everett agreed that the cemetery would serve as an ideal case study for applying subsurface imaging. He offered to bring out his class in an upcoming semester, and his students eventually helped supply an accurate mapping of a cleared area to the extent possible given the difficult circumstances of the soil, vines, stumps, various bits of metal fencing, and other detritus. His daughter, Laura Everett, also helped produce a more detailed geographic mapping of the cemetery several years later. Their work offered many insights into how such research could be conducted and demonstrated the mutual benefits of collaborating with the academic community.

As clearing the cemetery continued into summer, the work began to become even more difficult. There was little breeze in the more open areas, and none back in the dense undergrowth. The distance the cleared brush had to be hauled to reach the road increased as we got deeper in, and the sloping ground seemed to grow even steeper with the heat of the day. The number of volunteers began to decline, and the work ahead seemed to stretch on and on.

In late July, Bob contacted Rolling Thunder TX2, an advocacy group and motorcycle club consisting of veterans "committed to helping American veterans from all wars." Since there were many veterans buried in Camptown Cemetery, members of the Houston chapter came down to help dedicate the cemetery and place flags on veterans' graves. Some of these were still deep in the dense undergrowth, and Rolling Thunder understood the neglect and lack of respect we were seeking to rectify. In response to this challenge, they organized the "Camptown Cemetery Heritage Ride 'For Honor & Respect'" on September 28, 2013. It was a "Community Wide Clean-up effort to Restore Camptown Cemetery as a place of 'Honor and Respect,'" drawing on members not only from Rolling Thunder TX2, but also the Combat Veteran Motorcycle Association and the Houston branch of the Buffalo Soldiers Motorcycle Club.

This event brought out many volunteers to work on clearing the cemetery, as well as much-needed equipment to speed up the process. This included a Bobcat for hauling the cut brush to the collection site, where the city had a dump truck to pick it up, and a Gradall grappler to load it. Many of these volunteers and their equipment returned time and again, and work on opening up the cemetery began to accelerate. With more ground being cleared, the amount being surveyed by the geophysics students and their equipment increased as well. And even up to the final day, new gravestones were being found and names added to the cemetery census.

The Texas Historical Marker finally arrived from the foundry after several delays. It replaced the "Dead End" sign that had so long stood in the same spot. A dedication ceremony was held for the marker on March 22, 2014. It was attended by the largest crowd the cemetery had seen in this century, filling Mangrum Street with visitors in chairs and on foot. Residents of Camptown and Brenham also attended, as well as the local press and members of Rolling Thunder and the Buffalo Soldiers motorcycle clubs, who were helping out with the final bit of clearing even as the ceremony was taking place. Buffalo Soldier reenactors, in full period uniform, were also there to unveil the marker, and Dr. Dietrich, who had played an early role in gaining historical recognition for the site, gave a speech, as well as Eddie. All the volunteers who had given so much time and energy into seeing the project through attended, including Reggie Browne, Doug Price, Cynthia Eben, Ray Mildren, Bob Wishoff, and many others.

Camptown Cemetery, still in the final stages of cleanup, was finally showing itself off as the beautiful and peaceful place it was meant to be. After fourteen months of work, what had been a forgotten, overgrown, and overlooked segment of early Texas history at last had been given a new chance to reveal its stories.

The entire cemetery eventually was cleared, and with the help of a renewed Camptown Cemetery Association it continues to be maintained. Ray Mildren, who was one of the first volunteers working on the cleanup, continues to help maintain the grounds and keep Mother Nature from taking over again. As he said:

> Once we had cleared most of the area we wanted to clear, I made a commitment that I would not let the Cemetery get into disrepair as long as I could work on it. Although I did have a heart attack while working at the site, I still have that commitment as the heart attack did not slow me down. The goal is to make the Cemetery an historic site that people in and around Texas will want to go see. It is a beautiful site with many large trees providing shade and a breeze usually blows thru the cemetery. It is a great place to sit on one of the benches and contemplate your life, past, present and future.

Investigating the historical significance of Camptown and other Black communities in Brenham, Washington County, and surrounding communities continues as well. The Texas Ten Historical Explorers was set up as a nonprofit corporation "to identify historical and cultural contributions of African Americans, Germans and other cultures that impacted the development of Washington county communities...provide a more inclusive and accurate events leading to development of Washington County, Texas" and "...recognize the contributions of African Americans and others that were not included in the written history of our community."

By working from the names found in and associated with Camptown Cemetery, a previously untold history is being revealed. Very little written history on Black communities previously has existed, and this has been certainly true for Brenham. But research growing out of the work at the cemetery is beginning to uncover a surprisingly rich understanding of the post-Emancipation community of Camptown, Brenham, and Washington County.

History of the past is ephemeral, as is its documentation. Left to itself it can become hidden beneath the overgrowth of the relentless rush to the future. Without the constant pruning of memory, it begins to wither and fade as surely as Camptown Cemetery was beginning to disappear. But cemeteries are meant to be the custodians of a community's remembrance and should be treated with a corresponding dignity and respect. Their markers are there not so that we should forget, but rather that we should remember those who have come before and the world in which they lived. In resurrecting the cemetery it became possible bring some of these memories back to life. My desire is that these stories show Camptown Cemetery can become a place where doors are not closed to the future but opened onto the past.

Chapter 2

# WILEY HUBERT:
# BUILDING THE CAMPTOWN COMMUNITY

*Photo courtesy of Amy the Spirit Seeker*

One of the first burial plots after entering Camptown Cemetery is the Hubert plot. Long covered by brush and forgotten for many years, its neglect belies the importance of one of the patriarchs in early Camptown, Wiley R. Hubert. Hubert's life was closely intertwined with the land on which the cemetery lies. His family plot in the cemetery occupies a prominent position that seems fitting given the significance of his place in early Camptown.

Establishing the facts of a Black man's life in the late nineteenth century can be difficult, but for Hubert many important clues were already known. Many of his family members still live in the area and carried on the story of this ancestral patriarch. Eddie Harrison, one of the prime movers behind restoring Camptown Cemetery, spent many long afternoons on fishing and hunting trips along Yegua Creek with Hubert's grandson, Roy L., and great-grandson, Ray. Wiley Hubert and his community contributions were the main topic of discussion. Roy often spoke with pride about the "good old days" when his grandfather helped support the well-being of Blacks grappling with the many challenges they faced in the early decades after Emancipation, as well as how his former enslavers later helped support independent Black citizens.

Additional documentation reinforces these oral traditions, offering a broader picture of Hubert's life and highlighting one of the great untold stories of early Camptown history.

Wiley Hubert was born into slavery in Mississippi on January 26, 1833, as were both his parents. This information comes from his death certificate and census data, but he didn't enter the public record until he was about eight years old. His slave holder, Ann H. P. Noble, granted him and thirty other slaves to Noble's cousin as a gift "in consideration of the love and affection" they shared.[1] This "deed of gift" to Mary Ann Hubert was filed in Washington County on January 1, 1842, to acknowledge the original deed filed on August 8, 1839, in Canton, Mississippi. The document indicated Noble was "of the State of Louisiana and the Parish of Madison," which was across the Mississippi River from Mississippi's Madison Parish, of which Canton was the seat of government. Further compounding the provenance of this document, Noble had been granted a land grant for by the Republic of Texas 640 acres in May of 1839. Mary Ann and her husband, Fletcher Watt Hubert, were also from Mississippi before arriving in Texas in 1837, settling on a 1,280-acre land grant.

The difference in these two dates compounds the uncertainty about whether Wiley's age of eight is from the 1839 or 1842 date; judging from internal evidence in later records, it seems to have been the later date. The Noble document also suggests an interesting insight into the community in which grew up. Comparing later slave documents from the Hubert family indicate many of the slaves received from Noble were kept by the family over several decades. In 1848, following the death of her husband, Mary Ann was active in settling his affairs, and after marrying Thomas J. Allcorn in 1855, a division of the Hubert slaves was formalized. The Hubert's only son, Frank H. Hubert, received twenty of the slaves—men, women, and children—whose names and ages were given, as well as "Barney and one or two children who have died since said partition was made." Among those mentioned in the Deed of Release to Negro Slaves was "Wyllie," whose age was given as "23 or 24."[2]

Frank Hubert was one of Washington County's prominent citizens, a position secured at least in part by his marriage to Sarah Ann, the daughter of Dr. Asa Hoxey. Hoxey had been born in Georgia, and after obtaining his medical degree in New York had moved to Alabama. In 1833 he moved to Texas, along with thirty slaves and $40,000, eventually settling in Washington County. He owned four plantations, two on the Brazos River bottom, which he gave up due to flooding, and eventually became the second largest slave owner in the county. By 1860 he held title to over a hundred, keeping a careful record of not only the dates and names of all slave births, but also of dates and causes of deaths.[3] He played a role in establishing the Declaration of Independence of Texas from Mexico, and his home was frequented by many politicians, including luminaries such as Sam Houston, Stephen F. Austin, and Mirabeau Lamar. His library was considered one of the largest and finest in Texas, and he contributed to educational endeavors such as Baylor University, which was located near his home in Independence at the time.

After his marriage to Hoxey's daughter, Hubert became a wealthy man himself, eventually accumulating over $15,000 in real estate and $50,000 in "personal estate," with much of the later value probably the result of slave ownership. He owned a store that sold, among other items, "ready-made clothing, of every size, quality and price," including "negro clothing and plantation supplies."[4] He was engaged in politics, serving as a Washington County representative in the Eighth Texas Legislature. As a supporter of secession, he joined the Confederate army as a captain, securing military positions in South Texas before he died in 1861.

A rare firsthand account of life for slaves working for the Huberts came to light early in the early part of the twentieth century. It is a from the WPA-commissioned "Slave Narratives" story of Yach Stringfellow, "borned in Brenham" and whose "massa and missus was Frank Hubert and Sarah Ann Hubert."[5] Stringfellow spoke of living "in little log houses all kind of group together, and us eat in a long lean-to builded on to the big house. Us chillen had a long, scooped-out dish on a split log table. What we had to eat was dumped in dat trough and us ate it like slop. But it sure taste good when been huntin' for eggs or calves or gittin' in chips or breakin' bresh...Us eat bacon and cornbread and greens, but de white folks had more'n better. Dey didn't have to eat string victuals like us; us have to eat something to stick to de ribs. Right 'bout de time dis state come to be de United States, and de Mexicans raisin' de old billy, us cook most usual on de fireplace and have ovens by de side to make bread, and cranes for de pots. Us slaves used pine torches and sometimes a little bit of candle. De women make all the candles demselves for de white folks. Us didn't need much light at night, 'cause us tired after de long day, workin' from can see to can't see, and git in de bed early."[6]

This dismal account of daily hard life existed for many of the Hubert slaves, but it may not have been quite the same for Wiley. In 1858, while Frank Hubert was involved in running for a seat in the legislature, he sold twenty of his slaves to John Day and James McDade, including the same Yach mentioned above, for $15,000. He retained use of them until early the next year to harvest the 1858 crop and plant for 1859. The same slaves were rented from McDade and Day by Hubert's mother the following year, and several of them were bought at a forfeiture sale at the doors of the Washington County courthouse. In 1862 Hubert's mother then gave five of these slaves to her son's widow.[7]

Wiley Hubert was not included in any of these transactions. In 1858, immediately before them, Wiley was sold to Asa Hoxey for $2,500, along with eight horses, two mares, six mules, and a hundred head of cattle. The deed record included the description of "Wylie" as "a negro man…about twenty five years of age and of yellow complexion which negro I warrant to be a slave for life and my property." This sale to an individual owning over a hundred slaves was rather unusual, and even more so because a year later, Wiley was gifted by Hoxey to his daughter, now married to Frank Hubert, along with the livestock, for "one dollar in hand" and "in consideration of the natural love and affection for my daughter."[8] As to why Wiley was chosen by Hoxey as a gift to his daughter, it seems that he saw special qualities in him. Judging from later events in Wiley's life, such a perception of his special qualities would have been well justified.[9]

Life on the Hoxey plantation exposed Wiley to a household that played a pivotal role in early Texas history. He surely met Uncle Ned, a slave who had already been with the Hoxeys since he was ten years old. An 1888 article in a Brenham newspaper described him as "Tall and erected and retains the strength and vigor of manhood…He remembers well the 'run-away scrapes' and the hardships incident to those days. He talks familiarly about Davy Crockett, General Lamar, Kaufman, Austin, Houston and many other noted men who figured in Texas at that early day, having made fires and saddled horses for many of them. Is very proud of having saddled Gen. Houston's horse for him the morning he left the settlements to meet Santa Anna at San Jacinto. He attended a company was with it when the Indians were driven back out of the village of Waco."[10]

Ned continued to live on the Hoxey plantation after Emancipation, renting land "on which he has made a good living."[11] He remained on good terms with Sarah Ann, who had remarried after Frank Hubert's death, and appeared in 1887 for "his accustomed Christmas dinner." To his surprise, for his many years of "faithful and hones" service she gave him, as a Christmas gift, "the land, houses, etc. he has been occupying for the remainder of his life free of rent. Uncle Ned is now pleasantly situated and it is to be hoped he may live long to enjoy the fruits of a good black [sic] land farmer."[12]

Another fellow slave that Wiley would have met was Uncle Moses. Moses was born in Virginia in 1778 and had been "present at the capture of Washington City by the English" in 1812.[13] He was purchased by Asa Hoxey in Alabama and was one of the thirty slaves who accompanied him when he moved to Texas. During the Texas Revolution, Moses served as "the valet of Major Hoxey, one of Rusk's aides and considered himself one of the staff. While serving he was court martialed over some wine he had drunk while the officers were gone and defended himself by testifying that 'I can afford to get drunk, but you can't, too much responsibility resting on you.'"[14] He was "honorably acquitted, and promoted in the estimation of his General and the staff." He went on to serve alongside Hoxey "through all the trying scenes of Texas, having been on all of her battle fields."[15]

In his final years Moses was "permitted quietly to repose upon his honors, and his past services" and resided in a "comfortable cottage, a short distance from his master's mansion."[16] He died at four o'clock in the afternoon on November 2, 1858, the same year Wiley was bound to the family. A family friend wrote that Moses was "full of years and covered with faithfulness and honors, leaving a humane, kind and affectionate master and mistress to remember his virtues and to mourn his loss. I was on a visit to the Doctor at the time of his death, and with emotion in my own breast, witnessed its melancholy tendency upon the house."[17] After the funeral "the Dr. called in one of his servants and feelingly gave orders for the temporary enclosure of his grave, remarking that at some future time he would erect over it an appropriate monument."[18]

This exposure to mutual respect, despite an inherent power differential between the cultures of slave and master, was not lost on Wiley Hubert. It is also possible that witnessing the death and burial of Moses in a place of honor with "an appropriate monument" may have played a part in own role in establishing the first dedicated cemetery for ex-slaves in Camptown twenty years later.[19]

Wiley Hubert's early life after Emancipation remains largely a mystery, but he does begin to emerge in the public record in January 1867 as a man of some means. Washington County Public Record #148 of 1867 is a deed listing the purchase of property from John Wadkins by Paul and Wiley Hubert for $770, $400 "in coin," and the rest to be paid twenty-four months later. Paul Hubert was likely Wiley Hubert's younger brother born in Mississippi a year earlier. Wiley made an additional land purchase with his brother in June 1867 and was involved over the next decades in multiple real estate transactions, many of which helped establish the character of Camptown.

In October 1868, Wiley married Alice Crutchville and began his own family. The following year their first child, a girl named Savannah was born, followed by a son, Roy, in 1874.[20] Hubert was becoming a prosperous man for the time, and by the 1870 census his personal estate was valued at $500. He also became adept in real estate dealings, owning real estate valued at $2,000. Dozens of real estate transactions, usually listing both Wiley and Alice in the documents, are recorded in courthouse records and published lists in the newspaper over the following years, both with white citizens and with prominent Black citizens. At one point he even sold a street to the city of Brenham.[21]

One of the early property deals shaping Camptown took place on February 4, 1869. The deed describes Hubert, Matt Parker, Theodore Stamps, Charles Childs, and James Basey as "authorized agents of the colored peoples of Brenham," purchasing for $400 "in coin" a tract of land with a building on it formerly owned by Hubert. The building had formerly been "used as a sutler's store used by the Federal troops stationed" at the former Post of Brenham.[22] It was "expressly understood" that this property was to be used "for the said educational interests of the colored people of Brenham except that the same may be used by the said colored people as a house of worship" with the consent of the trustees," and "when used strictly as a house of worship no preference will be given to any particular denomination."[23]

The board of trustees included several prominent freedmen in the Camptown community such as Stamps. He was soon to be elected a city alderman in both 1870 and 1872. Childs was a carpenter who already had been involved in education by renting schoolhouses to the Freedmen's Bureau. Hubert also had done work for the Freedmen's Bureau as well. The bureau operated a hospital for a short period of time in Brenham, financed by $1,000 advanced to the governor, E.M. Pease. On a list accounting for that money, among the costs of medicine, doctors, coffins, graves, and services from other citizens, Hubert's name appears three times for reimbursements "in coin" for a total of twenty dollars.[24]

The Freedmen's Bureau had established various schools in Brenham since April 1866, but had been in rented buildings and churches, most of them unsuitable for the purpose and subject to closure after only several months in use. But, as one teacher, a one-armed Civil War veteran by the name of Thomas Huff, informed the bureau, it had "been reported around the colored people that if they bought their land and forwarded a certificate to the headquarters that the government would furnish them with the funds to buy the lumber." [25] For this purpose, the land had been purchased from Hubert, and during a "mass meeting of the freedmen of this community" in October 1869 a Board of Trustees of the Freedmen School was formed. The board consisted of five white men and five Black men, including Matt Parker, Wiley Estes, and Hubert.

The board hired a teacher, W. G. Zealy, thirty-one years old, born in South Carolina and a "gentleman in every respect and worthy to fill the function," who had moved to Brenham with his wife and four children. He taught fifty children, most females who attended regularly and who paid a monthly tuition of $1.50 collected in advance by the school board. Among the students was a young boy who was working for Captain James Biddle, then-commander of the U.S. Army's Post of Brenham. Biddle reported favorably on the school: "I have a freed boy in my employ who attends, and from the manner in which he has progressed in his studies in the last three months, and the promptness and readiness displayed by him I am satisfied as to the efficiency of the teachers."

While it also was reported that "the citizens of Brenham have contributed liberally to buy the house in which the school is taught and is nearly paid for," there was still work that needed to be done on the school. The Freedmen's Bureau eventually accepted a four-hundred-dollar contract repair and furnishing of the fifty-foot-by-thirty-foot school building, including "four hundred feet of lumber for making desks…30 seats, 8 feet long, with backs 20 inches high, made of cedar," six windows, a ceiling, a teacher's desk and a tin framed blackboard, although the president of the school board had to put up $200 in gold to pay for the lumber. The building was used as a school, a church, and a public hall for many years.

Although the contract had been let to a man named Stacy, much of the work, including putting up the ceiling, was done by the freedmen. Hubert likely contributed to this labor, since he also was an accomplished carpenter. While it is not clear if he first learned his skills as a workman in wood before Emancipation, Hubert became a sought-after carpenter and builder in Brenham. Among his many customers were the city council of Brenham and the Washington County Commissioners Court. Over the years his work for them included repairing the courthouse, the schoolhouse, and "the engine house." When the September 1900 hurricane that devastated Galveston reached as far inland as Brenham, "two of the churches in Camptown were so badly damaged that it was thought they could never be made to serve the purpose for which they were erected." But funds were raised and "repairs were done under the supervision of Wiley Hubert, who sustained his well-earned reputation for doing satisfactory work."

Hubert excelled not only in repairing and building houses but also moving them. One of his more outstanding works was moving a large cotton gin in 1893. This feat was covered in the local papers, which reported that "a fine piece of engineering work has been accomplished by Wiley Hubert, a colored carpenter and builder. It was the moving of the big iron-covered gin at the oil mill. The house is two stories in height, is 42 x80 feet and the distance was 150 yards across a railroad track and a deep gully, and then over very rough ground...Wiley had to crib the building up and then place it on rollers and false sills and pull it with horses. He accomplished the undertaking in two days and a half, and it was in every way satisfactory. There was not a strain or break in any part of the house when it landed at its destination."

When he moved the studio of Netta Botts from the southern part of town to downtown, the press account stated that "Wiley Hubert did the work very successfully." When a storm in Chappell Hill blew the city hall off its blocks, Hubert was contracted to place it back on those blocks and repair the damage.

Established as one of the most solid and respected Black citizens in Washington County, Hubert also was a valued member of his church. His role in helping establish the first freestanding Freedmen's School extended to its use as a church building, with Sunday schools as an important educational adjunct to the church's services. His financial acumen, as well as the trust he had developed among members of the white populace, were important skills he used to advance the role of the churches in Camptown.

A cemetery near Mount Rose Baptist Church had been present since at least the 1860s, as noted on a map of the Post of Brenham from 1867. In April 1873, trustees of the Mount Rose Cemetery Association bought the property from its previous owner for "100 gold dollars." Hubert was one of the prominent Black citizens serving as trustees, along with James Parker, Daniel Allgood, Anderson Hallum, Henry Milton, Samuel Love, and Waltman

Bynum. This was later to be known as Camptown Cemetery, where Hubert would be laid to rest in a place of honor near the entrance. Parker was a preacher who taught school and served as treasurer of the Grand United Order of Odd Fellows; he also was involved in local politics and served on grand juries and as a jury commissioner. Milton was a well-to-do carpenter and neighbor of Hubert. Love was a beloved educator who had been teaching in Camptown since the early days of Freedmen's Bureau schools and engaged in local politics. Bynum was a successful businessman and store owner who would be elected city alderman, but he would die while in office. He was "highly respected by all the white people who knew him and hosts of friends among his own color," and his funeral at Camptown Cemetery was "attended by the mayor and city council, as well as an immense concourse of colored people."

In November 1876 the "colored Methodists" began erecting a new church building on Sandy Street (now Alamo Street) in Camptown. It was described as "60 x 40, 18 feet ceiling, self-supporting roof, weather boarded, with shutters to the windows…it will be commodious in size, and tasty in design and finish." Although "the frame is now up and the weather boarding nearly all on…the windows, doors, shutters, etc. etc. are all on the ground." In anticipation of having it ready for the holidays, Hubert took out a notice in the Daily Banner "to call on the public for aid." Although such an appeal for financial assistance was not uncommon, it was not without peril. Later that year Hubert had to place another "card to the public" in the paper warning that "certain persons have been fraudulently representing themselves as agents of our Church, and under that pretense swindling, or annoying, many of the benevolently inclined among our white fellow citizens; this is to inform the public that by a vote of our church Mr. Wiley Hubert has been appointed our agent, and that he and the pastor in charge...only are authorized to solicit or receive donations for our church."

Affiliation with the A.M.E. church and advancing educational goals continued to be important in Hubert's life. His daughter Savannah became a schoolteacher herself, teaching music in Camptown. There she met Professor Calvin J. Anderson, the principal of "the colored free school at Camptown." Anderson was a graduate of Fisk University, and for a time had served as an assistant at Prairie View Normal School, now Prairie View A&M, working with his two brothers who had served as its first and second principals. In 1885 he became principal of "colored schools" in Brenham, where he was not only well liked in the community, but also had a well-paying job, making $600 a year (though this was still $150 less than white principals). The two fell in love and married in July 1886. The reception was held at the home of the bride and was described as "the event of the season in Brenham colored society." A newspaper reporter who covered the wedding noted that "the *Banner* was duly remembered with wine and cake."

The following year Anderson, as principal, had to suspend a student, Ella Bigsby, for an incident of unspecified misbehavior at school. Her father (and Hubert's neighbor) Willis Bigsby took exception to this, and when the two met at the post office Bigsby, described as "considerably less than average size, but...wiry and stout," beat Anderson, described as "small and rather sickly" with a cartwhip. Although exonerated by the school board for the expulsion, Anderson eventually succumbed to his overall sickly nature, dying of tuberculosis in Austin three years later.

Hubert understood the significance of enfranchisement in advancing the newly emancipated black community, and he appears in the first voters registry in 1867. Many Blacks were running for office and winning, with Brenham having had at least three Black city aldermen and the county electing a majority of Blacks serving as county commissioners. Black constables and city policemen also were common. Although Hubert never became a political figure himself, his stature as an outstanding citizen led him to be on many juries. In contrast to some other Southern communities of the time, Black citizens in Washington county frequently served on local juries. Hubert was no exception, and he served on both petit and grand juries, as well as a jury commissioner responsible for choosing panels of potential jurors. He was well known and trusted among local politicians, having borrowed and repaid large sums of money from Brenham's preeminent leader and politician D.C. Giddings, and having sold property to local Black state legislator Matt Gaines. His reputation as a competent juror continued into his later years, serving in 1897 on a federal grand jury held in Austin. But during a period when many Black citizens were actively participating in local Republican politics, the closest Hubert became involved was in 1881. A citizen's meeting called by Giddings complained about "the present slip-shod manner of choosing city officials" and created a committee of three from each ward to "agree upon a ticket that would prove acceptable and command the respect and support of all." Hubert was on the committee to nominate candidates for the Second Ward serving Camptown.

Within the next five years the political atmosphere in Brenham and Washington County began to take a nasty turn. The Democrats began to realize that with nearly half of the voting populace being Black and immigrant German Republicans, a new approach was needed to regain electoral power. This led to a mixed People's ticket meant to shift these voters away from the Radical Republicans with an implication that it would be more amenable to improving local government, together with numerous charges of malfeasance by Republican officials.

Violence increased at "Black belt" polling places where the electorate was primarily Black and Republican. At the Chappell Hill polling station in 1884, three black precinct officials, including former state representative A.W. Wilder and county commissioner H.H. Knoxson, were shot by masked intruders, with Knoxson later dying from complications. In 1886 the violence intensified, with ballot boxes stolen from three Black belt polling places and the Chappell Hill location not even being opened. To make matters worse, Dewes Bolton, a white candidate's son, was shot and killed in the process of stealing one of the ballot boxes and eight of the witnesses were held in jail even after the murderer had been apprehended. Although the People's ticket had succeeded in winning most of the seats, outrage in the white community over Bolton's death was followed by rumors of mobs of Blacks gathering to release the witnesses. Longtime white Republicans viewed as scalawags and the publisher of a German language newspaper were driven from town at the threat of their lives, and a month later three of the witnesses were kidnapped from the jail and lynched. This incident led to a hearing in the U.S. Senate the following year that produced no meaningful results.

Although Hubert had been only peripherally involved in the political arena, this overt neutralization of the Black vote seems to have been too much for him. He had seen Blacks in his community go from slaves with no civil rights to enfranchised citizens with a voice in their government, growing into a thriving community in Camptown. But with the right for a meaningful vote so severely eroded, Hubert left Texas with his family for Kansas.

This period of his life was addressed in 1906 in a letter to the editor of *The Galveston Daily News* by Stephen A. Hackworth, one of the white men who had been forced to leave Brenham after the election outrage of 1886. Hackworth had moved to Topeka, Kansas, soon afterward followed there by Hubert. The letter is surprisingly informative, including a physical description of Hubert, his stay in Kansas, and the influence it had on his life:

"...In 1887, Wiley Hubert, a colored carpenter of Brenham...whom I had known since his boyhood, came to Topeka to secure permanent employment in the carpenters' department of the Atchison, Topeka & Santa Fe Railway shops. He was a skilled carpenter, polite, industrious and reliable. He possessed the respect and confidence of all who knew him, and came to Topeka with written recommendations from Col. D.C. Giddings and other leading white citizens of Brenham. He is a quadroon, or only one-fourth negro blood, and having a bright yellow complexion, high cheek bones and long straight hair, seemed to indicate he is an admixture of white and Indian blood. He called upon the superintendent of the carpenters' department of the Atchison, Topeka & Santa Fe Railway shops, to whom he gave his recommendations and applied for employment. The superintendent said he needed a few skilled workmen and then asked Hubert if he was part Indian. 'No,' replied Hubert, 'I am part negro.' 'I am sorry,' said the superintendent, 'you are part negro, for I cannot employ you, because I have 200 white men in my employ who will not work with negroes, or anyone who has part negro blood, and if I were to employ you they would all strike.' Hubert at once reported the incident to me and I called upon the superintendent to see if I could induce him to reconsider his decision. He politely said that under no circumstances could he be induced to employ a negro, or anyone who had part negro blood, because if he should do so his 200 white employees would strike. I then asked if his employees were all Democrats. 'No,' said he, 'there may be a few Democrats among them, but about nine-tenths of them are Republicans.' I informed him that Hubert had often worked with white carpenters who were Democrats. To this he replied that Hubert ought to lose no time in returning to Texas, for, said he, negroes are not wanted here, and they ought to remain among Southern white people, who are accustomed to them. There was a real estate 'boom' in Topeka and hundreds of new houses were under construction, and contractors were daily advertising for carpenters. Hubert visited all the contractors and vainly applied to the white contractors for employment. He finally secured a contract from a well-to-do colored farmer to build a neat residence, and with the money he thus earned he paid railroad fare for himself and his family back to his old home at Brenham, where he now resided, and is able to earn a living. Before leaving Topeka Hubert declared his people could vote the Republican ticket safely in Kansas and have their votes fairly counted, but, said he, the Northern white people will not give us equal chances with white labor to earn a living, therefore, said he, I had rather live among the Southern white Democrats, who will give me a fair chance to earn a living."

Once back in Brenham, Hubert returned to the life he had left, working as a carpenter and dealing in real estate. He also continued to move houses, and it was after his return that his move of "the big gin house" made the news. The press was on friendly terms with Hubert over the years, a close relationship that can glimpsed in a front-page article from May 1900: "A ripe peach was brought to the *Banner* office Monday afternoon by Wiley Hubert, who lives in the eastern portion of the city. The peach, which is from a seedling tree, was of medium size and delicious flavor. It is perhaps the first of the season and the grower took great pride in exhibiting it."

When he was injured on a job site, it was reported that Hubert was "nursing an exceedingly sore arm from the effects of a cut from a chisel that fell from over a window on which he was working." Hubert also found a place in print as a man willing to bet on his horse in a race. An out-of-towner named Hargraves had a "little bay mare" named Dollie, and offered to compete with Hubert, "who owns a fast horse" with a side bet of $20 on the outcome. But when Hubert heard of the defeat of a favored local racehorse by Dollie, he stood down from the race.

These frequent mentions in the paper provide insight into other incidents in Hubert's life, one of which showed him to be a man of considerable bravery. One of his neighbors, Louisa Mangrum, was also a woman who dealt in real estate, doing quite well for herself; she sold the land to the city council for the second dedicated black school in Camptown (later Pickard High School), and the road on which it sits, as well as Camptown Cemetery, was named after her. Her home in Camptown was infested with ants, and she had doused them with an ant killing fluid. At the same time, she had hired Henry McDade to clean out her well. Some of the ant tunnels opened into the well also, and McDade was overcome by the heavy poisonous fumes that had settled into the well. Another man named Prince Edward attempted to rescue him but was nearly overcome by the fumes himself. At this point Hubert descended into the well and was able to fasten a rope around McDade, who was drawn out of the well and eventually revived by a doctor who had been summoned.

He had less luck with horses one night the following year when driving his "road cart team" south of town. A "double horse team" collided with him, "the result being that the pole of the first mentioned vehicle penetrated the breast of Wylie Hubert's horse." Such injuries were often usually fatal to the injured beast.

Fires were all too common in any community where almost all structures were constructed of wood, and Camptown was no exception. Following devastating fires in 1866 and 1873 that destroyed large portions around the city square, a series of waterlines and cisterns were established downtown. A regular fire brigade, the Brenham Hook and Ladder Company, was organized in 1867, even though it was considered "ostensibly…a volunteer fire company, but in reality a military company whose duties were to protect the town from the soldiers" who were involved in the 1866 fire. Camptown was served by its own fire company "composed of citizen of Camptown," Hook and Ladder No. 2, which sought to be "admitted into the fire department as a special fire company to extinguish fires and protect property in the immediate vicinity of Camptown" by the city council, though "not to have any voice in the election of chiefs of the Brenham fire department." After polling the town's fire company, the wholly white members refused to admit members of "the Colored Hook and Ladder Company, of Camptown" and threatened to disband the department should they be allowed to join. Nonetheless, Hook and Ladder No. 2 was an integral part of the Camptown community, buying its own fire engine, participating in the June 19th Emancipation Celebrations, parades and funerals, and assisting in the burial of a Black member of the Hubert family in their plot at Camptown Cemetery.

In 1898 Wiley Hubert found himself at the scene of one of Camptown's many fires. The home of Albert Milton, the son of fellow Camptown Cemetery trustee Henry Milton and assistant secretary of the Hook and Ladder No. 2, was engulfed in flames. Hubert was one of the many nearby neighbors who rushed to the scene as Hook and Ladder No. 2 sought to bring the fire under control. To their horror, a "fearful and heartrending spectacle met their startled and anxiously inquiring looks, on the person of Catherine Milton, who was wrapped almost from head to foot in seething flames and was struggling in agonized haste to free herself from the fiery raiment." Hubert and his neighbors rushed to her aid and stripped the burning clothing from her, ministering "to her hurts as best they could until a physician could be summoned." Her back, shoulder and hips were so badly burned that the doctor feared that she might die, but Catherine survived.

After the death of her husband, Savannah Hubert began teaching music again at Camptown. Each summer the Black teachers from the schools in Washington County and surrounding areas would hold a normal school or institute for teaching and training teachers. In the summer of 1892 Savannah was participating in an "entertainment" given by the normal school for over a hundred schoolteachers, in which she sang in duets and trios between speeches on topics such as "Woman as a Teacher" and "Opportunity." The concluding address was given by Samuel C. McCoy of Galveston, who found himself quite smitten by the comely young, widowed vocalist.

McCoy was an up-and-coming young political figure in Galveston, serving at the time as Norris Wright Cuney's private secretary. Cuney was the chairman of the Republican Party in Texas at a time when the Black electorate held its greatest political sway. McCoy was at his side, having first served with him in the U. S. Customs Service and later as assistant city clerk of Galveston. McCoy traveled extensively with Cuney and was with him when Cuney's doctor ordered him to Hot Springs, Arkansas, for his health. They were denied a sleeping berth on a Pullman car during the rail trip, and when Cuney sued the Pullman Car Company for discrimination, McCoy filed suit as well. It is not surprising that during the normal school address, McCoy "discussed the negro race, holding that it was wrong to bring them here originally, and that ever since their advent here they had been the bone of contention with the two parties." Considering her father's recent experiences in Kansas, it is not surprising that Savannah might have found McCoy, who was attracted to the intelligent young widow, an appealing man of promise.

In April 1893 the two were married at Hubert's house in Camptown. Although Cuney was not there, his wife attended the wedding, and afterward she and McCoy's sister accompanied the newlyweds back to Galveston. A week later Hubert was back to his life as a Camptown carpenter, preparing the rollers for moving the two-story gin house across the railroad tracks. His son, Roy, would learn the trade of carpentry from his father, and it would remain his occupation throughout his life. Roy apparently had somewhat of a temper, nearly landing him in jail with a murder charge just months after his sister's wedding. An argument over a pick arose between the nineteen-year-old Roy and a man named Ed Parker. Parker had borrowed the pick and lost it, leading to a fight between the two. In the heat of the fight Roy pulled out a pistol and, after hitting Parker over the head with it several times, shot at him several times as well. Fortunately, being a better pugilist than marksman, the shots missed, and Roy avoided arrest. He eventually settled down and married Emma Barton, with whom he had a son, Raymond.

Although Wiley Hubert was known as an upright and well-respected citizen not generally drawn into the local political scene, he seems to have been influenced by his overtly political new son-in-law. In 1896 a dispute erupted in a Republican convention to elect delegates from Precinct 3, which represented Camptown. McCoy, as a member of the local Republican Executive Committee, was instrumental in calling a meeting in Camptown to elect new delegates to the county convention at which Cuney "was present and made one of his rousing speeches." As an outcome of this meeting a new slate of delegates was selected, including Hubert and McCoy, the only time Hubert was ever mentioned as being directly involved in politics.

In 1896 Cuney also lost his position as head of the Texas Republican Party. As his political influence waned, McCoy began to shift careers. By 1900 he and Savannah had moved back to Brenham, along with their one-year-old daughter Alice, and was teaching school. The following year he was elected by the school board as principal of the high school in Camptown. He remained in that position for almost a decade, aside from a short period in the spring of 1905 when he left to teach in Houston. A few interesting incidents from their home life can be found discerned from short newspaper entries.

While McCoy taught, his wife stayed home with their daughter. One Tuesday morning while he was at school, Alice was at the dining table and Savannah was out of the room. While out of the room "a white tramp entered and cleaned the table of the victuals thereon." A less frightening encounter with another white being came into their life when a long-haired white puppy with brown ears was found at their house.

Wiley Hubert remained active, moving houses when he was seventy-five years old. However, cancer of the bladder was beginning to affect his health and on October 6, 1909, took his life. That afternoon, his obituary appeared in the Brenham press. "Well Known and Prominent Colored Man Dead. Wiley Hubert, colored, age about 75 years, died at his home in Camptown, at 8 o'clock Wednesday morning. He was a well-known carpenter and house mover, having moved many large houses around Brenham during the past few years, was an energetic, honest old man, greatly esteemed among his own race and had many warm friends among the white people." He was buried in the family plot next to the entrance in Camptown Cemetery, the same cemetery he had been instrumental in creating thirty-six years earlier. His family took out a "Card of Thanks" in the paper "to express our sincere and heartfelt thanks to the many kind friends who ministered to Wiley Hubert during his illness by words of condolence or deeds to the family and assisted at the funeral obsequies." His wife lived in the family home after Wiley's death with their son and daughter-in-law. She died on August 9, 1917, and was laid to rest next to her husband in Camptown Cemetery.

The marriage between Hubert's daughter and McCoy had begun to unravel before Hubert's death, and she had filed for divorce. Two weeks before his death, the divorce was granted. Savannah already had been teaching part time, filling in due to "an increase in the colored attendance, since the close of the cotton-picking season of 122" from a previous 224 students. By 1910 she was teaching school full time, with McCoy having returned to Galveston to live with his sister Mary until his death in 1916. In that summer following the divorce, Savannah also had taken out an ad offering "massaging, manicuring, shampooing, hair bleaching and dyeing, scalp treatment," and within a few years she was teaching music full time at the school in Camptown. She continued teaching there until at least the time of her daughter Alice's graduation in 1915. She continued to live and teach in Brenham, but by 1930 she went to live with her daughter and her husband, Henry C. Clark, in Marshall, Texas, until her death from a stroke on February 2, 1952.

Roy continued to work as a carpenter, but his temper and gun toting ways caught up with him. He was arrested for aggravated misbehavior in 1912 and for carrying a pistol in 1915, which carried the hefty fine of $100. But he remained married to his wife, Emma, with whom he had their only son, Raymond. He owned a home worth $800 during the Depression and eventually had his own business as a building contractor, much like his father. Roy died on December 2, 1935, and was buried in his family's plot in Camptown Cemetery. When Emma died on October 11, 1950, she also was laid to rest in the Hubert plot, followed in 1997 by Alice Hubert. Ray Hubert, great-grandson of Wiley Hubert, and his wife, Listene Graves Hubert, have since been interred in the Wiley plot following his death in 2022, and they will be the last who are buried there in the cemetery his great-grandfather helped establish a century and a half earlier.

Chapter 3

# SAM LOVE: A "SELF-MADE" MAN

Sam Love was born into bondage in Texas sometime around 1843, according to 1870 census records. He likely was enslaved by Robert S. Love, a wealthy farmer in Washington County who held sixteen slaves in 1850, including at least one male in this age range, according to that year's federal slave schedule. Robert Love enlisted as a private in 1863 at the age of forty-three under Brigadier General Jonathan Sayles in Company G of the Second Brigade. Although little else is known about his youth, in 1889 a judge who had known the enslaved Love for more than twenty-five years made some comments about him in a newspaper article, indicating that he had seen some service in the War Between the States: "The judge had known Sam for more than twenty-five years; Sam had served in the army with him and had cooked for the soldiers with whom he messed."[1] Although it is not made clear from this slim reference, it seems that as a young man he had followed his enslaver to serve as a manservant.

Sam Love first appears in the public record in October 1869, teaching at the Freedmen's School in Brenham. His reputation as a well-educated man is already clear, and this is the first of many times his work as an eminent Washington County teacher is found.

A "Report of Schools for Freedmen" he filled out at this time is a little confusing, but enlightening.[2] It is a preprinted form with spaces to fill in for "Day School" and for "Night School." It gives a categorized report for male and female students, though the entries in the "Day School" section are crossed out with two single lines. The "Night School" section has the word "Night" crossed out and "Day" written above it, but the categories are filled out. It is possible this was done to conserve paper, filled out at two different times and used the "Night" section for a later period. This would seem to make the most sense since the numbers in most of the uncrossed section have increased over the crossed-out section and official forms frequently in short demand.

The total number of students enrolled increased from twenty to thirty-eight, always more girls than boys, with an average attendance increasing from seventeen to thirty-four over the same time period. The number who paid tuition also grew, and the number who are "Always Present" (which equals the number who are "Always Punctual") increased from seventeen to twenty-three. The number of students who were over sixteen climbed from only two females to four males and five females, reflecting an increased interest in education and a challenge for Love, who was teaching writing, "Primer and First Reader," "2d and Advanced Readers," geography, arithmetic, "Grammar and History" and writing. None were white, none were "Free before the War." None are entered under the category "No. on Needle Work," which is understandable since Love probably was not a very good seamstress.[3]

By July 1870, the twenty-seven-year-old Love was married to twenty-two-year-old Angeline and living in Brenham with her and their two children, a three-year-old son named Thomas and a three-month-old daughter named Caroline. It is not clear if he was still teaching at this time, but he had branched out from

64 | VOICES OF CAMPTOWN

education into the grocery business. His occupation is in the 1870 census was recorded as a grocer, with a later newspaper article noting that "he kept store for some time in Camptown."[4] In April 1873 his name appeared on the deed for the purchase of the land, on which Camptown Cemetery now sits, for the Mount Rose Cemetery Association. Others on the deed were many of the same prominent Black citizens who four years earlier had purchased the land and building that became the school.

In December 1871, Love became involved in another financial enterprise with other prominent Black citizens from Brenham. Together with nine others, including Matthew Gaines and Allen Wilder, who were to serve in the Texas Legislature, The Dollar Savings Bank of Brenham was incorporated. Its purpose was to "receive or deposit or entrust such sum or sums of money as may, from time to time, be offered therefor by tradesmen, merchants, clerks, laborers, servants, and others," a service which would have presented a valuable economic force for the black [sic] community.[5] However, it seems to have been an idea well before its time, and there is no indication that it developed far beyond the stage of incorporating with a state charter.

But Love's associations with the local Republican Party remained intact. In August 1878 he was elected secretary of the local county precinct meeting, which was attended by some 500 Blacks. There were also a number of white Republicans of the "Black and Tan" party persuasion, as opposed to the "lily-whites," who resisted Black participation. Two factions formed in opposition over who would serve as delegates, with a fight breaking out between Love and Captain Jack Lands, a Black former state policeman who had also served in a local law enforcement capacity.

The local paper, the strongly Democratically leaning *Brenham Banner*, delighted in carrying the story, as it did when reporting on any disparaging news about the local Republican Party:

> At the wind up a fight took place between Capt. Jack Lands, colored and Sam Love. No serious damage done. The above is one half of the story of the meeting. At the conclusion of the Lands-Love engagement, a general scrimmage ensued...During the scrimmage a pistol or two was drawn, benches were broken and sticks freely flourished...The proceedings are said to have borne a striking resemblance to Pandemonium. The number of fights that occurred cannot be ascertained with any accuracy."[6]

It was a scene that was, unfortunately, to be repeated in later years.

Love was getting involved in more than politics. He had returned to teaching, with his occupation in June 1880 in the census listed as schoolteacher. He was still married to Angeline, and Thomas was still living with them and "at school." While Caroline was no longer listed, there were two new daughters in the household, three-year-old Rhoda and five-month-old Alfie. He also was strongly involved in his church, serving not only as a deacon, but also as superintendent of the Sunday school there, as noted by the local press. "Caned—Rev. Sam Love, colored, superintendent of the African M.E. Sunday school at Camptown, has been presented with an elegant gold-headed walking cane, by the children of the school, as a testimony of their appreciation of his services."[7]

In August 1881 he was appointed by the school board as assistant teacher, and the following month as first assistant to Principal J.W. Johnson.[8] A month later the *Banner* printed a glowing article on Love as "A Self-Made Colored Man," authored by a correspondent going by the *nom de plume* "Q":

> As an example of what colored men can do, we point to Samuel Love, of Brenham, who passed a very creditable examination recently, and received a first-class certificate. Mr. Love is an indomitable student; possesses a library of 200 volumes. When not at work you can find him at home, book in hand solving the knotty problems. He is also studying Latin and making commendable progress. He is now in his fortieth year. There are a large number of other colored teachers in the county who, if called for examination would pass with a tight squeeze; they should emulate the example of Sam Love – reach for the highest prize.[9]

Having set high standards for himself, Love expected them of others. His son, Thomas, was first in his class of fifteen in 1882, and traveled to Austin to continue his studies at the Tillotson Institute, which later became Huston Tillotson University. The average daily attendance of the "colored Grammar school" in Camptown, at that time under the leadership of Professor J.W. Johnson, was 285 students, with two male and three female teachers. Several of the students were doing extremely well in mathematics,[10] and when a new principal was instituted at the school in Camptown, Love expressed his doubts about his new boss's capabilities as an instructor. "To the Board of School Trustees and Honorable Board of Aldermen: Mr. Robinson having been appointed principal of the colored school at Camptown, we have reason to believe that he is incompetent, and ask that he be examined in the higher branches of mathematics. In behalf of myself and others. S.L.

Love."[11]

Love also was involved in buying and selling some real estate in Brenham, based on transactions reported in the *Banner*. He also was involved, along with Waltman Bynum, a Black Brenham alderman, Wiley Hubert (who had owned the house used as the Freedmen's school where Love had taught), the trustees of the Mount Rose Cemetery Association, and others in purchasing the land on which Camptown Cemetery now sits and in which Bynum and Hubert now rest.

The election of 1886 was one of the most contentious is Brenham history, with the formation by local Democrats of a People's ticket designed to draw away previous Republican members of the electorate based on allegations of local corruption by Republicans at the county level. When the county's Republican convention was being held, Robert Sloan jumped up on the table and began a vigorous defense of the People's ticket candidates. When he was pulled off the table by George Lands, the brother of Jack Lands, who Love had previously had troubles with at the 1878 convention, a fight ensued, drawing Jack Lands into the fray. As Sloan rose up and found himself surrounded by "...a crowd of negroes there, which gathered around him, and Sloan had a pistol in his hand and started to strike a negro over the head, and some other negro struck it out of his hand and it fell on the ground, and another negro named Sam Love picked it up and kept it."[12]

This testimony comes from a United States Senate investigation of the "alleged election outrages in Texas." This investigation was spurred by the theft of numerous Black Belt ballot boxes and the murder of a People's ticket candidate during the attempted theft of another ballot box. Eight Blacks were arrested and held for the murder, though not the man who eventually was convicted of the crime. Three white Republican politicians were threatened with death, forcing them to leave town. A month later but before their trials, a crowd of masked white men subdued their jailor and abducted three of the prisoners. The three were then taken out of town and lynched from a pecan tree.[13]

The predominantly Black and German immigrant Republican Party had suffered a defeat from which it never recovered. But Love had more pressing problems at hand during these shifting political tides. One of the issues raised by the People's Party regarding county corruption was the forgery of school vouchers, which required the signature of the county judge for their approval. Five of these vouchers, totaling $300, had been forged, two of them bearing the signature of the newly elected Democratic county judge, Lafayette Kirk.[14] Kirk was up for reelection in 1886, and he charged Sam Love with obtaining money on forged vouchers. Love went missing in September that year after several real estate transactions, and despite a ten-dollar reward for his arrest, he had not been found by October.[15]

By April Love had been apprehended and was found guilty of embezzlement. He was sentenced to two years in the penitentiary. A week later, he was granted a motion for a new trial on the charges and released on bail when a $125 bond was posted by two fellow Black citizens.[16]

In July the citizens of Brenham were surprised by the news that Sam Love had been lynched in East Texas. He had been arrested for the attempted "outrage" of the two young daughters of Guy Parker and was being held in the San Augustine jail. A crowd gathered there of "...about forty thoroughly disguised men. They assembled at the jail about 12 o'clock...and in an orderly and systematical way broke open the door, took the prisoner to the court house and hanged him to an iron bar that extends out under the upper door, and then quietly dispersed."[17]

Brenham's own Sam Love was just as surprised by this news

when he heard about it. He knew from personal experience that he hadn't been lynched and saw an opportunity in the possible confusion of identities over just who had suffered this unfortunate fate. He had been out of town looking for work until his trial but realized that this was an ideal situation for him to escape his legal problems. He moved to Austin where he remained a while before moving just south of there to teach at a private school in Manchaca, where he taught for five months. After this he then moved farther west where he worked on farms for a while. When the Oklahoma land rush opened land in that territory, he was one of the first there to stake a claim. After witnessing the death of fourteen men there over claim disputes, he "concluded that it was no place to stop at." He then moved back to Texas, eventually arriving in Fort Worth.[18]

He had been there a day when Washington County Sheriff N.E. Dever received a short telegram. It was from a former Brenham attorney named Randle, and simply read "Do you want Sam Love?" Sheriff Dever had previously written to the sheriff of San Augustine County shortly after the news of the less fortunate Sam Love's death and was already aware the Love he was after was still alive. He quickly responded that he did indeed want what Randle had to offer, and within three-and-a-half hours received a reply from Randle: "Have Sam Love under arrest awaiting your orders." [19]

Sheriff Dever traveled by train to Fort Worth to pick up Love himself, returning the following evening to find "...(a) large number of colored people, both male and female, were at the depot to see him brought in and gazed upon him with wonder, as if they were beholding one who had returned from the dead, as it was believed among a great many that he had been killed. Sam looked pretty badly hacked, but on the way up town recognized and spoke to several of his acquaintances."[20]

He attempted to make bail several times after his return but unsurprisingly was denied bond. In September 1889, two years after he had been accused of forging the school vouchers, he entered a plea of not guilty at the fall session of the district court but was found guilty of embezzlement. He was tearful at the sentencing, where the same judge who had been served by him in the Civil War twenty-five years earlier served to him a sentence of two years in the penitentiary.[21]

In early October, a large crowd of Brenham's Black citizens came to see Love depart on an evening train bound to Fort Bend County. An officer escorted Love and fellow prisoners Bud Morgan, a Black burglar with a two-year sentence and Charles Cooper, a white horse thief saddled with ten years, to E.H. Cunningham's convict farm in Fort Bend County.[22] Cunningham leased prison labor from the state to operate his 5,000-acre plantation, 3,500 acres of which were in sugar cane. It produced up to 400 barrels of sugar a day, and to help produce and get it to market it had "four miles of train railway and two miles of portable railway, which is moved about to all the obscure corners of the place from the main train."[23]

Harvesting sugar cane is extraordinarily difficult work, as Love, who had previously avoided manual labor, was soon to find out. Within a month he was suffering not only from the labor, but also from being punished with twelve lashes for "indolence" as well.[24] "He had never done any work, and his hands became blistered and very sore. And now that they are too sore to work the convict guards are said to be in the habit of whipping and beating him. Some of Sam's white friends have written in his behalf to the guards to be more lenient with him."[25]

All the county officials in Washington County filed a petition with Governor L.S. Ross, who granted a pardon on December 22, 1890, "in consideration of the high character of the signers of the petition for clemency in this case, which induces the belief that the punishment has been ample to vindicate the Law."[26] Love was back in Brenham in time for Christmas.[27]

After his return from prison, Love soon took up teaching again, including at the Peter Wilkinson community three miles west of Brenham.[28] He also was serving with Washington County's Colored Teachers Institute as early as 1893. This gathering of colored teachers was referred to by different names at different times in the press, and Love served various different roles in it, including as a member of the executive committee and the committee on by-laws and constitution.[29] He also would give history talks on the Civil War, perhaps even drawing on his personal experiences in that conflict.[30]

In July 1898, Love suffered a stroke. He received medical care quickly and was improving the next day. From here the existing records become unclear. His wife, Angeline, appears in the 1890 census as the mother of ten children, with only two surviving. She was living with one of them, their daughter Ella, who had married and was now known as Ella Anderson. But Angeline was listed as a widow. A death certificate has not been located for Love, but his stroke was fatal, and a short note in a Brenham newspaper indicates he died on July 11, 1898.[31] There is only one further reference to him in the Brenham papers after the notice of his stroke, a real estate transfer to an S.L Love in 1901.

Sam Love makes one final appearance in the official records as the father of Ella Love Anderson on her tombstone. In 1955 she was buried in Camptown Cemetery, the same cemetery her father had played an instrumental role in establishing almost seventy years earlier.

Chapter 4

# ROBERT S. SLOAN: "TEXAS IS FULL OF OPPORTUNITY"

*Robert, Ketchum and Mattie Sloan*

*Photo courtesy of Gesenia Sloan*

Robert Sloan was born in 1858, probably in Washington County to Maria Dick and a man named Sam, both of whom had been born in Tennessee. In August 1870, when his mother was working as a cook to support Bob and his younger brother, Joe, she married Willis Jordan, whose last name Joe took. Maria and Willis may have had a longer standing relationship, according to genealogist Nick Cimino, though it is unclear how Sloan came to choose his last name. Little else is known about his youth until August 23, 1877, when he married Mattie Knox, a twenty-three-year-old mulatto. By 1880 they were living next to his mother and brother, although Willis doesn't appear to have been there, according to that year's census records. Their first son, Ketchum Allen, was born in 1881, followed by their second son, Samuel, a year later.[1]

The year 1883 marked Sloan's first appearance in the *Brenham Banner* (apart from a notice of his marriage to Mattie), the beginning of almost fifteen years of news accounts. They provide a window into his life as one of the most renowned nineteenth-century Black lawmen in Washington County. Although no Black man ever rose to the level of sheriff in Washington County during the nineteenth century, when Sloan was elevated to the position of constable he was frequently employed to assist the sheriff and local police, including the care of prisoners. In December 1883 the county commissioners approved payment of $10.10 for feeding Ike Crawford and another prisoner. Although allowed $18.25 the following February for feeding prisoners, Sloan's bill of $23.10 for guarding those prisoners was "rescinded and account rejected." This was followed by an order by the court that "all officers, including justices of the peace and constables, will be held to a strict accountability for cash received and prisoners in their charge," apparently an ongoing problem since another constable and two Justices of the Peace also had their reports rejected because reports were "not in conformity with the law."[2]

The duties of a constable were not just confined to the care and feeding of prisoners, and the consequences could go far beyond not being paid for improper paperwork. Seven years after Emancipation, Charley Wilson spent another twelve years in bondage in the state penitentiary. He was from Burton but when he sold some stolen hides in nearby Grimes County, he had learned enough from his years in prison that he was willing to do anything to avoid going back. When and taken to the county jail at Navasota in 1884, he somehow managed to escape and made his way back home by way of Washington. Sloan's jurisdiction included the town of Washington, and that October when he was made aware of Wilson's presence attempted to arrest him. Wilson resisted and in the ensuing struggle was fatally shot, "the ball taking effect in his side toward the back and coming out at the nipple." As a result, Sloan was then charged by the state with murder later that year (later changed to assault with intent to murder), although the charges were only dropped after three years of keeping him in legal limbo. It did not, however, cost him his job as constable.[3]

The office of constable is an elected position, which inevitably involves an immersion into local politics. Sloan was active in the Republican Party in Washington County during the most tumultuous decades following Emancipation. The overwhelming majority of Blacks at the time belonged to the party of Lincoln, and as nearly half of the voting population they wielded considerable political influence. At least three Black men had served as city aldermen, and in 1884 half of the four county commissioners were Black, with other elected offices at the local and state having also been held by Black Republicans.

An essential element of local Republican politics were the late-night party meetings to choose candidates, generally referred to in the press as "owl meetings." The local newspaper defined an owl meeting as a "political gathering of colored voters, held at any time between 8 or 9 p.m. and 4 a.m., at which white office seekers appear and state their claims to the colored voters and are assisted by colored orators, most of whom work for a consideration. The owl meeting is secret in its proceedings, and democratic candidates are vigorously excluded. Wherever there is a large negro population the owl meeting flourished when a canvass is at hand."[4] The night meetings were essential to reach a Black population primarily engaged in agricultural pursuits by day, and provided not only a means of political, but also social engagement. They often included barbecues and music, and liquor often fueled heated debates.

The *Banner* dispatched reporters to cover owl meetings, even "if it has to hire a whole platoon of special owl meeting reporters. So long as the boss owls hold secret meetings, so long will special reporters be kept in the field. The people want to know what the owls are doing."[5] These journalists not only reported on the proceedings but delighted in a good story whenever they got out of control. One such occasion took place in downtown in October 1886 during a particularly contentious meeting when the Republican Party faced losing voters to the recently formed People's Party, also known as the Populist Party. The People's Party was formed in part as an attempt by a primarily Democratic white electorate to draw away Black and German immigrant Republicans with a promise to fight corruption on the local level. The meeting turned violent, as a reporter from the *Brenham Daily Banner* gleefully noted.

> "On Tuesday night there was an owl meeting at the corner of Ant and Quitman streets. Elder Bryan made a very good speech in [sic] behalf of the People's ticket. Hon. Guy then mounted the stand and was expounding the virtues of the Schutze ticket when a row occurred between Manuel Taylor and Gus Hopkins, leaders of rival colored bands. Horace Lindsay went to the assistance of Taylor; knives were brought into requisition and Taylor and Lindsay were both very severely cut; at this writing it is not positively known who did the cutting. Someone on the outside fired a gun: Gus slipped down from the stand like a turtle dropping off a log into the water. The parties are all colored and the fuss was over band matters, having

no political significance whatever.[6]

This was the volatile political environment in which Sloan was submerged in 1886. In early August he spoke in favor of a straight Republican ticket at a gathering that "became quite disorderly and Mr. Chairman Blont left in disgust...After the meeting broke up a good many of the delegates, having no means with which to stay in town all night, mounted their plow 'critters' and started home."[7] Later that month he found himself in court on a charge of disturbing the peace, related to "one of the shindies at the alleged Republican convention." He was found not guilty.[8] Two months later he "was tried for rudely displaying a six-shooter at a public meeting and fined $25 and costs." The newspaper account of the case commented that "this should be a warning to all officers not to make any objectionable display of their six-shooters."[9] This event may well have been related to a political rally, but it was not the first time guns caused a problem at political campaigns or during the actual process of voting itself.

The previous election of November 1884 was one of the first serious challenges presented by the People's ticket. Thirty-nine-year-old A. W. Wilder, who had previously been elected as a state representative in 1872 and may have been the first Black lawyer to practice in the state of Texas, was running for county attorney.[10] Hubert H. Knoxson, a twenty-nine-year-old school teacher from a politically active family, was a county commissioner running for re-election. Both were at the Black schoolhouse on the outskirts of Chappell Hill on November 5, 1884, to witness the counting of the ballots. Each had previously been elected as Republicans, and it was generally felt that Chappell Hill would again vote primarily along those lines.

Just before four o'clock on the morning after the election the votes were still being tallied by the election officials, a small of crowd gathered in the schoolhouse, including Wilder and Knoxson. Another group of Black men sat around a fire a short distance away. Suddenly the back door of the building was forced open and two white men, their faces blackened in disguise, drew pistols on the crowd. After firing a dozen or so shots, the assailants fled, leaving three men wounded. Wilder's left elbow was badly shattered, and Knoxson was struck in the back, with the ball exiting the front of his body. A third man, Lewis Maxey, had also received a "very dangerous" shoulder wound.[11]

Wilder's arm reportedly was amputated as a result of his wounds, and one of the men "died afterwards…in consequence of the wound received at that time."[12] It is not clear if it was Maxey or Knoxson who died, since Maxey is absent from the historic record after this single mention. Knoxson, after winning his re-election bid, died less than a year later after a lengthy illness, possibly because of his wound. The morning after the shootings, Sheriff James Moore arrived with a posse of men and returned the ballot boxes to Brenham, where they were counted under guard. Although law enforcement authorities tried to track down the shooters, none were found before the sheriff went out of office a month later. The search waned under the newly elected sheriff. As a result of this unresolved violence at the ballot box, political violence resurfaced two years in Washington County elections, leading to a threat on Sloan's life, and his involvement, however inadvertent it may have been, would be investigated before the United States Senate.

The election of 1886 in Washington County once again involved the use of firearms, but with a major difference. When a Black candidate and two others were shot at the polling place in 1884, the investigation into the attempted murder went nowhere.

In 1886, several ballot boxes from polling places in the "Black Belt" were stolen and the son of a white candidate shot in the process of attempting to steal another. However, several of the Black witnesses to this attempt to literally steal the election were subsequently jailed and lynched before they could testify to what they had seen.

Polling at Robert Turner Flewellen's house in the Black Belt was quiet and stopped at 6 p.m. on November 2, 1886. Tallying the votes went late into the night. The ballots were counted, each tallied on three separate sheets and then threaded on a string before moving on the next ballot. They included yellow diamond-shaped ballots designed for illiterate voters who were choosing a straight Republican ticket. Late into the process, Lafayette Kirk, the People's candidate for county judge, came by to check on the counting. "Boys, how are you getting along?" he asked. Receiving a positive response, he looked over the tally and walked back over to the bedroom to talk to A. H. Rogers, who had been taking a nap during the count. After talking quietly in private to Rogers, Kirk walked over to the door and called the white election judge to step outside to speak with him. Kirk then left and did not return.[13]

Thirty minutes later, four men showed up at the back door, dressed in yellow slickers with kerchiefs over their faces and white hats pulled low. They drew pistols on the unarmed men in the polling place, demanding "Hand's up!" Amid the commotion as the masked men gathered up the ballot box, several of the Black observers scattered. One of them, Polk Hill, slipped out a door opposite the one the intruders had entered and onto the gallery where he and several others left shotguns. Stepping back in, he shot one of the men in the left side of his face. The rest of the intruders scattered with the ballot box in tow. Left dead on the floor was Dewes Bolton; Hill, nervously laughing that he had killed a man, ran out of the building.[14]

Bolton was the son of a wealthy farmer, D. D. Bolton, who was running for county commissioner, and the son-in-law of the late Judge J. D. McAdoo, one of the most prominent citizens of Washington County. He lay on the floor, covered with a blanket until the next morning. When the sheriff arrived, eight of the witnesses were taken to jail. All were Black and were held without being charged for the next thirty-two days. Polk Hill had escaped.

Shortly after Bolton's death, a coroner's inquest was held, with each of the imprisoned witnesses, as well as the election judges, giving statements. For the Black men being held in conjunction with a white man's murder, the proceedings were frightening. Felix Kinlaw described the inquest and how his deposition was influenced: "I was scared, and I had a right to be scared...They were all around there with guns and pistols, and I was going to talk the best way I thought it was for me to talk, because I was alive and I aimed to live always." Lewis Pennington, a Black election official present at the murder, was also questioned at the inquest, but initially denied seeing Bolton either in disguise or with a pistol. As he explained it, "Well, there were double barreled shotguns and six-shooters around there until I was naturally afraid to tell the truth."[15]

The proceedings concluded that Bolton was killed by Polk Hill, and that the Black men previously jailed as witnesses "were accessories to the killing of deceased; and further believe that deceased came to his death by the advice of Ed. Lockett."[16] Lockett and A. L. "Lonny Gilder" were known as local "scalawags," a derogatory term used to describe white Southerners who supported the Republican Party and Reconstruction efforts. They fled the county in fear for their lives.[17]

Three additional polling places in Republican-dominant precincts had their votes invalidated in the election. Ballots from Lott's Store were being transported to Brenham when three armed men stole them at gunpoint outside of Independence. At the Graball polling place, where Republicans had a five-to-one advantage, three armed and masked white men destroyed the ballots and ballot boxes. At Chappell Hill, the election judge, who was a member of the People's Party, declared that not enough literate and intelligent men could be found to act as election officials, so the polling place was never even opened.[18] In addition, many of the yellow diamond-shaped Republican ballots in Independence were thrown out because the incumbent People's Party candidate, Lafayette Kirk, considered them invalid even though the Texas Supreme Court had declared them legal the previous year. As a result of losing these Republican votes, the People's party won an overwhelming victory, opening the way for later Democratic wins and the demise of the Republican Party as a political force in Washington County.

The day after the election, crowds of armed white men from surrounding towns began to pour into Brenham for an "indignation meeting held at Eldridge Hall" of mounted men armed with shotguns fearing "an anticipated negro insurrection."[19] Lafayette Kirk, the same judge who was at the Flewellen polling place thirty minutes before Bolton's murder, charged that Lockett and Gilder "had sent down to the Graball and Flewellen boxes on the day of the election, had gone there and instructed the negroes to be armed, and to shoot any white man that they found 'monkeying' around the box." It was also rumored that Stephen A. Hackworth, Carl Schutze, James L. Moore, and other Republicans were the ones who had sent Lockett and Gilder out with these instructions.[20]

A Galveston news story captured the meeting's tone. Bolton's murder was laid at the doors of six or seven white Radicals [sic] who made incendiary speeches during the recent canvass, and two of whom instigated the negroes to commit the murder… The committee made a report charging the responsibility for the murder...upon the making of the incendiary speeches to the ignorant and vicious colored people, and condemning in severe terms the owl meetings which were so common during this canvass...The sentiment of every man present was that secret meetings and that seditious speeches to the negroes should be stopped. They believe in free speech and a free press, but they will no longer tolerate incendiary talks to cornfield negroes." Emotions at the meeting were so heated that "the mob was ready to use hemp, and had it not been for cool heads and good counsel violence would have been committed."[21]

Hackworth, a former justice of the peace, real estate speculator and one of the Republican activists who was being condemned at the indignation meeting, later described that afternoon:

> "When these armed men began to pour into Brenham, friends came to myself and Joe Hoffmann, who was in my office, and they warned us to get away. They thought we had better go down to my house, and that we had better not show ourselves on the streets. We went on down to the house while the meeting was in progress, and I do not think we had been there more than twenty-five or thirty minutes before we heard yells. I knew what that meant. I knew it meant danger. I live nearly half a mile from where the meeting was held. In a few minutes after that my son came hurriedly to me, pale and frightened, and said there was great danger; that he was fearful they would come down there. He said he did not know what they were going to do; that Judge Kirk had offered a resolution expelling myself, Moore, Gilder and Lockett from Brenham within twenty-four hours, or from the county; and if we refused to go we were to be put out at the muzzle of shotguns."[22]

After this meeting "threats were generally known there that they were going to kill him"[23] and a fellow Republican, Paul Fricke, stayed up with him for five nights to help protect him when Hackworth refused to leave town. Fricke, who was also white, described the time after the election as "a fearful time there. Why, the Republicans were not allowed to talk to one another. I suppose I had fifty men to come to me and tell me of notes they got not to be caught talking with Republicans; they would not allow them to talk together, and even plenty of Democrats there themselves were afraid to say much." Attempts by Republicans to express their own outrage at the threats and the ballot box thefts were advised against.[24]

For Hackworth, Schutze—publisher of a German language newspaper—and Moore, a former sheriff, the threats on their lives were credible enough that all sold their properties in Washington County at a loss and fled with their families. Shortly after the indignation meeting rumors had spread that Black militias armed with bayonets were threatening to storm the jail house, and the local state militia was called out by the county sheriff. Fearing the rumor was a ruse to expose the jailed witnesses, a portion of the white mob was left to guard the jail house, while the others rode out to find no evidence of an armed insurrection. The following day the eight witnesses were taken from the Washington County jail and housed in Houston for their own safety. Appeals were made to drop the charges against them, but before they could be heard the prisoners were brought back to the county jail in Brenham where, for at least part of the short time they had left on Earth, they were under the care of Robert Sloan.

Around 1 a.m. on December 2, a mob of over seventy-five masked and armed horsemen surrounded the jail, with sentries posted at all the surrounding roads. Under the ruse of having a prisoner to deliver to the jail, they brushed the night guard

– a man named Schley, not Sloan -- aside and stormed inside. Demanding three of the prisoners by name, the mob tied Schley up before locking the remaining five back in their cells. The three kidnapped men, including one who was sixty-five years old, were forced to Sandy Creek just outside of town, where they were lynched and left hanging from a pecan tree. When they were returned to the jail in shrouds later that morning, the other prisoners were allowed to post bond and leave the jail. No effort was ever made to bring any member of the lynching party to justice.

This affront to the political process, which came to be known as the Texas Election Outrage of 1886, led to complaints to the United States Senate. It initiated an investigation that lasted from February 1887 to March 1888. Many witnesses, including Black, white, Republican, and People's party members, traveled from Washington County to Washington, D.C., to participate and give testimony. Among these was Sloan. A correspondent to the Brenham *Banner* commented that he also saw Hackworth, who had coauthored the "memorial" that led to the Senate investigation. The reporter noted the Washington County witnesses also included "a number of 'niggers,' Bunt and Robert Sloan being of the party."[25] Although Sloan never gave any testimony included in the 800-plus-page transcript published by the Government Printing Office in 1889, Hackworth and others who knew him well from their former involvement with the Washington County Republican Party commented on him in considerable detail.

Asked about Sloan, Hackwork referred to the pending charge for the murder of Charley Wilson:

> "He killed a colored man and was indicted three or four years ago for the offense. Up to three or four months

before the election he was an active Republican, acting in good faith with me. He came to me one day and said he had had a talk with H. M. Lewis, the county clerk, with Mr. Herbst, the district clerk, and they had notified him that unless he turned and went over to their side, they would fix up a jury that would convict him. He said he was compelled to go over, and he did so, and became one of the best tools they had…He was stationed at Graball to watch the vote and to report to the Democratic leaders in other parts of the county how the vote was going, so that in the event it was necessary to destroy the ballot boxes they could send Kuklux [sic] down there and destroy them, as was done."[26]

During the course of the investigation, a telegram sent from Sloan to a Democratic lawyer on the night of the murder was admitted into evidence. It read: "Graball gone against the People's ticket four to one. What must we do? Let us hear from you to-night. Flewellen box overflowing against us."[27] It was signed "Robert Sloan." Further corroboration of Sloan's involvement came during the testimony of Lafayette Kirk, who described him as "a negro who supported our ticket. He went around in the canvass; he had been a constable in Washington precinct, and worked down in that precinct, and helped to support our ticket…he was an active supporter of the People's ticket, but he was a Republican. I do not know but two negroes in Washington County who are Democrats, who come out and say so."[28]

Kirk introduced into evidence a note that had been received by Sloan less than a month after the lynching. It was addressed to Bob Sloan and read, with the original language preserved: "Dear Sir: We have cought two of the Dimocrat Chickins, and you and Algie Hunt is our next choice. We expect to kill Dimocrat nigers until we got tow for every one they have killed, yours, most respectfully, Dead [sic]."[29]

During the Senate investigations, a separate trial was held in Austin, with charges filed against Lafayette Kirk and eight others named as defendants in conjunction with the ballot boxes thefts. Hackworth testified that Sloan was named and stated that "it is already proven that he was one of the men in the indictment." Sloan's name did not appear in the indictment, unless he was among the "certain other evil-disposed persons."[30] Using the original transcripts from the trial, in which Kirk and the others were found not guilty, proved problematic. When the transcripts were subpoenaed by the Senate, only fifty-two of the 240 pages of testimony were found after a search by the district clerk in Austin.

Little came of the Senate investigation, except for the surprising level of detail about the events surrounding the Election Outrage in the published congressional records. But shortly afterward, in April 1887, the murder charges against Sloan in the Wilson case were dropped. That appeared to give some validity to Hackworth's testimony that they had been held over Sloan's head in exchange for his cooperation with Kirk to ensure the election of the People's Party candidates.[31] Despite this unfortunate involvement, Sloan remained deeply involved in the fractured Republican Party, serving as chairman of the county's executive committee in March 1888 when they called for a meeting to elect delegates to the state convention.[32] Sloan's willingness to use bellicose means to resolve political disagreements did not seem to have waned. By May he encountered John Cain, a Black lawyer who had been on the other side of the Republican split two years earlier. A disagreement between them deteriorated into fisticuffs and Sloan, whom the newspaper account described incorrectly as a "democratic darkey," got the better of Cain, who was described as "badly worsted."[33]

Business affairs gone bad also tended to be resolved through physical means. In 1889 Sloan had a side business selling firewood, delivering a load for the Levitansky brothers, two traveling salesmen renting a house on the north side of town with another man. They promised payment the following day, but when Sloan came to collect, they tried to convince him to accept shirts instead of cash. Sloan, who "thought he had a sufficient supply (of shirts) on hand," disagreed, and "abusive language" ensued. The three itinerant salesmen thought their numerical advantage could settle the matter and "all three of the peddlers pitched into the darkey, who, although unevenly matched, came off victor. One of the peddlers received a pretty severe scalp wound." The result was a jury trial in which Sloan was fined $5 for assault and $1 for the abusive language. In turn, he filed similar charges against the Levitansky brothers, although they were acquitted of the charge of abusive and offensive language, with the charge of assault dropped.[34]

Selling firewood was not the only job Sloan has after the Election Outrage. Although no longer serving as constable, his experience with the criminal element came into play in caring for prisoners in the county jail. On July 27, 1891, he closed up the jail for the evening, a procedure described in the paper the next day: "It is the custom of the jailer, Bob Sloan, to leave the individual cells open at night and only lock the outside or corridor door. This door is fastened with a heavy lock and a bar which is operated with a lever. This lever is surrounded by an iron box fastened to the outside of the cages and is opened by a combination lock. In this box the cell and corridor keys are also kept."[35] One of the three prisoners who had been released that night from his separate cage within the larger barred enclosure was Lee Hughes. Hughes was awaiting trial for the brutal murder of his wife earlier in the year. He had just been returned from the Lee County jail while new and improved cells were installed. Hughes managed to open the outer door with a looped section of wire and escaped, only to be captured the next day. He was tried, found guilty, and was hung on gallows across the railroad tracks from Camptown Cemetery, a hundred yards from where Sloan's grave would be located decades later.

Together with Robert Kerr, Sloan opened The Black Elephant Saloon in December 1892, a name recognizing its Republican ownership and clientele. It was located on St. Charles Street in the rough-and-tumble red light district of Brenham known as Hell's Half Acre. Located near the train station, it was frequented by a white and Black clientele attracted to the gambling that went on in the back room. The crowd could be rowdy, with a gun being drawn on the white dealer at least once and other patrons having to be policed by Sloan. Several months after opening, it fell victim to a county attorney who "declared before high Heaven that he would enforce the gambling laws for the next two years if the jurymen of the county would stand by him." Kerr and Sloan were arrested for "pursuing an occupation without license" and permitting gambling on the premises. They were released on bond, eventually paying a $10 fine for allowing gambling and the other charge dropped when they took out a license for operating their bar.[36]

That July, Sloan opened Hyde Park, a five-acre plot of land on the northwest side of town to be used as a park "exclusively by colored people." A Hyde Park Association of six directors, including Sloan, was formed to sell "stand privileges" to subsidize the park, which was free to visitors, with baseball games by teams like the Famous and the Sunday Sun. The first weekend the park was open the attendance was relatively small, and the visiting baseball team "failed to appear." Over the coming week crowds gathered there nightly, drawing the editorial ire of the local press over "the disgraceful orgies there nightly. When this park was first opened to the colored people it was announced that it was to be a Sunday resort, but instead it is the nightly gathering place of a crowd that make the nights hideous for the people of that entire section of the city. Of course, Saturday nights are generally the worst, but until long after midnight Wednesday night there was such a hurrah out there that no one in that section of the city could sleep." To make things worse the following night an argument "in which pistols were drawn and lives threatened in language that could heard blocks away" resulted in charges against three men for pulling guns as well as cursing, which was also a criminal offense at the time. The disruptions over the next few days calmed down enough that the *Brenham Banner* took "pleasure in giving the colored management of Hyde Park credit for keeping good order...and trusts that it will never again have occasion to score them for disturbances." At least part of the calming effect was due to a mayoral appointment of Sloan and fellow manager Gus Hopkins as "special police to keep order."[37]

Sloan had run for constable but lost the previous year. Despite this he remained effective in maintaining order, as signaled by his mayoral designation as a special policeman for Hyde Park. It apparently was a trait that ran in his family, with his brother Jordan also serving as a peace officer in adjacent Brazos County. In September Jordan "became involved in a quarrel with a crowd of young white men" and was attempting to arrest one of them when he was shot by another, the bullet passing through his chest in a flesh wound but exiting to break his arm. Although one of his assailants was charged with attempted murder, two of the others were released on bond. Jordan feared they still wanted to "do him up" and telegraphed his brother to come stay with him, returning with Sloan to Brenham a week later.[38]

Two days after Sloan brought his brother home, his son,

Sammie, was mangled under the train, dying a week later. Sloan was no stranger to loss, having just three years previously lost three sisters to consumption, the last being his sixteen-year-old sister Malissa Jordan, who had been buried at a largely attended service in Camptown Cemetery.[39] The loss of his son must have been even more painful for him, especially as he pursued his lawsuit against the railroad over the coming years, having to relive the moments leading up to his tragic accident over and over again. As likely as not it further fired his sense of the need for justice and the righting of wrongs in the years to come.

Samuel Sloan was delivering dinner to a prisoner in jail, a man by the name of Bluman who had been there for almost a year awaiting an appeal, convicted of having burned his store in Giddings in a fire that grew to consume a block of adjacent buildings. His wife, who was described as having a nervous nature, was at home taking care of their two children, the youngest who had been born while her husband was in jail. So, she had hired eleven-year-old Sam to deliver morning and evening meals in a basket complete with plates and a pitcher of drink to her husband, paying him $1.50 a week to do so. At four foot tall and about seventy pounds, the first-born son of Robert and Mattie Sloan was energetic and enterprising, making money after school waiting tables, washing dishes, and running errands for white folk. He also helped his mother open the church where she was a sexton and sweep it out. When she was taking in laundry for washing and ironing, he would help her pick it up, setting the fires for the washtubs, emptying them, and then delivering the clothes back to her clients and picking up payment. He cared for his father's horses and other stock, taking over the job and doing better at it than the man his father previously had been paying the same amount. Reliable and well mannered, Sam was well respected by family, friends, and employers.

Being diligent, he also was anxious to deliver Bluman's Sunday evening meal on September 24, 1893. It was around 5:30 in the afternoon, and he had picked up the meal from the Bluman house 500 yards south of the railroad track on Market Street. But across from the Central Depot he found his way blocked by the Houston and Texas Central train that was stopped on the tracks. By city ordinance trains were not supposed to stand on the tracks for more than five minutes, so Sam waited for it to pass so he could go to the jail on the north side to deliver the supper. Growing impatient after ten minutes of waiting, he asked one of the brakemen on the train if he could cross between the boxcars to the other side. Not receiving an answer the first time, he asked the brakeman again and received a gruff response. "Go on across, you damned kid, and get out of my way."[40]

Sam had just slid between the cars and had almost made it across when they suddenly lurched forward, knocking him down to the tracks. As he fell his left leg was caught between the outer flange of the wheel and the rail, mangling it. Split open from the knee to the ankle, the bone was chipped and exposed. Several other men who had been waiting for the train to move on were at first struck with horror at what they had just witnessed, then ran around the train to his side. Seller Tolan was one of the first there, recognizing him as Robert Sloan's boy. He picked Sam up and carried him to Sloan's father's saloon, the Black Elephant.[41]

Bringing him back home, Sam's mother, Mattie, and his father cared for him day and night, his father hiring a man to tend to his saloon. Two of Brenham's leading physicians tended to the young child, and though Sam was in excruciating pain and desperately needed surgery on the leg, the doctors couldn't operate for fear that he couldn't tolerate it and would die from shock. After almost a full week of this suffering, Sam quietly passed away at 4:15 in the morning the following Sunday.

He was buried later that evening, with services conducted by Reverend P. M. Carmichael of the African Methodist Episcopal Church. The funeral was well attended by family and friends, including Sam's younger brother, Ketchum Allen. Also present were members of the Pleiades Lodge Number 6, to which Sam had belonged. The lodge was comprised of young children and associated with the Seven Stars of Consolidation, a fraternal organization widely popular in Brenham's Black community at the time and devoted to benevolence and charitable causes, including assistance to ill members and assistance with funeral costs. While is not clear from records where Sam was buried, it is reasonable to assume he was buried in the Sloan plot at Camptown Cemetery.[42]

Normally, little would be known now about Sam and his tragic death aside from the single short notice about his death and funeral in the local edition of the *Brenham Daily Banner*. Yet the details of that fatal encounter under the boxcars and his entrepreneurial spirit come to light because his father sued the Houston and Central Texas Railroad for their negligence in the death, an incredible undertaking at a time when railroads were powerful corporations and even more incredible because he eventually won the suit. His father also was fearless enough that he later sued another railroad when he was denied seating to make way for white customers. That persistent courage made him one of the most revered Black lawmen in Washington County at the time of his son's death. Sam must have been very proud of his father, Robert S. Sloan, known to his friends as Bob.

Two months after his son's death, Sloan was once again serving as a deputy under Sheriff Dilmus E. Teague. On December 19, he arrested John Hood in Brenham and placed him in the Washington County jail. The marshal of Bryan had offered a $25 reward for his capture on a misdemeanor charge and for default on a court judgment. Later that same week, Sloan accompanied Sheriff Teague to St. Louis in pursuit of Henry Voss, who had been indicted on charges of a murder near old Washington and the alleged rape of his daughter, then jumping bail before his case came up before the courts that fall. Voss eventually wrote a letter to his wife, apparently thinking he was safe from apprehension, but was arrested by Teague and Sloan on Christmas Eve, his Christmas gift being a free trip back to Washington County.[43]

More events in Sloan's life begin to emerge in press accounts as he again operated as a deputy sheriff. Some offered sketches of arrests, such as the apprehension of Jim Brown, an out-of-towner from Robertson County for "obtaining money under false pretenses" and the all too common crime of carrying a pistol in public. Others were lengthy newspaper articles about Sloan's career and exploits. One such story involved Willis McIntyre, an ex-convict who had served twelve years in the penitentiary and clearly did not care to return to a life of incarceration.[44]

After serving his prison term, McIntyre once again got on the wrong side of the law. Wanted on warrants for default of court judgments in Burleson County, he was discovered by Sloan and Constable Boyd, who had defeated Sloan in a previous election for constable, at the home of Ida Looscan. He refused to surrender, saying he'd rather die than to be arrested, drawing his pistol and pointing it at Sloan before changing his mind, eventually surrendering it to Boyd. Instead of being returned to Burleson County, McIntyre wound up serving out a sentence on the Buchanan brothers' county convict farm on the western bank of the Brazos river. It notorious for "the bad treatment of county convicts.," and when W.P. Doran had been sent there to investigate conditions he reported that "there is no better material in the State than the denizens of Hell's Half Acre in Brenham...send the hoodlums to the convict farm and make Christians of them, or they will soon lapse into African barbarism."[45] But McIntyre not be there for long.[46]

One evening around 6 o'clock two months later, he and another prisoner, John Anderson, made their escape from the convict farm. Although bloodhounds picked up their scents, they had to be called off because the farm's guard couldn't leave other prisoners alone. A courier had to be sent to inform the sheriff, but it wasn't until early the next morning that the chase resumed through the Brazos River bottom, giving the escapees more than a ten-hour head start.

The next morning, the escapees were discovered hiding in a cabin north of Brenham and twenty miles from the convict farm. They protested that they wouldn't surrender, and Sheriff Teague, Bob Sloan, and a posse of nine others set out to capture them. Surrounding the two-room shanty, three members of the party quickly entered with a six-shooter and a shotgun; Sloan remained outside with the others to prevent any escape. As they attempted to enter the second room, McIntyre managed to get off one shot, narrowly missing its target before the room was filled with lead from the posse, wounding Anderson but miraculously leaving McIntyre unscathed but much more willing to negotiate a surrender. As a three-time loser, he was sent back to prison for life.[47]

Acting as a "special deputy sheriff" for the sheriff's department in July 1894, Sloan was instrumental in solving a long ongoing theft that was uncovered at Haubelt's Bros. Store in Brenham. A Black employee had been making sure he was inside the store when it closed at night and then passing goods through an open window to his accomplices, another young Black man with the unlikely nickname of Jack-in-the-Bush and a white "race rider." They never touched the cash drawer, and the items of clothing they had been stealing were in small enough amounts to remain unnoticed. But one evening a woman passing by noticed them and "supposed it was some of the proprietors or clerks, seeing they were so bold as to hold a consultation at the window and pass out the stolen items."[48] The crime was discovered after she mentioned this peculiar event to one of the store owners, but it was impossible to determine what was missing out of the store's large inventory.

When Matilda Values heard of the arrest of one of the suspects who had stored some of the stolen items at her house, she "at once reported their whereabouts to Robert Sloan, as she did not want to be connected with the burglary in any way." Upon solving yet another case and recovering the stolen property, the *Banner* soon reported that Sloan "has shown considerable proficiency in working up theft cases among colored people." He also made a favorable impression on the Haubelt brothers, one of whom was a city alderman. That soon would work in his favor.[49]

Earlier, in April of the same year, Sloan had been circulating petitions among both the white and Black populations. "The one among the colored people asked that the city council appoint a policeman for Camptown, reciting that it was necessary for the protection of that portion of the city, and the churches there, and that if the council acceded to this demand, that Sloan be appointed to fill the position. The other petition presented to the white voters was for his appointment in case the city decided to have a policeman there." The *Banner* endorsed him at the time for such a position: "Robert Sloan has done considerable work in this line in the capacity of special deputy for Sheriff Teague and Constable Boyd, and has always proved worthy of the trust reposed in him…he will no doubt make as good an officer as any they could get."[50]

When the petitions were received by the city council, they then referred them to the finance committee, which included

Alderman Haubelt, co-owner of the store whose burglary Sloan had helped solve earlier that year. But when no further action was taken on their petition, the clergymen of Camptown, acting on the behalf of their community, submitted another petition. It reasoned that "there are frequent and oft repeated disturbances down there which endangers the life and property of the residents and is obnoxious to the better elements of the citizens," again requesting Sloan be given the position of policeman there.[51]

Sloan finally was appointed policeman at the rate of pay of $30 a month on September 6, 1894. However, his appointment did not last long. Two weeks later, the same council "discontinued" him and had their secretary cut him a check "for amount due... owing to the financial condition of the city" in the wake of the depression of 1893, which led to one of the country's worst economic downturns from 1893-1897.[52]

Sloan remained active in the Camptown community outside of law enforcement and politics. At Mount Rose Baptist Church in May 1894, he was elected "worthy marshal" of the Seven Stars of Consolidation, the same benevolent organization that had come to his aid upon the death of his son Sam the previous year. He continued to play a role in organizing the annual Emancipation celebrations held annually in Brenham, serving as one of nine special policemen sworn in especially to keep order during the festivities. When Camptown's Common Toiler and Excelsior Clubs met at the Odd Fellows Hall a block north of the church to form a McKinley and Reed Club, supporting the eventual nomination of the Republican candidate who became the twenty-fifth president, he was appointed to the executive committee.[53]

In February 1896 Sloan also spoke at the Knights of Pythias Hall at an "indignation meeting" of over 500 Black citizens following the infamous murder of Thomas Dwyer, one of the wealthiest and most well-respected citizens in Washington County. Dwyer had been murdered at his office, which had been rifled through and his pocketbook found open. His body had been thrown down a cistern and recovered by "a negro boy" who ventured into the deep waters to bring the body to the surface. Dwyer had been beloved among the Black community as someone who "was affectionate and always gave work to those who would seek it and would often seek the poor and give them work." He was also a staunch Republican who had "always championed the cause of his party among his political opponents anywhere and always maintained the best relations with them."[54]

Sloan also remained active in the turbulent churning of the local Republican party. Before the elections of 1894, several prominent white Democrat candidates spoke before a large Black crowd at the Goodwill Baptist Church and schoolhouse. They were introduced by R. J. Moore, a former Black state representative from Washington County who had been elected on the People's ticket in 1886. Sloan expressed his support for the candidates on a split ticket. Though no longer a chairman, he was elected a delegate in an alternate 1896 Republican convention called in response to a prior convention chaired by Sloan's old nemesis, lawyer Joe Cain.

This was also a period when Sloan finally began reaping some benefit from his political career. In 1895 he was appointed to the position of porter in the state senate. The *Banner* stated that this was because he had "worked hard for the Democratic ticket during the last campaign and his friends have not forgotten him in the division of spoils," a curious statement in light of his long-standing work in the Republican Party and membership in the McKinley and Reed Club. He did, however, present a cane on behalf of the senate porters to the Democratic president of the state senate, "who gracefully acknowledged the compliment." Sloan also served in 1897 as a senate porter, and in 1899 as a senate mail carrier.[55]

By the late 1890s Sloan was becoming increasingly involved in the Baptist church. He had been working with Rev. Mose Johnson, head of the Mount Rose Baptist Church, for some years at civic events, and in 1896 the two of them served as delegates at the Good Hope Western Baptist Association in Marlin. In 1896 Sloan was named as the president of the reorganized Baptist Young People's Union, which was meeting at Mount Rose and remained active in the B.Y.P.U, serving as president numerous times and participating until at least 1915, a year before his death.[56]

At some point Sloan was ordained as a Baptist minister. The 1900 census listed him as living in McGregor, Texas, and his occupation described as clergyman. His name is also given as "Ketchum," as is his nineteen-year-old son, who was described as being "at school." He was still listed as living with Mattie, with a Walter Sloan (25), and his sister Lennae (15) living two households away. It is unlikely they are Sloan's children since Walter's parents' birthplace is listed as unknown and Lennae's as Louisiana. However, it is tempting to think there may be other relationships that could shed light on the unknown origins of Sloan's chosen last name.

The press reported that Rev. R. S. Sloan spoke at the General Bowen Baptist Association in 1903, and his "address was a telling blow to sin and ignorance."[57] He also is referred to as being from McGregor, a small town just southwest of Waco, and affiliated with the Central Texas Academy as "financial agent." The academy, located in Waco, also was referred to the Central Texas Colored Industrial School and later as Central Texas College, which was founded by the General Baptist Convention of Texas in 1901 and supported by tuition, the Baptist Association, donation, and other sources. In the 1904 Texas Almanac and Industrial Guide listing for McLennan County, the Central Texas Academy is listed as being exclusively for girls and located at 600 North 6th Street, with property valued at $12,500. Sloan had been there since at least 1902, when he was working to raise $500 toward paying the school's old debt, as well improving the school's building and grounds. The fundraising efforts on his behalf were reported as being "met with good success in every town in the state where he has visited." The following year the cornerstone was laid for a new girl's dormitory, presided over by the grand master of the Free and Accepted Masons.[58]

Being quite successful at fundraising for the Central Texas Academy the 1905 Negro Baptist Missionary convention, "Rev. R.S. Sloan, financial agent of Central Texas academy, rendered a very creditable report. Rev. Mr. Sloan has worked wholly among the white people of Texas and showed over $1000 given by the white citizens, especially of the small towns of Texas."[59] He was identified as associated with the Central Texas Academy as late as 1907, serving on the board of endowments for the Negro Baptist Convention of Texas. In 1912 he expressed his deep faith in the usefulness of this church work in furthering education when he addressed the Baptist Young People's Union: "Texas is full of opportunity for every man, woman and child, and you have only to prepare and take them up. You need not expect to make any headway without work. There are too many idlers in this country, men who do nothing but find fault with creation – they never do anything themselves and get in the way of others. They complain about the negroes, they complain about the white people, they complain about the weather, in fact, they are just in their own way and should be transported to heaven or some other port. Let us educate the young people in church work, educate them for usefulness, and we will be kind to ourselves as well as to the communities in which we live."[60]

It is not clear when Sloan joined the Masons, but it was most likely before the cornerstone for the girl's dormitory was laid at the Central Texas Academy with ceremonies officiated by Grand Master of the Free and Accepted Masons. The Rev. R.S. Sloan was there when "the Most Worshipful Grand Lodge of the colored Ancient Free and Accepted Masons" held its twenty-ninth session in Houston in July 1904, with members including "the leading professional and businessmen of the race, and any number of sectarian and secular teachers and preachers representing the different denominational schools and colleges throughout the state." He was appointed to serve on three committees, dealing with education, temperance and the third a "special committee." He was clearly proud of his membership, since in an undated photograph of Sloan one can make out a Masonic pin on his left lapel.[61]

By 1910, Sloan was living in Houston, though his occupation was listed in the census as "manager." The industry appears to be "Farm" and employment type as "Emp," which leaves it unclear if he is the employer or employee. The census also lists him as living with his wife, Mattie, and his son Ketchum, who had completed three years of college at Prairie View Normal School. Afterward, he had been working as a railway postal clerk on the Fort Worth and San Angelo line. In 1904 Ketchum was transferred to the Houston and Shreveport line, earning as a federal employee the princely sum of $,1000 a year. Following President Wilson's "curtailment of the privileges of the Negroes employed in this service," Ketchum became active in the formation of the National Alliance of Postal Employees in Houston, following President Wilson's restrictions on Black employees in the federal government.

The household also had two additional young children in the family – Bessie, twelve, and Mabel, seven, both listed as daughters. Bessie does not appear in the 1900 census for the Sloan family, so they may have been adopted. The Sloans were living in Houston at 3614 Chenevert Street, with the family matriarch, Maria Jordan, living around the corner at 1816 Holman, which indicated that Sloan was still very close to his mother.[62]

Another event demonstrating the strength of Robert Sloan's character occurred when he was fifty-four years old. In 1889 Texas enacted a separate coach law that required railroad companies to maintain separate coaches for Blacks and whites, a law that was further strengthened in 1891. In 1907 similar statutes were enacted covering street cars, and in 1909 separate depot waiting areas also were mandated. The laws had been challenged, but Sloan played an instrumental role in mounting another legal challenge to the railroads about how these laws were being implemented. On July 19, 1911, he and eleven others purchased tickets from the Galveston, Harrisburg and San Antonio Railroad to travel back on the train from Liberty to Houston for a religious function. The conductor refused to allow them on board the train, while allowing other white passengers on board. Each of the eleven filed suit against the railroad, claiming they were "greatly humiliated, outraged and mortified" and "that the agent of the defendant railroad company discriminated against them because they were colored and permitted white passengers to ride on the same train and at the same time."[63]

By December 1912, the case of R.S. Sloan vs. Galveston, Harrisburg and San Antonio Railway Company had made its way to Harris County Court, with Judge Clark Wren presiding. Earlier appeals had been overturned, and this time Sloan's motion for a new trial was overturned, too. The other plaintiffs already had lost their cases to the unassailable power of Jim Crow laws in Texas at the time, but Sloan showed an unwavering willingness to stand up for what he knew was right despite the odds. In 1913 nine of the cases finally were settled with the railroad paying a judgment of ten dollars, and the cases dismissed.[64]

The few remaining newspaper accounts of Robert Sloan's life mostly were related to his ongoing work in the Baptist church and with the Baptist Young People's Union. He moved to Stafford, Texas, where he was still living with his wife and still active as a Mason, serving as the a founding member and first "Worshipful Master" when the Attentive Ear Lodge was established in Stafford in July 1911, the stated purpose being "to aid widows, orphans, to give college scholarships to need students and assist the community at all times."[65] His last reported occupation was "gospel minister," which was listed on his death certificate.

On Saturday night, October 21, 1916, Sloan was "attending a negro supper and standing close to a dancing platform" in Richmond, Texas. Around 11 o'clock he was shot in the chest at close range, the .38 caliber bullet penetrating his heart and killing him quickly. The case was presented to a grand jury, and though little testimony came from people who had been in the crowd about the motivation, Sherman Allen was indicted for his murder even though the case never came to trial. However, on April 21, 1917, Frank Robinson, a Black farmer from nearby Stafford who was known to drink a bit was found guilty of murder for Sloan's death after he tried to implicate "three other negroes who were released after giving bonds of 1 cent each." Although he was sentenced to forty-five years in prison, Robinson was pardoned in 1926 after serving nine years of his sentence.[66]

This tragic death was noted in the Brenham newspaper with a short obituary. "Old Negro Resident Dead. Bob Sloan, Lately of Stafford, Was Once Active in Local Colored Politics. Bob Sloan, negro, for many years a resident of this city, died at his home in Stafford, Saturday, and the body was brought to Brenham for interment today. Sloan was active among his own people and took a leading part in the colored politics of the country, voting the Democratic ticket straight. He had the respect of all the white citizenship."[67]

Sloan was returned to Brenham for the last time for burial in the Sloan plot in Camptown Cemetery. This plot, surrounded by a simple wire fence, was probably the same one where his sisters and son had been buried, but his is the only grave marker there. It simply gives his name, date of birth and date of death, above which is engraved the gates of heaven opening with a dove carrying a pennant reading "At Rest in Heaven." Atop it all is an open book, symbolizing either the Bible, the significance of education, or perhaps both. For now, it can also signify the story of his life, now opened to those who care to remember him.

Robert Sloan was survived by his son Ketchum, who had married Susan Gladys Ball in 1913 and fathered four children. On December 4, 1921, Ketchum bought some property in Brenham with the assistance of a promissory note from Louisa Mangrum, the namesake for Mangrum Street, where Camptown Cemetery is located. However, the loan was eventually defaulted on. He eventually moved to New Orleans sometime before 1940 and was working part time as a painter before his death in 1958. After her husband's death, Mattie moved in with Ketchum and received a payment of death benefits to her in 1917 on behalf of her husband's dutiful service as a member of the Prince Hall Grand Lodge of Texas.[68]

*Photo Credit: Charles Swenson*

---

**Acknowledgments**—*This story owes an immeasurable debt of gratitude to Gesenia Sloan-Pena, whose efforts to find out more about her great-great-great grandfather led to his story coming to light, and for her kind permission to use these photographs. I'd also like to acknowledge Nick Cimino for letting me know that I had left Robert Sloan out of an early census of Camptown Cemetery and his many valuable additions to this story. I could keep on going on and on in gratitude, but I would be remiss if I didn't also mention Eddie Harrison, whose devoted work in preserving Camptown Cemetery and the rich history it holds have been my inspiration throughout this project.*

## Chapter 5

# THE LONG, STRANGE JOURNEY OF HIRAM WILLIAMS

Like those of so many others buried in Camptown Cemetery, Hiram Williams' journey began in slavery and the forced progeny of white and Black blood. After a stint in Brenham's short-lived black militia, the Brenham Blues, he took on a life of fighting and gambling, winding up in one of the most dangerous and violent areas of Brenham, Hell's Half Acre. To escape a charge of attempted murder of a police officer and possible lynching, he led a life on the run through much of the American West before he was exonerated of that crime. He participated in the Spanish-American War as part of an all-Black volunteer regiment in Cuba before eventually returning to remarry his wife and make his final home in Brenham, just a few blocks away from Camptown Cemetery.

On December 20, 1858, Hiram was born into bondage in Louisiana to Malissa and Clark Williams.[1] Little is known about his early childhood, his parents or how he came to arrive in Texas. His first appearance in the records is the 1870 census, at which time he was living with his mother next door to Wiley Hubert, a well-to-do carpenter and one of the prominent Black citizens of the Camptown area of Brenham.[2] Although his father is not mentioned in this census (his name only appears on his death certificate), he was a mulatto, which brings up questions of parentage for those born into slavery. In 1894 a reporter for *The Galveston Daily News* described him as "rather a good-looking man, almost white, with black curly hair."[3] His mother is listed as a mulatto, thirty-nine years old, as well as all his siblings. She owned her own house worth $200, as well as personal property listed with a value of $200. Also in the home were four other siblings; Mary, a seventeen-year-old laborer and the only child born in Texas; Pierce, a fifteen-year-old news boy; Henry, seven; and another sister whose name is not clear in the census. Hiram was employed as a domestic servant, and attended school within the past year, with later records indicating his education only reached to the third grade.

Hiram's first appearance in the Brenham papers came with the announcement of his marriage to Rhoda Rodgers on December 12, 1878.[4] This marriage did not last long, and seems to have ended with some acrimony, since in the 1880 census, eighteen months after their marriage, Hiram is listed as widowed, with a ten-year-old son, Clark Williams.[5] This makes it unclear if they were just divorced or separated instead, with the census possibly making assumptions because she wasn't present. They were eventually remarried some forty years later.

Shortly after Hiram's first marriage, a Black military company of Texas volunteer guards was formed in Brenham, in accordance with the militia laws at that time. They were called the Brenham Blues, and after the filing bond was granted, the forty-eight members received the Springfield rifles that had belonged to a former militia group, the Brenham Greys. Under the leadership of Captain C.C. Coleman, Hiram was named first lieutenant. Around 10 at night on July 31, 1880, he and the rest of the company paraded under torchlight down the streets of Brenham, accompanied by a brass band. The company proceeded to Camptown, where they gathered at the school house for a fundraising dinner that helped acquire uniforms.[6] It is not clear how long Hiram remained in the militia, but the Brenham Blues disbanded within a year of their participation in the Emancipation celebration parade -- in full uniform and with muskets -- in 1881. [7]

Following this account, newspaper reports regarding Hiram reveal a darker side of his nature. From 1880 to 1881, at least eight articles in the *Brenham Banner* reported his fights or court cases for fighting, assault, being drunk and disorderly, or use of abusive language. Most altercations were with fellow Blacks, such as Dick Riley, Bill Price, or Injun Bill, but Hiram was not beyond carrying the fight to whites as well.[8] As a Galveston newspaper later reported, "(h)e was raised in Brenham, and from early youth his name has been frequently found on the criminal dockets of the courts. Having a little education, he was always stirring up mischief between the races, and never hesitated to show his enmity for the white people."[9] At the Central Railroad passenger depot in January 1881, he got into a fight with a white man who insulted a Black woman. Another white man pulled a gun on him, and although it "for a time looked as if it might become interesting,"[10] the police stepped in to prevent an early end to the story of Hiram Williams.

Larger problems loomed as he continued to broaden his horizons. His travels frequently took him to Houston, where he once again became well known to the police. But in April 1882 he was arrested in Waco for involvement in the robbery and murder of a white man.[11] He was still being held there in 1883 when he and two other "jail birds" attempted an escape. They had nearly cut their way through their prison bars with files made from a kitchen knife and a pocket knife before they were caught.[12]

Although still in jail in Waco as late as June 1884, Hiram eventually was released and found his way back to Brenham, where he once again was in legal hot water, despite his increasing skill in getting out of trouble.[13]

The *Brenham Banner* reported that December 11, 1884, "was a day that will long be remembered by the colored sports of the city. The police went fishing for them; they set hoop nets, trammel nets, wing nets and also draw a long seine; when the nets had all been taken up and the seine drawn it, it was found that fifteen able-bodied colored gamblers had been caught." Two had their case continued and twelve of the fifteen were fined, although five of them used their winnings to pay "$5 and trimmings each." Seven others were confined to jail to work off their fines working on street repairs. But only one case, that of Hiram Williams, was dismissed, according to the report: "Hiram proved that he was so sharp a gambler that no one would play with him, consequently he had done no gambling."[14]

Hiram again frequented one of the most notorious areas in Brenham, Hell's Half Acre. Like many sizable cities, Brenham had a red light district specializing in drink, gambling, and prostitution. Its exact location was unclear and probably somewhat fluid, though it seemed to center around several blocks south of the town square, bounded on the south by the Buzzard's Roost[15] and on the west by Coon Flats.[16] A general proximity to the railway depot assured an ongoing stream of clientele looking for a good time and colorful but shady characters willing to make them think they could find it there. They provided a ready way into town when business was thriving and a quick way of leaving during periodic attempts to clean up the area. It was also conveniently located near to the calaboose, or city jail, located on Quitman Street behind the county jail.

One of the earliest references to Brenham's version of Hell's

Half-Acre is found in a Galveston newspaper from 1876. It tells of a number of Black and white citizens who had been arrested there for gambling:

> These prisoners have all been committed in due course of law, and it is the duty of the Sheriff to keep them safely in jail until lawfully released; but the *Banner* is informed by the night policemen that a number of the gambling gentlemen have been turned out after dark and allowed to go where they please. A policeman says on Saturday night he saw four or five of these prisoners around town generally, a party of them in their old tramping ground—Hell's half-acre [sic]; and that with some difficulty he succeeded in capturing one of them—a very bad one—and succeeded in landing him in the city bastille. As the case stands, these men are simply being boarded at the expense of the county and allowed unrestricted liberty going and coming at will.[17]

The city fathers periodically felt pressure to clean up the area, especially when other newspapers began to give it unwelcome publicity, such as that found in an Austin paper, *The Weekly Democratic Statesman:* "Fanny Watson, a dusky queen of the Hell's Half Acre of Brenham, was fatally shot Friday night…Jim Simpson, colored, is the head devil of hell's Half Acre at Brenham…It was too cold for "Hell's Half-Acre" in Brenham to bubble up very fiercely Christmas week, and even whisky froze in some of the dens of the ghastly suburb."[18] From January to October 1877, at least three separate and apparently unsuccessful efforts to clear out the "denizens of this sink of iniquity" occurred, usually by offering the choice of jail or leaving town.[19]

Getting rid of Hell's Half-Acre turned out to be uncommonly difficult, at least partly because of the continuing appeal of its illicit pleasures to so many local citizens and visitors. In one account, a white visitor in February 1885 lost money and valuables after making a stop in Hell's Half-Acre:

> Thursday an old man named Tom Flippen, who formerly lived in this county, was robbed of $130... Flippen was drunk and fell into the hands of thieves. He was steered to a negro bagnio in Hell's Half acre, a notorious locality and later to another house of the same character in Coon valley, a settlement two or three squares south of the union depot. He went to bed in one of the houses after dark and after staying two or three hours he emerged only to find that his wealth had vanished. A copper-colored negro named Frank Brown aged about 25 years, acted as steersman and ran Flippen into the dens. After the "loot" had been obtained the accountant of the mob divided it up by long division, he obtaining a liberal share. He was first robbed of his silver at Caroline Sweetning's in Hell's Half acre, and later of his currency at Becky Vaughn's in Coon flat. Late on Friday evening, Rena Vaughn, Becky Vaughn's daughter, was caught in an up-town saloon with Flippen's fine plain gold ring ornamenting one of her dingy left fingers. Frank Brown, the pilot, Becky Vaughn, the bagnioist, and Ed Shelby, a one-legged white man, who has for some time been gate-keeper at the union depot, were arrested Friday... After dark Caroline Sweetning and Rena Vaughn were arrested and jailed. There seems to have been an organized band of colored hyenas, who for a long time have been preying on unwary strangers who had picnicked on rifle whiskey,

and who after they had been robbed would rather stomach their losses than to "squeal."[20]

Murder was a frequent crime in Hell's Half Acre, leading one Galveston newspaper to comment that "(t)he mere fact that one negro has shot and killed another is so common as to excite no more comment than the wringing of a chicken's neck by the family cook."[21] But an underlying hostility towards attempts at law enforcement in the area were growing. In February 1887, a particularly dangerous character named Jim Smith was murdered there, possibly as the result of "a conspiracy...by five or six negro prostitutes and three or four negro men to make away with Smith." There was an effort to blame the murder on Ed Inge, a Black policeman in Brenham who had killed several other Blacks in the line of duty, though he was cleared by the results of a postmortem examination.[22]

Hiram was caught up in one of the most notorious backlashes against attempts to police Hell's Half Acre. Around one in the morning of October 1, 1887, John Lockett, a white night policeman, was breaking up a fight there outside of a late-night dance. He was set upon by three men, and while one held his arms so another could bludgeon him, another cut his throat from ear to ear, severing his windpipe as well as slashing his mouth and head. When Lockett attempted to pull his pistol to fend off the attack, it was wrested from him, and he was shot in the wound that had been opened up in his throat. Fortunately, Marshal Swain had been already summoned, and Lockett was rescued, although it took him over five months to recover from the assault. Hiram was soon implicated.

As soon as assistance could be procured, Lockett

was removed, and all that the combined medical skill of the city could do was at his service. He could not speak and Marshal Swain immediately started in search of his assailants with such clues as he could get. Strangely enough one of the negroes whose name Lockett afterwards gave [sic] as one of his assailants offered his services very officiously to the Marshal and was very certain that he could render valuable assistance in hunting down the perpetrators of the outrage. As soon as he was able the wounded man with blood streaming from his hands traced the names of Hiram Williams and Sam Rucker as two of the men and described the other one fully not knowing his name. They were soon found and taken in. The third one calls himself Henry Bassett, and was identified by Lockett. He is a strange negro. Hiram Williams is a gambler and one of the most vicious and dangerous negroes in town. He figured in a killing in Waco a year or two ago and has been in innumerable scrapes in various places.[23]

Talk of lynching the prisoners quickly began to circulate, and the sheriff moved the prisoners to Bellville in Austin County for their own protection.[24] "...(H)ad not wise precaution been taken by the sheriff of the county to remove the wretches charged with the cowardly crime; the good name of this county might have again suffered at the hands of Judge Lynch."[25] This was a real possibility since less than a year earlier three Black prisoners being held in the Washington County jail were abducted and lynched in the middle of the night by a crowd of outraged citizens, as part of what came to be known as the Election Outrage of 1886 in later Senate investigations.[26]

A week after the attempted murder indictments had been

handed back by a grand jury against Rucker, Williams and Bassett, Hiram lawyered up early with two attorneys. Within two weeks they had filed a motion of continuance on the grounds of "...absence of witnesses, by whom the defense proposed to prove, that Hiram Williams was elsewhere when the assault was committed, that in fact another person, viz. Ben Hill committed the assault, that the razor found near the scene of the assault was Ben Hill's razor, that immediately after the assault Ben Hill fled the country and is now a fugitive from justice, and various other facts and circumstances."[27] Within three weeks Henry Bassett had been convicted in a separate trial and sentenced to the maximum penalty, seven years in the penitentiary, and was on his way to prison.[28]

Hiram and his lawyers kept up their legal maneuverings early, seeking to avoid the indictment being served because of the omission of the phrase "make an assault" in the copy.[29] At one time they even managed to have the original indictment thrown out on the grounds that the grand jury had thirteen jurors instead of twelve. There were even reports of threats being made against witnesses in the case.[30] Although he had been offered bail earlier and decided it was safer to remain in jail, after fifteen months in jail in Bellville his bond of $500 was finally secured by Mr. Ellis, a local banker.

Hiram jumped bail the day before his trial and disappeared for the next five years.

In August 1893, a curious letter arrived at the Houston office of George Ellis, the sheriff of Harris County. It was from Sheriff Matthews, the sheriff in Tacoma, Washington, "inquiring as to who wants a negro man, Hiram Williams, for murder committed about four years ago. Williams, he says, is understood to have escaped from jail somewhere in Texas, may be had if wanted for he is evidently in a safe place, though a long way from home," with a notice to that effect even being printed in a Galveston newspaper. The Brenham paper took note, but no further mention is found of this near-arrest of Hiram, and he apparently managed to evade arrest for the next ten months. [31]

On May 16, 1894, James Martin, a part owner of a barber shop in Los Angeles, California, was arrested. Martin's name turned out to be an alias used by Hiram Williams, although the details of his arrest are unclear from newspaper accounts. A local paper stated that he was arrested on a "minor charge" and detectives, "profiting from a remark of the prisoner, began an investigation and found he was wanted in Texas."[32] According to a Brenham paper, the arrest was the result of "information from a negro woman there, who gave away his identity."[33] Either way, it was clear that Hiram knew his life on the run was over, though not if he could help it. Williams attempted to gain his freedom by secreting a long iron in his cell in the city prison, with which he intended to use to strike the jailer when the opportunity arose. The weapon was discovered in time to prevent its use.[34]

Regardless of the events surrounding his apprehension, two days later Washington County Sheriff Teague received notice of it and, determined not to let Hiram slip away again, quickly sent his under-sheriff, W.L. Sallis by train to pick up the prisoner.[35] On May 24, after a four-day train trip, Sallis arrived in Los Angeles, and went around to identify Hiram the next morning. "He recognized Mr. Sallis and asked him about some of the people of Brenham, and if he intended to take him back."[36] It took several more days for the extradition paperwork to arrive from Sacramento, during which time which time Sallis toured San Francisco and Los Angeles. He also took time to compose a lengthy travelogue letter describing his journey, which was later printed in its entirety in the *Brenham Banner*. This letter also describes his encounters with Hiram, who apparently made no further attempts at escape, while at the same attempting to justify his flight from trial five years earlier:

> In regard to the prisoner, who is known here as being a desperate negro of bad character, I want to state that I found him to be as obedient and docile a prisoner as I ever went after. He never caused a particle of trouble or uneasiness on the whole trip. The handcuffs on his wrists made them sore, but he never complained, and in changing cars, and in getting off to eat he avoided making any more trouble than was absolutely necessary.
>
> Hiram said to Mr. Sallis after they had turned toward home that he was glad that he had not got a lawyer to prevent his return, as he was tired of being a fugitive from justice, and that it had always been his intention to return to Brenham if he could have ever made enough money to pay a lawyer to defend him and get him bond, that he had been afraid of the prejudice against him, unless prepared for it, and for this reason had evaded arrest…He has been a constant reader of the papers and was thoroughly posted as to what had been going on during his absence, even to being able to tell about the Brenham city elections here during his absence. He protests his innocence of the crime of which he is charged and believes that with a fair trial he will be acquitted.[37]

Shortly after being re-incarcerated in Brenham, Hiram was visited in his cell by a reporter from *The Galveston Daily News*, who found him sitting up on a top bunk, "smoking a cigar and reading a copy of *The News*." He seemed to relax into being the center of attention after so many years of hiding his identity, and launched into a lengthy account of his years on the run:

"I was kept in jail at Bellville for fifteen months and was then released on bond. I was afraid of being killed by someone or lynched by a mob if I came back to Brenham, because I was warned by a number of friends that it would not be safe for me and I had no money to pay a lawyer to defend me, so I thought best to leave. I first went to El Paso and then to Piedras Negras, Mexico. I was there two weeks and left for Chihuahua, where I also spent two weeks. I came back to El Paso, spent a day and a half and went to Silver City, N.M., where I remained ten days, then went to Los Angeles, Cal, by way of Deming N.M. I was in Los Angeles only two days when I concluded to go further [sic] north, so I left for Portland, Ore., and after nine days went to Seattle, Wash., where I remained a month. I then crossed the strait to Vancouver Island and spent two weeks at Victoria. From there I went to Winnipeg in the Northwest territory, remained two months and returned to Victoria and then down to San Francisco, remaining only four days at the Golden Gate. I went east again to Gallup, N.M., on the Atlantic and Pacific railroad, and remained there three months. I returned after this to Seattle, where I went to work as second steward on a steamship on Puget sound. I held this job about a year and then going to Vancouver I took passage on a steamer for Honolulu. I remained on the islands for three months, then returned to San Francisco. After spending three months there I went back to Seattle and Tacoma, Wash.; was there a month; then back to San Francisco for a three month's stay. After this I went to Fresno and remained for a month, I then left Fresno and went to Los Angeles, arriving February 22 of this year. I had bought an interest in a barber shop, and was doing pretty well when I was arrested by the California officers on May 17. I stayed in the Los Angeles jail until June 1, and at 8:30 o'clock on that morning I left in charge of Deputy Sheriff Sallis for Texas. Arrived in Houston Sunday night and reached the Brenham jail at 2 o'clock in the morning."[38]

He took the opportunity not only to protest his innocence, but also to announce that he had always intended to "come back and stand my trial whenever I could get money enough to pay a lawyer. I have been warned time and again that the Texas officers would get me and I would be brought back, but I came to the conclusion that they did not want me bad enough to spend all the money necessary to bring me back, so I was not much afraid I would be brought back until I got ready. I haven't any doubt about my being able to establish my innocence. All I want is a fair trial by an impartial jury." He had already an ex-judge from Dallas and his lawyer to represent him, showing he still a man of enough means to hire competent attorneys. Their advice was probably instrumental in his requesting a clarification of his account of his activity on the night of the assault.[39]

By the end of the month Hiram had once again been released on bond, which "was made in Houston and brought here for his release and was secured through the instrumentality of his brother."[40] This was likely his brother Henry, who at the time of the 1900 census was married and living with his wife, aunt, uncle, and cousin in Houston's Third Ward. Interestingly, his brother was also a barber, the same occupation Hiram was engaged in when captured in Los Angeles.[41] Despite speculation in the press that he would once again skip town, Hiram did stand trial for assault for murder. His case was heard in September 1894, but the case was ultimately held over until March 1895 when it was dismissed in district court, though for reasons not made clear in the newspapers.[42]

The next instance of Hiram's life in the public record comes in 1898. A Hiram Williams appears in the Galveston City directory working as a porter and living at 1312 17th Street, while a Henry Williams, the name of his brother, was operating a barber shop there at 505 24th Street.[43] While it is not certain that Hiram was living in Galveston at this time, another important chapter in his life began to unfold.

In 1898 the Spanish-American War had stirred the patriotic spirit in many Americans. Many volunteer militias throughout the country were answering McKinley's call in late May for 75,000 volunteers to serve. Although hundreds of Black Texans were ready to volunteer after the heroic performance of the Army's four Black regiments, including the state's Black militia units, Governor Charles Culberson refused to accept them in fulfilling the state's volunteer quota. A similar situation existed in all but four other states, with the only opportunity for Black citizens to serve was to enlist in one of the regular Army's Black regiments. This barrier to service was circumvented with the authorization by Congress of ten federal "immune" regiments.[44]

As in all wars, disease was a major source of casualties. An erroneous but widely accepted misconception was that Blacks were naturally immune to the tropical diseases that were devastating the troops in Cuba. Galveston's Republican House Representative, Robert Hawley, was instrumental in forming one of these "immune" regiments, referred to as the Hawley Guard or the Hawley Rifles in his memory. This was Company G of the 9th Volunteer Infantry, which Hiram enlisted in on June 29, 1898.

There were seventy-five men in Company G, and when they left for New Orleans, a crowd of 700 Blacks and whites appeared at the train station to see them off.

In New Orleans, Hiram's company met the other Black Texas volunteers, Company I (the Ferguson Rifles) from Houston, received their Springfield rifles and improvised marching ditties such as "Colonel Crane has arranged a plan/ To fight old Spain with a nigger man."[45] The Immunes moved to Georgia for further training at Camp Thomas before setting out for Cuba, arriving in Santiago on August 22. The fighting had ended in Cuba, and the Immune's first assignment was to relieve the soldiers at San Juan Hill who had been guarding several thousand Spanish prisoners there. The regiment that had been guarding them had been devastated by tropical disease. Within several weeks, the Immunes showed they weren't necessarily immune after all and also began suffering losses to these diseases, with over thirty enlisted men and one lieutenant eventually dying, including three in Hiram's Company G.

Hiram was one of those who suffered from disease while serving in the Ninth Volunteer Infantry, first falling ill less than a month after enlisting and before even leaving New Orleans. He may well have suffered from disease more than once, since the roster listing his "Date of First Illness" seems to indicate that recurring illness was not uncommon.[46] The Immunes remained in Cuba until April 26, when they left Santiago for Staten Island, where they were kept in quarantine for another two days before proceeding on to Camp Meade in Pennsylvania for mustering out. Hiram was discharged on May 25, 1899, and may have returned to Galveston; there is a Hiram Williams living at the same address listed in the 1899 City Directory.[47] The same name appears in various city directories in Houston, Waco and Fort Worth, but nothing is certain in the public record about him for nearly three decades.

On November 23, 1927, Hiram Williams was married once again in Washington County, this time to a Rhoda Johnson.[48] Since Hiram listed himself as widowed in the 1880 census, it is not unreasonable that this was either a misunderstanding on the part of the census taker or self-justification on the part of a recently divorced and disgruntled Hiram, whose later behavior makes it clear that he was probably far less than a perfect husband during this period of his life. There is a marriage record of Rhoda Rogers to Jordan Johnson, who worked at a cotton compress, in October 1884,[49] and they lived together on Bragg Street; Jordan died of dysentery in 1919.[50] It seems this is the same Rhoda Rodgers that Hiram had married in 1878, and she appears as his wife in the 1930 and 1940 census.[51] The 1930 records indicate they had been married while she was 18 and he was 20, which hints that her given age of 60 may have been incorrect.

Further evidence that this is the same Rhoda Rodgers he originally married is that Alex Rodgers is listed as a brother-in-law living in the same household in the 1930 census. Alex was Rhoda Rodger's brother and is listed in the 1880 Schedule of Defective, Dependent and Delinquent Classes as an "Idiot,"[52] defined as "a person the development of whose mental faculties was arrested in infancy or childhood before coming to maturity." Rhoda was possibly helping to care for her brother with diminished mental capacity, although in 1910 he had lived alone as the head of a house on Bragg Street.

Their residence at 223 Parker, one street east of Bragg Street, may have been the same home Rhoda had been living in for some time. Interestingly, Rhoda's mother's maiden name was Jane Bragg. In 1930 the house was valued at $1,000, and $500 in 1940. Hiram's occupation is listed as "none," while Rhoda (her name is given as Rosa in this census) was listed as a "laundress"

-- the same as in the 1910 census when she was living with Jordan Johnson, whose place of work was "in and out." Alex's occupation is given as "laborer" working at "odd jobs."

Ten years later, the Williamses were still on Bragg Street and had been there for at least the past five years. Alex was no longer living with them but boarding with a Louisa Brown. Although the census indicates that neither had worked over the past year, Hiram is listed as having unspecified other sources of income. One of these may have been as a cook, since this is the occupation on his death certificate three years later. But the indignities of old age were finally beginning to catch up with Hiram. He had been suffering from prostatitis for over a year, and his kidneys began to fail him in February 1943. At 4 o'clock on Tuesday morning, March 1, 1943, the long, strange journey of Hiram Williams ended.[53] His death was noted in an obituary on page four of the Brenham paper:

> Hiram Williams, a well-known colored man, died at his home in Camptown Monday. He is survived by his widow but had no children. He also leaves a number of nieces, nephews and other relatives. Owner of considerable property he was considered one of the most well to do negroes in this section. He was a veteran of the Spanish American [sic] War. Funeral services will be held Sunday afternoon from the Camptown Methodist Church." The funeral seemingly was delayed while awaiting the arrival of "relatives from New York, Chicago and California.[54]

Hiram was buried on March 7 in Camptown Cemetery, just two blocks away from his home on Bragg Street. In November Rhoda applied for an application "for a headstone or marker for the unmarked grave of a veteran." In April of 1944 an upright granite headstone was shipped by rail to Brenham; this is the marker that now stands over his grave.[55] Rhoda died in 1946 and is also buried in Camptown Cemetery.

Chapter 6

# FROM JAMAICA TO CAMPTOWN:

# GEORGE P. ISAACS

*George and Martha Isaacs,
from "The Negro Blue-book of Washington County"*

George Peter Isaacs was born in Kingston, Jamaica, on June 10, 1848, known at that time as the West Indies. Slavery had been abolished on the island of Jamaica in 1834, so it can be assumed that he was born free. It is not clear how or when he came to the United States, aside from a short biographical sketch that appeared in "The Negro Blue-Book of Washington County, Texas" in 1936 written by his daughter, Annie Belle Isaacs Estelle.[1] While still young he came to Galveston before eventually moving to Washington County to teach. His first position was near the community of Goodwill at Cole's Creek, near what is now Washington-on-the-Brazos and the old Cole Plantation.

When Isaacs first began as the school's sole teacher, it consisted of a one-room log cabin that had also served as the community's church. As Goodwill continued to grow, the school grew in size and number of teachers, with Isaacs eventually making as much as $60 a month for five months as principle[2]. After his death his daughter became principal and the cabin eventually was replaced by a four-room Rosenwald school. By 1936 it had an auditorium, library, and cottage for teachers on a fourteen-acre site.

On Christmas Eve, 1879, the twenty-five-year-old Isaacs married seventeen-year-old Martha Flewellen. His occupation was listed in the following year's census as farmer, working fifteen acres of land, although he had also been teaching at the Goodwill school since 1877. The newlyweds were living next to the bride's parents, Anthony and Sam Flewellen, as well as five of her brothers and sisters working on a hundred-acre farm. Anthony took his last name from the man who had previously held him in bondage in Georgia, Dr. Edward Flewellen.

Formerly known in Georgia as "Anthony Flewellen, the blacksmith," he had several children by another wife. He left her behind when he came to Texas, although he attempted to contact his family after Emancipation in 1885 when he heard they had moved to Texas.[3] He was not only accomplished as a blacksmith, but also a gifted mechanic and inventor as well. His daughter remembers him making "braces for deformed children."[4] Seven years after his marriage into the family, Isaacs witnessed paperwork for a patent granted for his father-in-law's "Combined Cotton Cropper and Cultivator."[5]

124 | VOICES OF CAMPTOWN

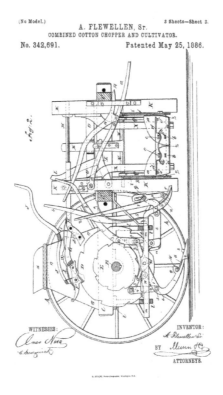

*Illustration from U.S. Patent Number 342, 691*

Although he operated a cotton gin a few miles east of Camptown, Flewellen's interests were not strictly agricultural. In 1893 took out an ad in the *Brenham Daily Banner* to help solicit funds for another of his inventions:

> Notice to the Public and Citizens of Washington County: I hereby call your attention to a Buggy [sic] I

have in preparation to be run without a horse. I am a poor man, and it requires a little money to complete the same. Therefore, I have resolved to put the said buggy on exhibition, at a small admission, in order to raise the necessary means to complete it, when I have completed the said buggy, I will warrant the same to run 1 mile in 3 minutes upon any road or street ordinary buggies run upon, up or down hill, and be guided at any turn or crook in a road, with perfect ease to the riders. The riders will have nothing to do or be put to any exertion, but guide the same. I will put said buggy upon exhibit in the City of Brenham, on the 28th, 29th and 30th days of December, 1893.[6]

A reporter from the local paper spoke with Flewellen shortly after the ads started running in it. The buggy was to be displayed under a tent for a small charge to raise money to finish its production, and while the inventor would not say exactly how it was powered, it was said that since "it was not steam, electricity, gas, horse or man power, consequently it must be a wonderful buggy," supposed to run at a speed of twenty miles an hour.[7] Unfortunately, the Brenham papers for that holiday period are not available, and it is not known how well this early horseless buggy fared at its introduction.

Though he was clearly close to his father-in-law and farm, Isaacs was primarily a teacher. He started teaching at Cole's Creek School, but eventually took a position at the Goodwill School about fourteen miles northeast of Brenham, teaching there for over a quarter of a century. Referred to as Professor George Isaacs, he frequently appeared in the local press, once as a result of having a student at a closing exercise arrested for drunkenness and creating a disturbance, resulting in a $15 fine for the student.[8]

Isaacs was active in the educational community and a founding member in 1884 of a Washington County "colored teachers" institute, serving as the treasurer. alongside J. M. Parker and Samuel Love, who were founding trustees of the first dedicated school building in Camptown, funded in part by the Freedmen's Bureau. Isaacs continued to remain active in local education, serving on the executive board of the county Summer Normal School.[9]

Benevolent organizations were an important component of the Camptown community, and Isaacs was a member of the Grand United Order of Odd Fellows (headquartered across from Mount Rose Baptist Church) and installed as an officer at the Fair Grounds during the Emancipation celebration that year.[10] Freemasonry had been big in Brenham since the 1870s, and Isaacs belonged to the Cachet Lodge No. 40 of Colored Masons and elected as the Worshipful Master in 1893.[11] He remained active in his church, attending the Mount Zion African Methodist Episcopal church, where he was referred to as Reverend George Isaacs.[12] In November 1893 he was appointed an alternate delegate for the Colored Men's National Convention called by AME Bishop H.N. Turner, to be held in Cincinnati later that year.[13] Serving as second vice president, he worked on several committees for a group of Black citizens meeting to help organize "a colored county fair association."[14]

Like many other prominent Black citizens in the county, Isaacs was involved in local politics as a member of the Republican Party at the county level. Though he never ran for any office, he was elected in 1894 as a delegate to the state Republican convention, as well as protesting in a letter to the local paper their coverage of that county convention.[15] Isaacs also was called upon to serve on juries at the county and district court levels.[16] In March 1897, Isaacs was called to be a witness in the trial of

Charles Kugadt, accused of murdering his sister. Although his testimony, as reported by *The Galveston Daily News*, seems to have been minimal, it indicates he was still teaching at Goodwill and commuting to school with fellow teacher Richard Mackey when they came across Kugadt and his soon-to-be-deceased sister along the road shortly before the murder.[17] In 1904 Isaacs was selected from a list of 150 potential jurors as one of two Black men to weigh in on a death sentence for one of two white brothers, John and Jim Yeldermen. The Yelderman brothers had been indicted for the murder of their father, Julius, several months after his divorce from their mother "to stop their father's giving away his property to Addie Laas or Williams, a negro woman."[18]

The Isaacs family grew with the addition of five children born to George and Martha. They moved from next to Martha's family into the Camptown area of Brenham, buying lots worth $200 from as early as 1882. They also bought property worth $200 from Wiley Hubert in 1884, which was to be the family home at 1619 East Alamo Street in Brenham. However, buying property and holding on to it could be two very different matters. In May 1887 one of Isaacs' lots in Camptown was seized by the sheriff for sale to the highest bidder due to back taxes of $4.20.[19]

Marital bliss may have existed for a while in the Isaacs household, but ultimately it did not last. In 1900 the census indicated that the Isaacs family, including two teenaged boys, were living with Martha's father (rather than next door to them) and working as farm laborers. In June 1901 George filed for divorce from Martha in the Washington County District Court, seeking an equal division of their property. In his petition he alleged she had engaged in an adulterous affair with a Reverend Carmichael since at least 1900. This was an explosive allegation, since Carmichael was also the presiding elder of their church, where Isaacs and his wife had been "ardent and zealous workers."[20]

When the case came to court that September, Martha had the chance to tell her side of the story, which was understandably quite different. Her deposition acknowledged that she and George had "lived together for many years, in contentment and happiness, and would have so continued, but for the fact that the plaintiff became smitten with one Mary Jane Jefferson" in January 1899. She said that after this her husband's affection for her "began to wane, and he then entirely abandoned her, and moved out into the country," refusing to live with his wife. Their five children were now with her and living in the two houses on the Sandy Street lot. She said George had "totally failed and refused to provide any support, for her self [sic] or children." She asked that she be granted the judgment and received the house and its effects, custody of the children, and a restraining order against her husband from interfering with her or the children.[21]

The divorce was granted that October, and their property divided. A week later George sold off another lot in Brenham, probably to help settle associated legal costs.[22] A year after George had filed for divorce, he married Sarah Jane Jefferson, the woman named in the divorce proceedings that Martha Isaacs had claimed he "became smitten with."[23] They apparently continued to live in Washington County for at least several years since Isaacs was still a citizen of the county when he was called to serve on the jury at the Yelderman murder trial. Martha lived on there as well for several more years before succumbing to stomach cancer on October 9, 1905.

Around this time Isaacs and his new wife moved to California. By 1910 they were living in a racially mixed neighborhood at 35 Peach Place in Pasadena, half a block from the city's Central Park. He appears on the city's voter registry (as a Republican) that year, and the couple was still at that address according to the 1916 and 1917 city directories. However, he was no longer working as a teacher; his occupation was now listed with the generic term of laborer and the general nature of his work as "streets," indicating he was possibly working for the city. Sarah Jane (whose name is variously given as Sarah J. and Mary J.) was working as a house cleaner. There is also a difficult-to-explain Los Angeles marriage certificate from 1912, which seems to involve the couple as well. The description of George P. Isaacs on the document (sixty-three years old, born in the West Indies) fits him, although the bride's name is given as Mary J. Jackson, a native of Texas.

To further muddy the waters, an affidavit of heirship filed in 1954 regarding the family home purchased from Wiley Hubert in 1884 states that George and Sarah Jane never had any children and that she died in 1915. This affidavit had other questionable information as well, such as stating that Martha and George "had lived together as husband and wife" until her death. Sarah Jane's fate remains unclear, though it seems George and his second wife were no longer together at the time that he had returned to Brenham.

The final legal document in George Isaacs' life indicates that he was still married, rather than widowed, in October 1918 and living in Brenham. He was one of the early victims of the pandemic that has come to be known as the Spanish Flu, and died on the morning of October 14, a day after first being seen by Dr. J. H. Porter, a mulatto physician who served the community of Camptown. Isaacs' swift demise was all too common with this particularly deadly viral infection, a suddenness that would leave the patient with no available medical recourse and families in a state of shock. His daughter provided the information on his death certificate, being sure to recognize his occupation as a teacher as befitted his primary contribution in the Camptown community and in her life.

The day after his death Isaccs was interred in the Camptown

Cemetery. The plot in which he is buried stands out as one of the most elaborate in the cemetery. Four beautiful head stones mark the location of George, Martha, their son. Lawrence, who had died in 1915, and Martha's sister-in-law Esther, who had died in 1912. When the headstones were encountered in 2013, they were set far back in the cemetery, with surrounding gravesites in far worse condition. Situated among overgrown trees and shrubs, the headstones showed the care, work, and money that had been expended to memorialize the family. But there are clear indications that these were not the original grave markers for the four, who likely were reinterred over a decade later.

The first inkling that there was something unusual about the gravesite came only after further restoration and inventory of all the markers in the cemetery. While clearing the dense vegetation surrounding the Isaacs plot, another marker was found in the immediate vicinity. It was a rough concrete marker with the names, ages, and dates of death for George and Martha etched in cursive script while the concrete was still wet, with a line dividing the two. This simple and inexpensive form of marking gravesites is not uncommon in Camptown Cemetery, at times with multiple names being found on a curb surrounding a family plot. This had undoubtedly been the site of his original burial. It was also likely Martha's as well, the two being laid next to each other despite the bitter divorce that had separated them fourteen years earlier. What is so remarkable about the Isaac plot is the evolution from a simple marker to a much more elaborate and costly site.

*The Later Isaacs Plot*
*Photo Credit: Charles Swenson*

An explanation for the change of the Isaacs grave site might be found by looking more closely at the life of Anna Belle Isaac Estelle. Annie, as she was known, was born on August 31, 1880, the first of five children born to George and Martha.[24] She was not living with her parents in 1900 when they living with Martha's father, probably because she was at college receiving her certification as a school teacher. In 1910, after her mother's death of her mother and probably the departure of her father, she was living with her two younger brothers, Edgar and Lawrence. They rented a farm in Washington County while she was teaching.

Although Annie Belle was almost ten years older, her sister Ruby was the first to be wed, marrying a college professor at Prairie View College by the name of Henry Estelle.[25] Annie Belle also became enamored of an Estelle, marrying J. L. Estelle in September 1918, just five weeks before her father's sudden death. The relationship between the two Estelles is unclear, as was J.L.'s location in 1920, when she appears in the census as living in a house she owned on East Main Street with two roomers, with her status as still married. They belonged to the Knights and Daughters of Hermon, which mentions their presence together at a meeting at Mount Rose Church in Brenham. Annie Belle served on a committee on education, while her brother-in-law was listed as a Supreme Home Officer. J. L. Estelle was there as well, serving as Supreme Scribe, from Galveston.

He and Annie Belle next appear in the Galveston census, providing valuable insight into the probable origin of the extensive and clearly expensive Isaacs plot that lies to the rear of Camptown Cemetery. By this time Estelle was a well-established undertaker in Galveston, owning a mortuary on Avenue L worth $10,000 and employing three helpers who lived on site.[26] With ready access to the funeral industry and the resources of her husband, Annie Belle would have been able finally to pay respects to the three people she had lost in the years before her marriage, as well as her father. This would go a long way toward explaining how a teacher born in the West Indies had come to his final rest in one of the best-appointed graves in a plot thousands of miles from his place of birth.

George Isaacs' devotion to furthering education in Washington County lived on after his death. His daughters were well educated, with Ruby receiving four years of college education and marrying a college professor. Annie Belle also taught at the same school in Goodwill where her father had and eventually taking on the position of principal there. But her life was not without troubles in marriage. By 1934 her husband filed for divorce on the grounds of cruel treatment, with legal notices published in newspapers demanding her to answer the charges in Waco. In 1940, when she was responding to questions for the decennial census, she gave her marital status as single, though she kept the last name of Estelle.[27]

Under Annie Belle's guidance as principal, in 1951 the Goodwill School received notice as an honor school in *The Texas Standard*, a quarterly publication of the Colored Teachers' State Association of Texas. She retired but remained active in education, organizing the Washington County Chapter of Retired Teachers in 1964 and serving as president of the organization.

In her later years she moved to Waco, probably to be closer to her sister and brother-in-law who had moved there around 1925 when he became an agricultural extension agent and supervisor. She outlived them both before dying from a stroke in January1982. She was buried next to them there in the Doris Miller Cemetery.

Teachers are all too rarely remembered for the important roles they play in their communities. Education in the Black communities of Washington County was pivotal in raising them up, and the significance of George and Annie Belle Isaacs' contributions touched hundreds of lives. Fortunately, she was able to share the previously untold story of her father's life so it could be honored. His love of education carried forward in his daughter, whose contributions equally deserve to be remembered.

Chapter 7

# AUSTRALIA GUY COMES HOME TO STAY

*Photo courtesy of Amy the Spirit Seeker*

A grave marker often commented upon at Camptown Cemetery is that of "Australia Guy." It lies in the Guy plot on the eastern end of the grounds, and although much of his life is now known, it remains unclear how he came upon his unusual first name.

Australia Warren Guy was born on September 14, 1894, one of eight children. His parents were Ellen and William Guy, who were born into bondage—Ellen in Texas and William in Louisiana.

Neither had learned to read or write. All of Australia's siblings, however, were granted the gift of literacy, thanks to a rich heritage of educational opportunities in Camptown that had begun shortly after Emancipation. Thanks to this foresight, his old sister, Bedia, became a public-school teacher in Brenham.

Australia graduated from East Side High School in 1912, which was immediately adjacent to Camptown Cemetery. The school eventually was renamed after Professor A.R. Pickard, the principal at the time of his graduation. The commencement exercises were held at the adjacent Mount Rose Baptist Church, and after the singing of the school anthem, "Tarry with Me," most of the graduating class of twelve presented songs, essays, and readings. Australia presented an oration on "Present Opportunities." It was said that each "essay and oration showed careful preparation and research and proved that the colored high school maintains a high standard" and "reflected great credit upon" the principal.[1]

The opportunity that Australia took advantage of after graduation was to use his education to work as a clerk at Clarence Scott's Grocery Store on East Alamo Street in Camptown. Scott was an ambitious young man who made use of opportunities himself, already owning his own store and one of the most successful Black merchants in Brenham for decades, at times even advertising his business in the newspaper.[2] He was also an active member of the Mount Rose Missionary Baptist Church. In addition, he belonged to several of the local fraternal organizations, the American Woodmen and the St. Luke Lodge of the Knights of Pythias. Guy was establishing himself as a responsible member of the Camptown community when events in 1917 caused him to leave it.

When the United States declared war and entered the European conflict that eventually came to be known as the First World War, patriotic fervor ran high in Camptown and other Black communities. On April 9, 1917, five days after Congress passed the resolution to declare war on Germany, a "colored citizens patriotic meeting" was held at the high school in Camptown where Guy had graduated. A committee chaired by Pickard, the principal, passed several resolutions:

> Resolved. That we, the negro citizens of Washington county, state of Texas, do hereby offer our services (as our people have done in every warfare against our country) to the President of the United States in vindication of peace and justice against the ruthless warfare waged by Germany...and that we urge our people everywhere to pledge their unqualified support to the American flag with our blood and that equal military rights such as are guaranteed any American citizen be guaranteed our people.[3]

Among the more than sixty prominent black citizens who signed the resolutions was Guy's employer, C. W. Scott. A "patriotic demonstration" also was organized for the following weekend at Chancy Williamson's Park, a Black-owned venue that also was used for local Emancipation celebrations. The event was preceded by a parade that included "practically every colored pupil in all of the various schools...attired in white and waving flags," as well as "teachers and all of the leading negroes of the city." The parade was "headed by the Brenham (colored) Band and a half-mile in length."[4]

To raise the necessary troop levels, a military draft was enacted, requiring all male citizens of Washington County between the ages of seventeen and thirty-one, both white and Black, to register. Guy registered on June 7, giving some basic information about his life. He was of medium height and build, not bald, married but with no other dependents. He was living with his parents on Bragg Street, a few blocks from Camptown Cemetery, while still working as a clerk for Scott's grocery. When the roll of 2,347 eligible young men from the county was printed in the press in July 1917, his was the fourteenth name on the list.[5] He was one of more than a million Black men who registered for the draft, and one of those selected for duty.[6]

Inducted in San Antonio at Fort Sam Houston on August 24, 1917, Guy likely did most of his early training at the adjacent Camp Travis. Following the large proportion of Black draftees filling the draft quota in the South, the War Department decided to transfer Black soldiers into camps further north. This included Camp Funston in Kansas, which became home to the 92nd Division. The 92nd was one of only two fully Black divisions that fought in World War One, taking its nom de guerre of Buffalo Soldiers from the legendary Black soldiers who had fought on the Western frontier forty years earlier. Camp Funston was a massive complex built after the declaration of war in the summer of 1917. Its 2,000 acres grew to contain about 1,400 structures, including two story dormitories, training centers, hospitals, workshops, general stores, arcades, pool halls, a library, movie theatres, and bowling alleys.[7]

The locals in nearby Junction City and Manhattan protested when they heard of the plans to move 14,300 white soldiers to accommodate the transfer of 12,000 Black soldiers such as Guy into the camp; at the time Junction City had no Black inhabitants at all. One astute newspaper editorial commented at the time that "Kansas people should have no trouble in getting along peacefully with negro troops; it is only in the south that a negro is lynched for trivial cause. If Kansas believes it is right to send negro and white children to the same schools, she should hardly draw the color line in the war game, since the last session of the Kansas legislature again refused to vote in favor of separate schools."[8]

Not everyone was put off by the influx of Black soldiers. By the following February there were 3,000 on base, with 6,000 more expected. A "community house" to accommodate friends and family members while visiting was funded by local subscriptions and built for Black soldiers, the first of its kind in the country despite $1,500 in funds being converted for personal use by a white captain.[9] This community house, constructed on the camp's eastern edge and known as the "negro zone," had "separate amusement places and exchanges."[10] It became even more important to these troops when General Ballou issued orders for the 92nd Division "enjoining officers and soldiers to refrain from going into public places where their presence is resented because of color," a move prompting a telegram of protest to President Woodrow Wilson from the National Equal Rights League.[11]

As one of the 50,000 troops stationed at Funston in the spring of 1918, Guy must have encountered some of the estimated 1,100 men who experienced one of the first documented outbreaks of the Spanish Flu pandemic in the United States. His training in the medical department as a hospital attendant placed him in the 317th Sanitary Train, specializing in medical transport as a private first class in the 367th Ambulance Company. The division gathered at Camp Upton in New York by train and on June 19th, when his family was back home in Brenham celebrating Emancipation on Juneteenth, Australia Guy set sail from for France.

Eight days later Guy and his company landed at Brest. After further training in France the 92nd finally moved to the front lines as part of the American Expeditionary Force. In September he was promoted to corporal. Later that month the Meuse-Argonne offensive began, the largest offensive engagement in U.S. military history, involving 1.2 million American soldiers.

It was also the deadliest, with over 26,000 deaths and 120,000 casualties. Guy served in the Defensive Sector transporting and treating the wounded with his division, which amounted to 1,300 before the hostilities ended on November 11. For his services, he was eventually awarded a World War I Victory Medal.[12]

After Armistice, Guy remained in France for another three months caring for the wounded and sick, including the growing number suffering from the influenza pandemic that was beginning to devastate not only the troops, but also millions of civilians throughout the world. On February 18 he departed from Brest on the troop carrier Olympic accompanying the sick and wounded and arriving in New York on the 24th. After returning to the states, Guy remained enlisted until April 11, when he was demobilized with an honorable discharge. He returned to Brenham, where his father, a worker cotton compress laborer, had died in March the year before. On June 19 he was married to Woodie E. Jones, the woman who was destined to be his wife for the rest of his tragically short life.

The newlyweds didn't remain in Brenham long. By January 1920 they had moved to Dallas to live with his sister Ada, who was living at 2507 Flora Street after divorcing her previous husband. The following year they moved across the Trinity River to live with his brother Terry on Dodd Street. Woodie was working as a waitress at the Modern Cafe, where Australia was also working. Guy was also a member of a branch of the Knights of Pythias that offered membership to Blacks. This fraternal order was based out of the red brick neoclassical building on Elm Street that recently had been built based on a design by the African American architect William Sidney Pittman. The building was the center of Dallas' Black community at the time, with stores, a pharmacy and a barber shop on the ground floor, offices for doctors, a dentist and other professionals on the second floor, and insurance offices on the third. The top floor was a ballroom that held dances, musical presentations, and lectures. The Knights of Pythias also offered financial assistance to its members in distress.

Australia also worked at the Adolphus Hotel in a position described as variously as a "porter," elevator operator, and "bellboy." It was to be the last job he would ever hold.

Dallas in 1920 was the second largest city in Texas, with a population of almost 160,000 and a vibrant Black community centered around Elm Street. Called Deep Elum, it featured blues and jazz bars with musicians like Blind Lemon Jefferson, Leadbelly, and numerous jazz and swing bands. Although Prohibition was in effect, alcohol was freely available there, especially at the jazz clubs. The area was a tremendous draw not only for Blacks but for whites as well, drawing comparisons to "the Jazz Age mecca of Harlem in New York City, pushing at race and class boundaries under the draw of music and white curiosity...The alcohol, risqué music, and interracial and cross-class socializing that typified Deep Elum at night."[13] This would have been especially appealing for the young Guy, who like other Black soldiers returning from Europe had experienced a degree of racial prejudice and inequity worse than what they encountered when they returned to the South. And this was all taking place within a few blocks of the Adolphus Hotel.

This easy blending between the races also attracted the attention of another group of Dallas residents. The Ku Klux Klan was undergoing a resurgence throughout the country following the war, and Klavern 66 in Dallas was growing as well. On a Saturday night in May 1921, a thousand Klan members outfitted in robes and hoods held a march down Main Street to proclaim their strength. The previous month they had made their presence known in a more ominous fashion, one that must have struck Guy as a little too close to home.

Fred Ball and Paul Jones, two Dallas newspaper men, at first thought they might be the butt of an April Fool's joke when they received a phone call on April 1, 1921, telling them to meet a mysterious stranger outside a local department story for an "important story." Finally convinced to make the meeting, they were persuaded by a well-dressed man to be blindfolded and taken on a miles-long late night journey by car. Once at their destination the blindfolds were removed and their story lay before them—a terrified Black man stripped to his waist and tied to a tree in the Trinity River bottom with a noose around his neck. He was surrounded by fifteen men dressed in the hoods and robes of the Ku Klux Klan.[14]

The man was Alex Johnson, who had been kidnapped from his house after midnight. Earlier that day he had been released from jail on bond on charges of being found in a woman's room at the Adolphus Hotel, where he worked as a bell boy. After twenty-five lashes with a whip and fearful he might be hanged, he told his interrogators what they wanted to hear, that he had engaged in "intimacy with a white woman." To further drive their point home as to who he was dealing with, Johnson then had the initials KKK branded with acid on his forehead. To add insult to injury, he was taken back to the city and "shoved out of the hotel where he worked and told to go in and tell the other negro bellhops what had happened to him."[15] Guy may have been one of those bellhops.

The Klan had a special affinity for the Adolphus Hotel. In 1922 the organization was working hard to influence the Democratic primary elections, obtaining a copy of the poll tax rolls sorted on index cards according to sex and race. These were distributed to local Klan leaders to help get out the vote for Klan-backed candidates. This campaign, including "a manager, a clerical staff of ten or so, typewriters, special telephone lines, and a mysterious detective who received $50 a week for unknown services," was headquartered in three rooms at the Adolphus.[16]

This was the environment in which Australia was working as a bellboy on November 30, 1922, his last day on that job. What happened next is documented in only one place -- his death certificate. The given cause of death was "internal hemorrhage," but there is more implied. The line for contributory or secondary cause for death read "fractured pelvis from fall 3 stories in elevator shaft" followed in parentheses by "(accidental.)"[17] It is hard to believe that someone who worked for years as a bellboy or possibly even at times as an elevator operator, frequently going up and down elevators, would make such a potentially fatal mistake as falling down an elevator shaft, especially considering the safety features built into elevators. The signing doctor's addition that the secondary cause of death was "accidental" casts even more doubt on how Australia Guy wound up at the bottom of an elevator shaft. It seemed likely to avoid any potential investigation of his death as more than an accident.

Guy didn't die immediately from his injuries related to this fall. Instead, he lingered on in agony for ten days in St. Paul Sanitarium. A change in his condition required an operation. Two days later, after bleeding extensively into his abdomen, he died at three in the afternoon.

After his death, Australia Guy's body was shipped back home to Brenham. The Knights of Pythias had helped his family during his hospitalization and with transporting his remains back to the town where he had been born. He had also been a member of the American Woodmen, which helped provide not only assistance during his illness, but also death and burial benefits. He was buried in the Guy plot in Camptown Cemetery, a few blocks from his childhood home and in sight of the church he had attended. The Adolphus hotel sent flowers to his funeral.[18]

Five years after he had left his hometown, Australia Guy had returned to stay.

## Chapter 8

# A HANGING IN CAMPTOWN

Charlotte and Lee Hughes lived together in a small cabin on the old Zurcher farm, just three miles west of Chappell Hill and seven miles east of Brenham. They'd been married six years earlier, when he was eighteen and she was several years younger. Although they had no children of their own, Charlotte already had a child that lived with her parents. Her mother said that during visits Charlotte rarely spent more than an hour with her child, sometimes just walking to their house and looking at it before turning around and leaving again. The child was the source of friction between Lee and Charlotte. At times Lee would become violent, often taking out his anger on Charlotte. After one such beating she had even run away, but their relationship had seemed to stabilize.

On the Friday morning of January 30, 1891, Charlotte was working near the fireplace in her home in Washington County. She had made breakfast for a neighbor earlier and was probably cooking more food because when she was found later that afternoon, a pan was still in her hand with a bit of uncooked cornbread in it and bacon on the table. It was the last meal she would ever prepare.

The press speculated that her assailant must have come up behind her, assaulting her with both sides of a club axe. The blunt end had caved in her forehead, while the honed edge struck the back of her neck with such a massive blow it nearly severed her head from her body.

Later that Friday morning, a relative of Charlotte's who lived nearby asked Lee if he knew where she was. He responded that she had gone over to visit a neighbor, but when the relative went there, he found was she not there and hadn't been there all day. When he came back by the Hughes residence again later that day, Lee brought him into the kitchen where her body lay still and cold on the floor, along with the uncooked meal.

The following Monday afternoon District Attorney Beauregard Bryan arrived in Chappell Hill for a preliminary hearing on Charlotte's death, with Lee as the main suspect. He was taken to the Washington County jail in Brenham that evening and held pending a grand jury hearing on his wife's murder.

It was a long winter for Hughes. The district court's spring session indicted against him and his case was set for March 20, 1891. The trial began less than two months after the murder only lasted until the next afternoon. After deliberating for an hour-and-a-half the jury returned a guilty verdict of murder in the first degree, to be punished with the death penalty. Hughes was to be held in the county jail until his appeal of the sentence could be heard.[1]

At some point Hughes was transferred to the Lee County jail in Giddings while renovations were underway at the Washington County jail. Its lower story was also the residential portion of the jail, housing not only Sheriff Dilmus E. Teague, but also his wife and three young daughters. A new addition was being built on the lower level, with a new coat of paint being applied to the entire jailhouse. At the cost of $4,000, four new "chilled steel" cages were being installed on the upper floors that housed the prisoners.[2]

Before Hughes was returned to Brenham, the Court of Appeals heard his case in June and upheld his guilty verdict. It was once again up to the district court in Washington County to affirm his death sentence and set a date for his execution within thirty days. The court would meet again in September, which meant the date of his execution should occur at some time in October. At this time execution meant hanging, and before 1923 the county where the prisoner had been sentenced was also responsible for his hanging.

Sheriff Teague returned with Hughes on July 9, 1891. While Lee was not an overly large man previously, he appeared to have lost at least fifteen pounds from his previous 135 pounds and seemed emaciated and ill. On the way back to the jail with his prisoner, Sheriff Teague visited Dr. Lockett and a pharmacist for medicine for Hughes, surrounded all the while by a crowd of curious onlookers.

Once safely housed in one of the new steel cages in the jail house, Hughes was interviewed by a reporter from the *Brenham Weekly Banner*, who said Hughes

> ...proceeded, as soon as he was safely ensconced in his cell, to ascertain how he felt in regard to his fate, since the decision of the District court had been affirmed by the higher courts. He did not know even that his case had been affirmed and when so informed by the reporter expressed surprise, and with a slight, twitching of the lips, said, 'I don't know what they will do with me, but that there is consolation, whatever they do, God in Heaven knows I am innocent of the crime of killing my wife.'

He seemed to take considerable interest in the results of the appeal and asked more about it after someone had interrupted the conversation between him and the reporter.

He was lying down on one of the cell cots munching a lemon during most of the conversation and said that he had a mighty close call during his confinement at Giddings, and at one time thought he was going to die. Someone asked him if he was scared, to which he replied, 'Oh no! no! not at all.'

Unless Lee Hughes takes a turn for the better, he will die. If he regains his health or even lives between 30 and 60 days from the convening of the next term of the district court in September, when he will be sentenced, he will be hanged, so little difference either way.[3]

But much to everyone's surprise, not least of all the reporter, Hughes would be walking out of the jail less than two weeks later. It was the second escape from a Brenham jail that month. In the first days of July, Morris Routt was arrested for stealing three dollars from a fellow "negro sport." He was being held in the "city prison" or calaboose (rather than the county jail) while the more secure steel cages were being installed. Routt had simply burned a hole in the floor of his cell large enough to crawl down and out through, making his way to freedom. Later that same month, on the morning of July 28, Hughes managed his escape from the freshly renovated county jail. At the time he was sharing the new "chilled steel" cage with two other prisoners, "...Johnie Jones, a white boy, charged with unlawfully carrying a pistol, and Al McIntyre, a negro boy, charged with shooting at a passing mixed train."[4]

His getaway from a newly built, state-of-the-art jail was a matter of considerable embarrassment for the county, but also indicated that Hughes was a man of considerable intelligence, manual dexterity, and careful planning. The following is an account in the *Brenham Weekly Banner* of how he effected a breakout from his with little more than a piece of wire, a stick. and a nail:

> There are four of the steel cages, the doors of which open into a corridor between them the corridor being closed from the outside by an iron door locked, and which has combination bars. On each side of this door to the corridor is an iron box, on which is a combination lock, on the inside of which the levers that work the bars that fasten all five of the doors and in which the keys to all of them are kept. On the back of this iron box was an unfilled rivet hole not large enough for a cedar pencil to go through, but it was through this hole that the prisoner had to work. The inside doors were all open, giving the prisoners the privilege of the four cells and the hall, and the other prisoners say that he worked the lever that unbars the door with the wire through this small aperture, which looks like a mechanical impossibility. But the door was locked also, and the key in that iron box. This he shoved of the front of the box with his wire, and with a stick and a nail commenced springing the door to the box, but inserting the point of the nail and then driving it up and inserting a larger wedge until he could get his stick in there, which gave him considerable power and sprung the door so that the keys dropped to the floor on the outside of the cage. This done, it was but the work of a moment to reach his arm through the bars, pick them up and reach around the bars and unlock the

corridor door of the cells letting himself out into the large room. Nothing but a thin brick wall was now between him and liberty, and a heavy window weight lying nearby and some large nails were as good tools as he needed to go through it, which he did just beneath a south window, the opening striking the iron window sill which dropped down several inches below where had calculated it reached but he didn't have to enlarge much, for being a small negro he squeezed through a very small opening. Before doing this however, he had fastened a rope to the bars of the window over his hole, of ample length to let himself to terra firma below. The rope was perhaps made prior to Monday night as the workmanship on it showed considerable skill, it being twisted so smooth that it could scarcely be told that it was made out of one of the jail blankets.[5]

Hughes' fellow cellmates decided not to take advantage of the situation to slip away themselves, though they weren't in any great hurry to inform the authorities either. When questioned about it they indicated that Hughes escaped between one and two in the morning but remained silent about the matter out of fear for their lives. The first indication that anyone else knew anything was wrong came around 7 a.m., "when one of the prisoners called an old negro woman in the yard and told her to tell Sheriff Teague that the jail was broken open."[6]

A posse was formed to pursue the escaped murderer and a $50 reward offered for his capture. Hughes had been seen around daybreak passing through a yard two miles east of town, and eventually made it another mile-and-a-half out of town before hiding in a tree on the farm of Steven Stanislauns. When the young Polish farmer discovered him there, he recognized Hughes as the infamous murderer and went back for his gun. Keeping him covered with his single-barrel, muzzle loading shotgun, Stanislauns led Hughes back to his house, where his wife tied him up and kept watch on him until Sheriff Teague could come for him. Handcuffed and under guard by the posse, Hughes was returned to same cell he'd escaped from earlier that day. His sister was there at the jail on his return, and he scolded her for crying for him.[7]

After this, the steel cages were clearly more effective. On Monday, September 20, Hughes again appeared in district court before Judge Bryan, who ordered him held without bail in Chappell Hill at the preliminary hearing three days after his wife's murder. Sentence was passed upon Hughes, who was to be hung by the neck until dead on October 3, between 11 a.m. and sundown, either "in the jail or some other private place in Washington county."

This was major news in Brenham, and once again the *Brenham Banner* covered the court proceedings and interviewed the prisoner:

> A *Banner* reporter was present when Sheriff Teague and Deputy Crockett escorted the prisoner into the court room and watched his every movement to note the effect that marching up to receive a death sentence would have on him. He came in and walked to a chair in front of the court at a good lively gait, swinging his arms with a careless air and sat down with the supreme complaisance of one who had nothing to fear, instead of a death sentence to hear. A meaningless smile played at the corners of his thick lips, and when the court asked him if he had anything to say why sentence should not

be passed upon him, he leaped up from his chair with cat-like agility, and answered clearly "Yes sir, I don't think it right dat I should suffer for somfin' I never done, and I didn't do it Jedge." The court then proceeded to read the sentence, and contrary to all precedent in the reporter's limited experience, didn't close with the sentence "and may the Lord have mercy on your soul." As evidence that Lee was not much impressed with the fate that awaits him, on the way back to the jail he remarked to Sheriff Teague that he had forgotten when the Judge said that thing was to come off.[8]

As the final days began to wane for Hughes, the *Banner*'s coverage became even less objective, as in this account: "Only ten more days until Lee Hughes…will be ushered from before the footlight of time behind the drop curtain of eternity, and according to his own statement, make his debut on the golden streets in the city of the New Jerusalem, transformed for the final act as an Angel in the robes of spotless white with shining wings, so innocent perhaps that he will think Christ ought to get up and give him His seat."[9]

The tenor of the *Banner*'s coverage seemed to be taking on a more ominous undertone, which would continue throughout the coverage of the hanging. Interracial relationships, never overly harmonious, had been fraying throughout the post-Reconstruction era, and most of the inhabitants of Brenham vividly recalled another jailbreak five years earlier that also was followed by a hanging.

In that case in the early morning hours of December 1, 1886, the jailbreak was by a masked mob of about seventy-five angry whites who kidnapped three Black men held after the shooting death of Dewees Bolton. Bolton, the son of a county commissioner candidate in that November's election, was involved in the theft of one of three ballot boxes stolen from the "Black Belt" precinct polling places at Lott's Store, Grabal, and Flewellen's Store. The three men taken from the jail were later found lynched in a pecan tree about a mile north of town. They were not accused of Bolton's murder, but simply had been witnesses to his death. Polk Hill, later convicted of Bolton's actual murder, was sentenced to twenty years in the penitentiary and moved away from the jail for his own safety.

Five years later public excitement was again heightend when Sheriff Teague announced the hanging of Lee Hughes would not take place at the jail. This led to speculation in the *Brenham Weekly Banner* of October 8, 1891, not only that "the execution will in all probability take place publicly" but also that "(a) public execution will bring a bigger crowd than the approaching circus."[10] The spectacle of a public hanging of two Blacks in Bastrop fifteen years earlier, in November 1876, had attracted a crowd of 3,000. To put this number of people into perspective, it's important to realize that the town's population barely topped 1,500 four years later, according to the 1880 census. And, as time would tell, although Brenham was a larger community, it would ultimately see an even larger audience at the hanging of Lee Hughes than its total population.

While the frenzy around the planned hanging could be compared with a circus environment, a real circus, the Forepaugh Show, came to town a few days before the hanging, giving the the *Banner* another chance to comment on it:

> The streets of Brenham presented an interesting scene on circus day-a moving mass of humanity, ⅔ of

which were negros who numbered no less than 10,000, but strange to say 300 covered their representation inside the circus tent. -- Austin County Times.' This is the lowest estimate we have seen of their representation, but it has been a subject of general remark on the small number that attend. The fact is they would have gone, but they didn't have the money and just came to town to see the parade.[11]

The circus arrived in Brenham on October 21, aboard fifty rail cars and pulled by four trains. The Great Adam Forepaugh Show was a true three-ring circus under fourteen tents, complete with trained horses on trapezes and jumping through hoops of fire, twenty trained elephants, five caged lions "riding tricycles, forming high pyramids, playing see-saw, carried in arms... harnessed to chariots and racing and riding," "200 wild beasts in the enormous menageries," a "realistic Wild West exhibition... illustrating the famous ghost dance...Wounded Knee Creek... Custer's last stand..." and, as if to warm up the crowd for later that week, a "hanging horse thief."[12]

But less than a week after the circus left town, preparations began for the next big show of the season in Brenham. Although the date had been set for the execution and the decision made to not have it at the Washington County jail, no citizen was willing to have the hanging on their property. The site finally chosen was a small triangle of city-owned land a mile east of town that served as a powder magazine site for the Brenham Field Artillery, a local militia unit.[13] But even this site was not without controversy, and "(i)n fact the citizens of Camptown, which is about 200 yards away, are threatening to sue out an injunction restraining the Sheriff from hanging him there."[14] Although not explicitly mentioned by the *Banner*, the location of Hughes' execution was directly across the railroad tracks from Camptown Cemetery.

When the *Banner*'s reporter visited the newly erected gallows several days before the hanging, he already found the site swarming with hundreds of visitors. It was an impressive structure, thirteen steps leading up to the ten-foot-square platform constructed of four by fours rising nine feet above the ground. The noose hung from the cross beam seven-and-a half feet higher. The trapdoor was held in place with a five-eighths of an inch thick rope, released when the executioner cut it through with "the single blow of a hatchet and Lee Hughes will have a clear fall of eight feet...before the footlights of time bend the drop curtain of eternity."[15]

The reporter also pointed out potential viewing options:

> The gallows is in a low place, the ground on the west side rising in amphitheater style, and facing the gallows on the north less than 40 yards away rises the Central railway embankment, while only a little further east Hogg Branch trestle furnishes a splendid view of the execution. From the situation of the gallows the hanging can be seen easily by countless thousands. In fact, no better place could have been found for a public execution, though the place was not selected with any reference to the advantageous position it furnished the public to see it...[16]

The *Banner* seemed to have hanging on its mind as the date for the execution of Hughes approached. Next to the column headed "Lee Hughes Gallows. The Place, One That Possess Advantages Unsurpassed for Viewing the Execution" was an article titled "Insurrection. Some Fool Negro Wants a Little Notoriety and he Might Get it if he Tries Hard" and consumed as much space. It dealt with "a notice stuck up on the corner of Ant and Sandy streets Monday morning, evidently written by some colored ignoramus who perhaps sought through this means to give himself some notoriety, but if he was to follow the bent of his harangue would soon take up in the penitentiary or at the end of a rope." Although the full contents of the notes (a second was found at the post-office) is not given, the allusion to another 'rope-stretching' as a solution is unmistakable from the concluding paragraph:

> No alarm is felt at the idle threats of the two fool negroes whose names appear on the paper. In fact, the names are probably fictitious, but if any negro in this country gets to believing that he is so badly oppressed as these seem to think he had better take a quiet dark night, sneak out of the country, and walk on the shady side of the lanes until he gets to a better place, where limbs don't grow low on the post-oaks and hemp is high.[17]

The day before Hughes was to be hung, the *Banner* had a reporter again visit him in his cell, where he was attended to by his two sisters and Elder Dickinson of the Mount Rose Baptist Church. He continued to deny any guilt in the crime, but acknowledged

> ...that he was not the first innocent man who had been jerked up and hung, and that he did not mind death and had the courage to face it unflinchingly, and that he had no doubts about the future. His confidence that the gates of heaven are standing ajar awaiting his arrival, and that a retinue of angels will attend him from the gallows to the great White Throne was as strong as words could express

it. He begged his sisters not to grieve after him, but to meet him in Heaven.[18]

Afterward, according to the news account, Elder Dickinson and Hughes' sisters prayed together

> ...a fervent prayer...for the soul of the prisoner, the sisters indulging in expressions of sorrow, an occasional Amen! and continuing a chant peculiar with negroes of the South when worshipping. At the conclusion of the ministers [sic] prayer the elder sister, in a burst of tears, said this may be the last time I can ever pray with my baby brother, let us again pray, and throwing herself on her knees upon the floor she commenced a chant, half prayer and half song, first low then louder, until with lungs thoroughly inflated, the occasion perhaps with her poignant grief furnishing the inspiration, she prayed as few women can pray, such a prayer as the reporter has never heard from an illiterate person, man or woman... The prayer was full of pathos, and the closing sentences really sublime, and only concluded when she was exhausted.[19]

After the sisters left to get a bathtub for an in-cell baptism by Elder Dickinson and Hughes was measured for a new black suit of broadcloth, the reporter tried again, in vain, to get him to confess. Baptism was performed, and by Hughes' account he slept from about midnight until two in the morning, spending the rest of that night praying. The next morning, the *Banner*'s reporter came calling again, offering both a smoke for Lee and breathless purple prose for readers:

VOICES OF CAMPTOWN | 157

The prisoner accepted a cigar and smoked it with as much satisfaction as if his hours were not numbered, his destiny sealed, the black despair-the shadows of a starless night gathering around him, obscuring hope, and him carelessly whiling away the moments that for him would seem to have been gliding too swiftly, yet he colored all without weakening in his assertion that he was ready and willing to go, to let out his life through the hangman's door, as unconcernedly as if there was nothing terrible in death, as if it was but to cast aside life like a robe, and sleep without a breath to disturb repose, till dawn, as if he had the golden key that opens the palace to eternity.[20]

The jail was surrounded by a mass of onlookers until noon, when the horse-drawn, still-empty coffin left for the hanging ground. The streets were "...almost impassable from 12 o'clock until the dray left with the coffin, enough of the crowd following it to then thin out some." Thousands were already estimated around by the gallows an hour later, "...scrambling for advantageous positions from which to view the execution, and at 2 o'clock a careful estimate of the crowd was easily placing it at 6,000, and still they were coming. The railroad embankment 50 yards away was strung with people for 200 yards."[21] Even the train traveling along those tracks stopped alongside the gallows to offer its passengers a prime viewing spot. When the eastbound train out of Austin passed by "...the train had many passengers and they begged the conductor to wait a few minutes to give them a chance to view a Texas legal execution. The conductor granted the request by waiting five minutes, and he was warmly thanked by his passengers."[22] The crowd that came to witness Lee's death was also estimated by a reporter from Galveston to eventually grow to between 3,00 and 8,000.[23] This is even more impressive considering that, according to 1890 census data, the total population of Brenham was only 5,209.

At ten minutes before three o'clock, the guards opened the way through the sea of people for the two-horse hack that brought Lee Hughes to the gallows. Physicians and newspaper reporters had preceded them and taken up a position on the scaffold. After considerable effort the guards cleared the way for the hack, which contained Sheriff Teague, Deputy Sheriff Sallus, and Constable Boyd, Lee Hughes, and Elder Dickinson.

Once these four finally arrived at the gallows, they left the carriage and ascended the thirteen steps to the platform. All were quiet as Teague read a summary of the court's judgment, followed by a reading of the death warrant. Hughes was then allowed to address the crowd. "Friends, I want to bid you all good-bye. Here is an innocent man going to be hanged, and I don't want anyone to grieve after me. I am not afraid to die. The Lord wants all his soldiers to be brave, and I go to meet him in glory. I have been fed with the word of God, and I want to feed you all, for I want you to go and live with Jesus."[24]

Elder Dickinson then led the crowd in prayer while the sheriff attached the noose to the cross beam:

> The condemned man walked to the other side of the scaffold and bid the crowd good-by [sic], reiterated the statement of his innocence and prayed the Lord to fulfill the vision he had shown him in his sleep, which was to the effect that when the trap door fell the Lord would send his angels down to bear his soul to heaven. He called on one Thompson and said "hanging ain't no disgrace, and while I am going to die Jesus will save the soul." He took

his position in the center of the trap door. Still not a tear at the parting, not a tremor of the voice to show that he was filled with emotion, a sardonic smile playing on his lips, as though grief was forced to life against her will. He shook hands with the officers, physicians, reporters, and told them good-by. His arms were pinioned behind him, his feet tied together, the black cap adjusted, the noose slipped over his head and drawn taut, and at 3:08 Sheriff Teague picked up the hatchet, asked Lee if he was ready and receiving an affirmative answer, the sharp edged tool descended swiftly, cleaving in twain the rope that supported the trap door, and the body of Lee Hughes shot through the opening to the end of the rope a distance of eight feet, his neck being broken by the fall. The reporter looked down at him, but he could not detect the movement of a muscle, not a struggle, seeming to be dead by the time he stopped.[25]

Eleven minutes later Hughes was pronounced dead by the three doctors brought along for the purpose. After the body had hung there for twenty minutes, it was cut down. Hughes' family had requested his body be released to Martin Johnson to be buried the next day. He was laid to rest eight miles east of town at the Miller graveyard.

Within the week, the ghost of Lee Hughes was reported seen by local Black citizens:

> The negroes living near the place where Lee Hughes was hanged have seen his spirit or "hant." On Friday night, between 11 and 12 o'clock, it was seen upon the scaffold just in the place Lee stood before the execution,

though the trap door had not been replaced after the rope was cut-still the spirit stood upon the air in the center of it-and then again on Hallowe'en the "hant" was there, walking around the place where the scaffold had been. The rope was around its neck and coiled around its body, but the hands and feet were not tied, and the black cap was pushed up off its face. Whether or not these stories are made of full cloth or whether some person has been actually seen around the place where the tragedy, matters not. The stories of Lee's ghost will find willing ears and there are very few negroes who would dare walk near the place of his taking off on a dark night."[26]

Within the next five years, there would be another hanging of young Black men protesting their innocence to the end before giving up their ghosts before record crowds at the same location in Brenham, immediately across the railroad tracks from Camptown Cemetery, "Washington county's own 'Tyburn,' to the southeast of town."[27] Brothers John and Brady Rutherford and Joe Goodson were hung on May 20, 1896, in a triple hanging for the murder of Thomas Dwyer, a prominent white citizens well respected among both the white and Black populace. As reported in the *Conroe Courier*, "(f)ully 15,000 people witnessed the gruesome sight of three men being executed on the same gallows at one time, many having come long distances. The crowd was very orderly, but after the bodies of the culprits fell and were swinging in the air numbers of the colored people gave vent to moans and several of the women shrieked considerably."[28] The bodies of the Rutherford brothers were turned over to their grieving families for burial, but the body of Joe Goodson suffered a different fate. In a grim echo of slavery, he had sold his body to Drs. Raysor and Langhorn of nearby Chappel Hill, "who had purchased it for the "purpose of dissection."[29]

## Chapter 9

# "YOU ARE GOOD FOR TWENTY YEARS YET!

# ASA RIPPETOE

One cold December night in the opening year of the twentieth century, Asa Rippetoe was roused from a deep sleep. He was astonished to find an angel had woken him and said, "Asa, you are good for twenty years yet!" Then, just as mysteriously as this unexpected visitor had come into his bedroom that evening, it vanished. Amazed at this wondrous revelation, Asa turned to Caroline, sleeping next to him, and told his wife of the gift that had just been presented to him.[1]

This episode in Rippetoe's life is certainly one of the most unusual. We only know about this peculiarly intimate moment because it was published in the same newspaper where other more mundane articles were published, giving us a broad outline of his life in Camptown

As is all too common with those born into slavery, little is known about Rippetoe's early life. The day of his birth, December 22, 1844, is known from his gravestone in Camptown Cemetery, which was erected by his daughter, Ada Hill. Born in Alabama, he moved to Brenham in 1867 and lived there until his death. The 1870 census showed him to be a farm laborer living with

Dr. Albert H. Rippetoe, a white physician, farmer, Mexican War veteran, and a former Master of the Graham Masonic Lodge #20. The relationship between the two seems to have been amicable and may be the source of his surname.

Asa Rippetoe eventually became involved with Caroline Basey, who had previously been married to a much older man and possibly became a widow. They were wed in Brenham in March 1879 and were raising Caroline's two children from her former marriage when they had their first child, Ada. They eventually would have four more children of their own – Lily, Mariah, George, and Talmadge.

The issuance of their marriage license received a brief notice in the *Daily Banner,* a local Brenham newspaper,[2] but it was not the first time Rippetoe was mentioned in the press. The first was in 1878, when he was the fifth assistant to the Grand Marshal in the Emancipation Day celebrations at the head of a parade that made its way down Main Street following the firing of a signal gun.[3]

By far the greatest number of references about Rippetoe were about his occupation, that of "one of the best-known draymen of the city."[4] A dray referred to a wagon without sides and a flatbed that was very low to the ground and used to transport goods from one point to another. Hauling freight on a low-slung vehicle over roads that were in notoriously bad condition was a skill much in demand at the time, and by all appearances Rippetoe was quite good at it. Items that he moved ranged from "transporting paupers to the county poor farm[5] " to bales of cotton weighing more than five hundred pounds each from plantations, coal, firewood, and groceries. His business brought him into contact with many of the local white business owners, with whom he developed good working relationships, including many hauling jobs for the city and county. Much of the work involved loading or unloading railroad cars. Usually it went smoothly, but mishaps became fodder for the press, as when a barrel of molasses rolled from his wagon and "was bursted [sic] by the force of the fall. Very little of it was lost, however, as a number of negroes soon rushed to the scene of the catastrophe with buckets and pans and other available receptacles and scooped it up."[6]

Horses were an integral part of Rippetoe's business and often played into press accounts mentioning him. When one of his horses was slashed on the hip "with an undoubted malice aforethought" and sustained a crippling large cut, Rippetoe was described as an industrious colored drayman who worked for a living and deserved better treatment at the hands of his fellow men than he received "in this blow to his livelihood."[7] He had a great affinity for his animals and when one of them was "taken very sick with colic," a crowd gathered around with numerous suggestions, "but Asa administered what he thought best and soon had the horse able to get on his feet and led him home."[8] The teams of horses he managed could be skittish amidst the hustle and bustle of city streets, and on one occasion his four-horse team "became frightened and dashed up Sandy Street at a lively rate of speed," coming to a sudden stop only when the tongue of the wagon they were hitched to struck another heavily loaded wagon, "throwing one of the horses to the ground, stopping the others."[9]

A more disastrous incident occurred in 1900 while unloading a carload of lumber. His team of horses and the wagon were on the tracks of the Houston and Texas Central railroad when "the local, which was switching in the yards, backed down on them. Both horses were killed, and the wagon demolished."[10] Rippetoe filed suit against the railroad, valuing his horses at $110 each, and the case dragged on for a year before he was awarded $175.[11]

As his drayage business continued to prosper, Rippetoe understood the power of advertising his services, taking out a series of ads in the local weekly paper in 1913 promoting "his cheaper" wood delivery services.[12] When he began to headquarter his business at the Gas Office on Main Street, he took out an even longer series of ads as a "Transfer Man" in the daily paper from 1913 to 1914, boldly listing his name, the location of the office and its phone number, which was simply 474.[13]

A few other details of Rippetoe's life can be gathered from the pages of the Brenham papers. In an incident in 1893, he filed charges against two other men for "using profane and abusive language."[14] This may seem an odd case to bring before a judge, but during that time such behavior was an offense subject to a fine and frequently enforced. We also know that he wore gold rimmed spectacles, since he ran ads in the paper offering a reward to anyone who found and returned them to him. These ads also mention that they were lost before his home and "the colored M.E. church in Camptown."[15] His affiliation with the church also is noted in an "Important Notice" placed in the *Brenham Daily Banner*: "People affiliating with all church organizations are urged to attend the services at the African Methodist church at 11 o'clock Sunday morning, May 4. I have a message to deliver than everyone should hear. Asa Rippetoe." There is no further indication as to what that message was, though it was twelve years after his nocturnal visit from an angel.[16]

The final article mentioning him is his obituary, published on the front page and titled "Well-Known Negro is Dead. Asa Rippetoe, for Years a Drayman in Brenham, Passes Away: Burial Services Wednesday." It went on to read:

> Asa Rippetoe, a well-known drayman of this city, died at his residence in Camptown Tuesday morning at 2:15. Asa was one of the old-time darkies –the kind

that is rapidly disappearing. He attended strictly to his own business and was always obliging. He was born in Alabama, came to Brenham in 1867 and has lived here continuously, engaging in the transfer business and had by his courteous bearing made many friends among both white and black. He will be buried from the St. John's A.M.E. church in Camptown at 2:30 Wednesday afternoon."[17]

Although he hadn't quite made the full twenty years the angel had promised in 1901, he did manage another thirteen years as one of the leading citizens of Camptown.

# Chapter 10

# ALEXANDER THOMAS: THE TWO ENDS OF SLAVERY FOR A BLACK LAWYER

Eli Ross was at his mother's house when Mrs. Grant[1] sent for him. She had heard groaning sounds out in the prairie next to her house, and she wanted Eli to go see what it could possibly be, possibly fearing the worst. Following the sounds into the undergrowth along Bray's Bayou, Eli found a nearly nude black man dressed only in bloody underclothes.

He later described what happened next:

> "I.... went after Louis Mays, and he went over to look at him. I also accompanied him. Mr. Mays and Hampton tried to talk to him. They found him speechless. Mr. Hampton wrote a note to Mr. Fant (the sheriff), and sent it by me to town. I went back with the sheriff and party, and when we arrived, we found life extinct. They then took the corpse to the city. This is all I know about the case. I never saw [sic] deceased before."[1]

---

1    No first name given

The body was brought to the undertaker's office, where the justice of the peace impaneled a coroner's jury, which was standard practice in March 1885 in Texas. As the undershirt was being cut away to reveal a massive shotgun blast in the left torso, Eli "slipped from the crowd and took to his heels. The absence of the main witness caused a suspension of the inquest proceedings."[2]

Deputies were saddled up in pursuit, only finding him the following day. It turns out that Ross had been frightened because when the underclothes (most likely a pair of long johns) were cut away it revealed a body and legs wrapped in damp, gray moss. It was possibly this unexpected finding of a moss-covered man that caused Ross to run, and likely the moss was an attempt at staying warm in the damp chill of late winter when dressed only in underwear.

The moss-covered dead man was quickly identified. Colonel E.H. Cunningham, who leased prisoners from the nearby state penitentiary system, had sent a telegram to Sheriff John J. Fant about an escaped convict who matched the body, including "the suit of underclothing":

> Shortly after the escape, Jack Rice, "an old negro who lives in the neighborhood of where the body was found, discovered a negro suiting the description of [sic] deceased in his kitchen. The old man accused the intruder of being an escaped convict, which he denied, at the same time picking up an ax. Rice ran into a room, armed himself with a shotgun that was loaded with No. 5 shot, and fired at the negro, who made his escape. Owing to there being no shot marks on the side of the room behind the spot where the negro stood, Rice believes that

the shots took effect."[3]

The dead man was five feet nine inches tall. He had a "projected" forehead, a missing front tooth, and a long scar visible on his left shoulder. He weighed about 140 pounds. His name was Alexander Thomas.[4]

One of the great ironies of history is that certain moments at the end of a person's life can be greatly detailed, while earlier events remain frustratingly obscure. This is certainly true of the life of Alexander Thomas.

His parents were born in Virginia, and he was born there as well around 1842. All were likely enslaved, judging from their race in that place and time. This scant bit of information comes from the 1880 census. Thomas next emerges in the public record in 1867 on the Voter Registration List for Washington County. According to this list, he had been in Texas for the previous sixteen years and in Washington County for the past three. Thomas ducked back out of the public record for the next eleven years, but not out of life. He took a wife, Clora Jane, who was nine years younger than he was. Following the birth of their first son in 1867, they had at least seven more children.

When Thomas next appeared in the written record, it was as one of Washington County's earliest Black attorneys. The event was mentioned briefly in the local paper as "rather a novel incident." He "stated in the out-set that he was young at the business and somewhat rusty, and therefore claimed the indulgence of the Judge and jury, then went straight to business. The effort is said to have been very creditable, and was listened to with attention."[5] His admission to the bar was based, at least in part, on the judgment of three county commissioners "that he was a man of good moral character, and also the report of three of the most prominent lawyers in Texas that he was learned in the law."[6]

However, life as a Black attorney in a legal system dominated by whites was not easy, and the press was more than willing to report on the difficulties inherent in such racial disparity. When Thomas was defending a client in district court, he "made a motion to quash the indictment, which motion was sustained by the court. The incident caused much amusement. The idea of the county attorney's indictment being quashed on motion of a colored attorney is regarded as supremely rich, and is highly creditable to Mr. Thomas."[7] The county attorney in this case was Carl Schutze, whom Thomas found himself up against two years later when running for the Republican candidacy for county attorney. "Thomas made an eloquent speech in his own behalf, and received 4 votes for his pains, Schutze received 65 votes."[8]

Few of his cases made the press. One, which referred to "Alexander Thomas, esquire, of Burton," was a divorce case "the parties to which were colored. Alexander succeeded in getting the golden chains of matrimony which had uncomfortably bound his client unlinked."[9] Another was for the murder of a young Black man by another over a woman, defended by Thomas in conjunction with a white attorney in front of a jury that included only two Black men. The case was lost, and the defendant was sentenced to fifty years in the penitentiary for second degree murder.[10]

Another murder in which Thomas had been legally entangled had occurred the previous year, one in which an acquittal had been obtained. It happened in Thomas's hometown of Burton, and the defendant was Thomas himself. The only record comes from a letter to the Brenham paper from a local correspondent reporting on "rather a novel procedure in Justice Court today, in which Alex. Thomas, colored lawyer of this city, was brought to trial for the murder of another negro." The letter described what happened:

> About two weeks ago Thomas gave a festival at his house; a disturbance was raised by the deceased sticking his knife in the cakes, promiscuously, at the supper table. Thomas objected to this and a general row ensued, in which Thomas struck deceased on the head with a rock, from the effects of which he died a few days ago. A coroner was notified and a jury of inquest summoned. The case was continued until today, the case called and the jury put in the box. The defendant called for his attorney, who conducted his defense, secured his acquittal.[11]

At this point in his career, Thomas seems to have been moderately prosperous. In addition to his legal practice, he also owned a working fifty-one-acre farm outside of Burton valued at close to $500, according to the 1880 census. He and his three sons grew enough cotton for three bales in 1879, as well as twenty-five bushels of Indian corn and enough sorghum for twenty gallons of molasses. They raised pigs, chickens, milk cows and other cattle. The cattle ultimately would lead to Thomas's death.

In late November 1884 Thomas was engaged in his final legal case, and he was again the defendant. Even though he raised cattle of his own, he had been accused of stealing "a yoke of oxen" in Fayette County, , and he not only lost the case but was sentenced to five years in the penitentiary.[12] He filed an appeal based on witnesses who had not appeared at the trial and lost his appeal, leading the Brenham newspaper to derisively comment that "his knowledge of the law must have been very defective or he would never have risked stealing cattle."[13] He was received into the prison system on February 23, 1885. According to prison records, at the time he was forty-three, slightly less than five feet, four inches tall and weighed 120 pounds. He had "a very high forehead" and his skin was reported as copper colored with over nine scars on his arms, legs, and back. He wasn't a smoker, had "temperate habits;" his "marital relations" status was listed as "no," which leaves open speculation as what may have happened in his home life.[14]

Once in the prison system as a convict, Thomas was leased out to Cunningham's plantation to work for the ex-Confederate general growing sugar cane. Conditions there had earned it the nickname of "hell-hole on the Brazos." It was described as "low, mosquito infested swamp and the sluggish bayous were habitats for alligators and noisome creepers. Convicts labored barelegged in wet sugar cane fields, dying like flies in the periodic epidemics of fevers. Civilian labor could not be kept on the place."[15] Convict labor such as this was slavery by another name, a bondage where men were leased rather than sold. Prisoners were subject to brutality with little concern for their safety. Mortality rates were appalling; in the years from 1890 to 1892, 10 percent of the prisoners died. It is not surprising that the rate of escapes during the same period was also 10 percent.[16]

For Thomas the thought of suffering life at the other end of a legal system he had sought to serve must have seemed unbearable. He would not be enslaved again; he would emancipate himself. Alexander Thomas escaped from Cunningham's plantation at night on March 9, 1885. It was never clear whether those witnesses who never appeared at his trial could have kept him from prison or how he spent those last three days of freedom after his escape before he died from that gunshot wound from a fellow Black man, but it was a tragically ironic fate for one of Brenham's first Black lawyers.

Chapter 11

# "IF IT WERE ALL KNOWN AND COULD BE WRITTEN:"

# MARY MARKS AND "UNIQUE STORY"

*Courtesy of San Antonio Daily Light, June 29, 1896*

In early 1896 in Independence, Texas, a frail old woman was reported dead after a fire erupted at the home where she was staying. The fire threw the small community into such a state of agitation in attempting to put it out that Sam Houston's grandson was run over by a horse and his leg broken. As the wooden structure finally burned to the ground, it was feared that Aunt

Mary was finally dead, having become bedridden the previous winter after she fell into a fire while trying to warm herself from the cold during a snowstorm.

Aunt Mary and her husband, known as Uncle John, never had any children of their own before he died sixteen years earlier. But they welcomed all the young people of the town with sweets and kindly words of wisdom, and in turn were treated as family. Aunt Mary had been a much beloved part of Independence for over sixty years, and many had fond memories of her. Her loss was so deeply felt that the news of her death was reported in newspapers throughout Texas, with interest in the stories spurred by the fact that she was said to be over a hundred years old.

But Mary wasn't dead.

Somehow during the fire, she managed to crawl away, a detail the press came to realize only several days later. Retractions were printed and the story seemed to die away for a while. Then in May 1896, a reporter, accompanied by a photographer named T. A. Holland, journeyed to Independence to get the story of "one of the oldest persons in the state—probably the oldest." They interviewed Mrs. Marks as she sat on the side of her bed at a cottage owned by Louis Perkins, a neighbor at whose house she had been living since her latest perilous encounter with flames. The story they came away with was captivating enough to garner two columns of print, with at least one incredible fact that spread her story to newspapers across the nation.[1]

Mary Marks claimed to be 119 years old, the same age as the Declaration of Independence. Centenarians are rare even today and were even more so at the turn of the nineteenth century, when there were only a handful throughout the country. Achieving a hundredth birthday virtually guaranteed press coverage, especially at a time when the average life span of women was barely over fifty. But the story of her life was every bit as unique as her age.

Mary's life, as she recalled it, began in what was then known as the Spanish Caribbean, on the island of Hispaniola. The island has a complex history of slavery, complete with slave rebellions and a brief period of slavery being abolished. Mary claimed to have been born in 1776, before either of these brief respites, belonging to a tribe of "Spanish Caribs" raided by Captain Thomas Parker and his crew gathering slaves for sale in the American South. Still an infant "at her mother's breast," Mary found favor in the eyes of the captain, "a dashing fellow, that Mary still remembers with a mixed feeling of terror and admiration."[2] Rather than selling her off with the rest of the captives, Parker kept her with him aboard his ship, the Black Cat, throughout much of her early childhood.

Mary still held "even now vague recollections of many sea voyages, the flap of sails, the creak of cordage, the wash of the waves, the cruelty of the captain," as well as "the waste of the seas, the hoarse commands, the groans beneath the hatches." Her life on the Black Cat ended after Parker died "of a fever contracted in the tropics" while he was "unloading a cargo, and Mary with the rest was sold into slavery."[3]

Her life became one of a slave caught in the grips of an economy of human chattel, sold and resold multiple time over the coming decades. But things began to change for her in 1821, when her last masters, James and Betsy Whiteside, brought her to Texas. They settled along the Brazos and opened a tavern in Stephen F. Austin's first colony at San Felipe. It was a wild frontier, "roamed over by buffalo, mustangs, deer by the thousands, leopard cats, wolves, Mexican hogs and wild cattle."[4] Marks served as the head servant for the tavern which also served as a hotel—of sorts. It consisted of "a double log cabin, with various sheds and lean-tos, built on from time to time as increasing demands were made upon its hospitality; the principal sleeping apartment was a low loft running the entire length of the building, unbroken by a single partition and reached by a ladder thrust through a hole in the floor."[5] Cooking the meals and serving the guests, "'Aunt Mary Marks' dispensed the corn 'dodgers,' game and coffee which constituted the usual menu." Over the course of time, she met many of the most important men who would shape the course of Texas independence over the coming years, including "Austin, Rusk, Houston and many other famous people."[6] As an "attentive waitress, (she) was thoroughly alive to the greatness of her guests and repeats with the keenest appreciation many of their sayings."[7]

Working with the Whitesides, Mary would meet the most important man of all in her life, John Marks. John had been born into slavery in Virginia but set free by "his young mistress" while still young. He committed his life to the ministry and became a Methodist preacher. In 1836 he "came in his wanderings to Texas, the outpost of civilization," staying at "Uncle Jimmy's Tavern." He was "a full blooded African, tall and very black, with long arms and a mouth almost from ear to ear. He had little education, but he preached with power, and the white people flocked to hear him, in the words of his relief, 'like birds.'"[8] The two clearly made an impression on each other, and they were soon married. Their "union was not the result of a sudden infatuation, for both John and Mary had long since passed the time when the fires of youth are supposed to burn. Theirs was a union of heart and mind; their tastes, religious beliefs and general characteristics were similar, and their married life was as clear as piety and true honesty could make it."[9]

Their marriage did face one major obstacle—John may have been a free man, but his new wife was still another man's property, at least until he was able to buy her freedom. Eventually, he was able to save up enough money to purchase her release from slavery, and several years later, after Texas had won her independence, the Marks "took up their residence...on ten acres deeded them by Judge John P. Cole"[10] on Cole's Creek, half a mile west of what was later became the town of Independence after being settled by Cole. This gift was "to revert to the Cole heirs at the death of the survivor" since the couple remained childless.[11] John and Mary lived on this tract of land throughout the transition of Texas from nation to state to state of rebellion, somehow managing to survive free in a time and place when virtually all other Blacks were slaves.

Or at least, this was the story that was reported. The truth seems to have been different in some ways, but even more rich and complex in others.

John Marks was one of the most best-known Black preachers in early Texas history, though known early on as simply "Uncle Mark." In Texas before 1840, there were few Baptist preachers in Texas, and they would often rely on clerics of other denominations. O. M. Addison, a pioneer Methodist preacher, was witness to the situation:

> About this time there came to Washington County a gentleman owning a negro slave, "Uncle Mark," a Methodist local preacher. These guileless Baptists, hungering for the true word, engaged from his master the services of this negro preacher. The first the writer heard "Uncle Mark" was on one of these occasions. Attracted to the novelty of a negro preaching to white folks he with a younger brother walked seven miles to Mrs. Katie Smith's whose best room was improvised into a chapel for the occasion. "Uncle Mark" was coal black, with a serious cast of countenance and a wide forehead. He was grave

and dignified, and his manner becoming and impressive. He read his opening hymn with marked emphasis and correctness.[12]

Uncle Mark also used to preach in Washington, the earliest capital of Texas. "In the early days, too, there used to come to Washington, a negro from Independence, by the name of Mark, who occasionally preached...to the negroes. This old negro was a prodigy. His discourses were delivered with as much ability as most of his white brethren could display. He used to preach in a grove, and his audience was frequently composed of more whites than negroes. The white people were very kind to old Mark, and their charities were so liberal that he purchased his freedom.[13]

Further evidence that Marks may not have been or stayed a freedman when he came to Texas is found in an obituary written by another prominent Methodist, R. Alexander. It indicated "that the 'deed' to John Marks was first held by a Masonic lodge, but on the request of Mark himself, who wanted the Church to be his master, the Texas Annual Conference, aided by several generous Methodists, purchased him and held the deed."[14] Dr. H. S. Thrall was a Methodist circuit preacher in 1848 when he encountered at Independence "one of the most able and influential preachers he has ever met," known as Uncle Mark:

> The planters paid for his time, and he traveled extensively, preaching, organizing churches and doing an excellent work for his people. About that time the owner of Uncle Mark removed to the West, and the planters, unwilling to lose his labors and influence among their slaves, raised the money among themselves, and purchased him; but as our laws did not allow

of emancipation, he was deeded to three Methodist preachers in trust for the Methodist Episcopal Church, South.[15]

Thrall witnessed Uncle Mark's preaching firsthand, leaving a few small hints at his preaching style. He "once heard Uncle Mark illustrate the conduct of unstable Christians. 'You,' said he, 'are in and out, joining the Church and backsliding. Bless your souls, the Lord don't count you in the crop! You belong to the 'Droop Shot Gang!'" (a gang composed of feeble women and children, not counted as hands in the crop). On another occasion he was preaching against pride, he said; 'You think a poor negro has nothing to be proud of; but on Sunday afternoon give one of these boys a red bandanna handkerchief and white cotton gloves, and he's proud as a peacock!'" He was eventually ordained as a deacon by the Texas Methodist Conference in 1853.[16]

The reported story of John and Marks living on land donated to them during their lifetime is difficult to substantiate, but after Cole's death it eventually was purchased by Moses Austin Bryan. Bryan was an early Texas settler, arriving in 1831 at age fourteen, and he remembered "Aunt Mary" well from his earliest days in San Felipe when he was a clerk in the town's first store. Bryan was also a prominent citizen in the early days of the struggle for Texas's independence, remaining well respected for his role in it. With the coming of secession, he served as a major in the Confederacy, but after the end of the Civil War he came to realize that race relations with new citizens who had previously been slaves were undeniably changed.

As a result, on August 27, 1866, Bryan deeded the "upper" five acres of land that John and Mary were living on to her "in consideration of the Kindness shown me by said colored woman

Mary Mark in the year Eighteen hundred and thirteen in the Town of San Felipe de Austin." In addition, "being desirous to aid and assist the colored People in and around the Town of Independence in improving their condition so that they better understand their new relations and changed situation," deeded the lower half of the ten-acre tract to the African Methodist Church. The land was given so that "the said Colored people may erect a church building and a schoolhouse and also lay off a burying ground for the use and benefit of the colored people."[17]

John and Mary remained in Independence, helping to stabilize the tumultuous relationship that arose after Emancipation. Their church and school were among the largely illiterate community of previously enslaved Blacks still dependent upon an agricultural economy dominated by previous slave holders, acting as a bridge between whites and Blacks while still being respected by those on both sides. John continued to preach until his death in late November 1879, "at a good old age." His funeral was held at the Methodist Episcopal Church in Brenham, where the funeral sermon was given by a "...negro preacher...never in the history of the town were so many colored people congregated in the town."[18] Following his passing, Mary received a pension of $30 a year from the African Methodist Episcopalian church where her husband had been pastor. Although she had grown "quite feeble," she was "taken care of by different neighbors, both white and black [sic], contributing cheerfully to her support."[19]

A Galveston reporter found her "sitting cheerfully" on the side of her bed as she "prattled on about Texas, life here at the early days of her first acquaintance with its prairies and forests, and her own extreme old age, which she attributes to the goodness of God. She is sustained by constant draughts of whisky and cannot survive many weeks, for her mind, which up to within a few days ago was clear, has begun to fail."[20]

But survive she did. Two months later a correspondent from the *St. Louis Globe-Democrat* visited her at the Perkins home, sitting on the edge of her bed, her mind clear "though her body is sustained by frequent draughts of whisky, a stimulant that only the necessities of age have induced her to touch." Again, she was the subject of a substantial news story that made its way across the nation, with most of the stories emphasizing her claim to have been born in the same year as the birth of the nation. Ironically, her story reflected what so many in the nation would later experience.[21]

Time began to weigh ever more heavily on Mary. The $30 she had been receiving each month from the A.M.E. church was no longer enough to support her. As early as May 1895 the county commissioner's court was being petitioned for assistance, and as late as May 1896 she had received allotments of $4 to help her. But eventually poverty won out, and she finally was committed to the poor farm. She died there at 7 a.m. on December 4, 1896, spawning a new wave of attention from the press because she died at the ripe old age of 120. But she was still yet to experience what was yet another remarkable events in her afterlife.[22]

Moses Austin Bryan had reminisced several times before his death in 1895 about Aunt Mary, whom he still recalled fondly from his days as a fourteen-year-old teenager arriving at the outskirts of civilization in San Felipe. In 1890, he was somewhat pained to say "that of all the people he knew when he first landed in Texas, which numbered between four and five hundred, Mary Mark[sic], an old mulatto woman who lives near Independence, is the only one who still survives."[23] These were stories his son, Beauregard Bryan, must have recalled, as well as probably knowing her himself. As a district judge, he exercised what power he had to propagate her memory. And "at the instance of her white friend, the chief promoter being Judge B. Bryan," it was decided that her remains be exhumed from the ignominy of the poor farm cemetery and "reinterred at the white cemetery in Independence." He even proposed "to erect a monument to her memory and to mark the spot where sleeps the remains of this interesting old character." And so, she was indeed exhumed and reinterred there, and it was reported that a "nice marble slab will mark the last resting place of the oldest person who ever died in Washington county."[24]

Mary rested there in peace and her story was almost forgotten until 1914, when she appeared in a story that mentioned that very marble slab erected at the behest of Judge Bryan entitled "Old Cemetery at Independence Is Sadly Neglected and Its Improvement Should Receive Attention of People of County." It described how "many people whose lives are very closely interwoven with the earlier and tragic as well as romantic history of the Lone Star State repose in this great Silent City on the hill" but "that the cemetery deserves better attention than it is receiving." It should be "one of the largest and prettiest in all the southland as it should be, instead of being overgrown and covered with a tangle of briers, bramble, and weeds."[25]

As the author wandered through the twenty acres of markers, "many of which are toppling towards the ground, we found one among the weeds and briers. A cricket sat on top of the timeworn and modest rock and sang its evening melody." The article continued:

> On the name of the old and weather-beaten rock, we read the name of "Mary Marks." Born 1796 and died 1896. We are told further that she was an old colored mammy who came to the Republic with the early settlers of Austin from Missouri, and was for many long years connected

with the family of General Sam Houston. The whole and true history and story of humble Mary Marks will, of course, never be known, but if it were all known and could be written, it would no doubt show a life of devotion and sacrifice to her people, among whom she lived, labored, loved and died. When the roll is called up yonder bye and bye [sic], and the saints answer the summons from this old hill at Independence, we believe that among the number will be Mary Marks whose life was given in the cause of duty and affection.[26]

I visited the same cemetery with my wife in 2018 and found no sign of the Marks headstone. Fortunately, her story had already been exhumed from the poor farm of crumbling old newspapers and reinterred so that those who pass this way may pay homage to the unique story of her life.

---

**Author's Note:** This story was inspired by a serendipitous find from Janel Jefferson of the Texas Ten Historical Explorers, a group dedicated to bringing forward untold stories from Washington County and the surrounding areas. The information on the deeds from Bryan to Marks was from the Washington County Public Records website, based on a hint from Jan Kelm, who also supplied the quote from *Sixty Years on the Brazos*. Most comes from newspaper databases, namely the Portal to Texas History and the Library of Congress's Chronicling America website, excellent resources for researching "the first rough draft of history," as journalism has been called. Addison's complete manuscript was found at the Dolph Briscoe Center for American History at the University of Texas in Austin. Every item in quotes above can be found in these sources.

I've chosen not to delve too deeply into the exact age of Mary Marks at her death, because I quite frankly don't think it can be determined, or that it is important. Claims of exaggerated ages were frequent topics for newspaper stories at the time. One article claimed "a centennial darkey" lived on the Filous plantation outside of Chappell Hill in Washington County. His age was said to be "140 or 155," his hair turning black to white and then back to white, working on his third set of teeth, and fathered eighty-five children by fourteen wives. There is no record of anyone with the name of Filous in Washington County at that time, but it is the plural form of the French word for trickster, rogue or rascal.[27]

Another aged person, Joice Heth, was on display by P. T. Barnum as the nursemaid of George Washington and reputed to be 161 years old. It does seem clear that Mary Marks was probably at least around a hundred at the time of her death, given her more clearly documented presence in San Felipe. The elder Bryan seemed to feel she was around 100 as well. Furthermore, the 1880 census, the only one she appears in, finds her living after the death of her husband with the Graves family and her age is given as "(72)." Yes, that's (72) with parentheses around it, the only time I've ever seen this in census records. The birth date on her grave marker as found in 1914 seems to more firmly place her age at probably around a hundred at the time of her death.

I was not able to find any record of a slave trader named Thomas Parker or a slave ship titled the Black Cat. It doesn't mean they don't exist, but the reality of the slave trade and its horrors certainly did. Regardless, one fact does certainly remain—that Mary Marks was a truly remarkable survivor.

Chapter 12

# THE LONG REACH OF THE CIVIL WAR

In 1861 the secession of the South quickly led to war, with the Union considering the Confederacy states in rebellion rather than a new nation based on the freedom to own slaves. But until the end of the conflict, slavery continued as an institution in Washington County. Many of the white citizens would go to war to protect their perceived right to own a human being of a different color. Service was voluntary at first, with many whites quickly signing on to local regiments lest they miss serving in what they were sure would be a short but glorious conflict. Ideas of chivalry ran high early on, with Chappell Hill forming a regiment of lancers, a concept spurred on by prewar tournaments complete with jousting.

But as the war progressed, the South's imagined easy victory rapidly evaporated and re-enlistment dropped. By April 1862, the resulting shortage of manpower forced compulsory service for all white males between the ages of eighteen and thirty-five. There were exemptions from service, but they did not include overseers. The fear of servile insurrection arose again, with only minors, women, and older men left to manage a slave population that was beginning to realize the possibility of eventual liberation. Within weeks of Lincoln's Emancipation Proclamation, a second conscription act was passed for plantations owning more than twenty slaves within five miles of each other, allowing an exemption for one white owner or an overseer.

The following year even slaves were being requested by the Confederacy to serve in the military. Following the two battles in which the Confederacy lost and then regained Galveston, General John B. Magruder issued an order requesting the planters of seventeen counties, including Washington County, to send 2,000 slaves for the purpose of building defensive fortifications at Galveston. The request was later clarified that "1/4 of the male Negro population between the ages of 16 & 50" were to report there with shovels and spades, and "must bring with them their bedding and cooking utensils. Clothing and shoes will be furnished them at cost prices. Comfortable quarters provided for them. Medical attendance, medicines and rations furnished free, and thirty dollars per month will be paid for their services. Overseers with 25 negroes will be paid $60 per month. Transportation to the Island and back home furnished free." It is unlikely that many slaves were sent since the total number working for the engineers probably never reached a thousand and was likely only 600 that spring. By December General Magruder sent another order to planters for able-bodied male slaves between the ages of sixteen and fifty, with those from Washington County now to be sent to Austin, with the planters once again to supply their own "intrenching tools, such as axes, spades, shovels, hoes, picks, grubbing hoes, etc."[1]

But not all planters were willing to listen to a government telling them what to do with their slaves, especially since they were actively fighting another government that had been telling them what to do with their slaves. And gentlemen planters, especially, were not so willing to head off without having a manservant along with them to act as valet, cook, forage, and ease the many other discomforts incumbent upon serving in the military. This the case with Benoni W. Gray and his three sons when they joined the Confederate army and brought along their slave, Dick.

Dick, named after his maternal grandfather, was born in March 1843 in Mississippi. His mother, Indiana, was a slave belonging to the Gray family. His family, including three sisters, moved along with the Gray family several times before he was sold off at age sixteen for $1,200 to Benoni W. Gray, a relative living in Washington County. His mother and sisters were sold separately, and he was not to see them again for many years. With the outbreak of war between the Confederacy and the Union, Benoni Gray went off to war, along his three sons, and Dick was brought along with them as a servant. Benoni and two of the sons died in battle, and when the youngest was badly wounded, Dick took him back to Texas to recover. When it was feared that he might be captured, Dick took the son to Mexico and returned with him, continuing to run the plantation for the family until several years after the war was over. Following Emancipation, he took the surname of Boyd and paid to learn how to read and write with the assistance of a white girl and later attended Bishop College. He eventually joined the ministry, serving various churches throughout East Texas before eventually founding the National Baptist Publishing Board. His family continues to run it as the R. H. Boyd Publishing Corporation.[2]

The sense of camaraderie that both slaves and whites experienced while enmeshed during the trials and tumult of the Civil War created deep bonds. This closeness lasted long after the war. Sam Love was a Brenham citizen who faced trumped-up charges of embezzling school funds twenty-five years after the war's end, eventually being found guilty years after fleeing to escape a certain guilty verdict. The judge who sentenced him had known him as a cook who had served in his unit, Company G of the 2nd Brigade under General Jonathan Sales. "In pronouncing sentence, the court referred to these old associations feelingly and told the prisoner how much he regretted to have to pass sentence on him, after which he wound up with some good advice to him. Love was moved to tears and wept bitterly."[3]

Plenty of books exist about the Washington County plantation owners and others marching out to do battle in defense of a way of life firmly ensconced in slavery. The slaves who formed the base of the economy supporting them felt quite differently about all this, leading a significant number of them to run away. Some fled to a tenuous promise of liberty in Mexico, others to an equally tenuous life in the North. Following the inescapable outbreak of hostilities between the northern and southern states, another opportunity arose for those who had taken their freedom into their own hands. As the Union forces began to accept Blacks into the military, they could fight not only for their freedom, but also for those still held in bondage.

Some of the men who found their way from Washington County to the North escaped slavery and could fight for the cause of their freedom.

Two former slaves, the Hewett brothers, were born in Washington County and served on the Union side in the Civil War. James C. Hewett was twenty-one years old, five feet, four inches tall and of a light complexion; his brother Thomas stood five feet, two inches and was two years younger. Their parents were born in Alabama, and while it is not clear when they arrived in Texas, later census data indicates the two brothers were born the Lone Star State. In 1863 the brothers enlisted in the 54th Massachusetts Infantry Regiment. Some records indicate that in 1863 they were in Xenia, Ohio, a way station along the Underground Railroad.

Along with four others ex-slaves from Xenia, they joined the 54th's company K after abolitionists—including Frederick Douglass, whose son fought in the regiment—began advertising for recruitment.[4]

The Hewett brothers joined as privates, with James quickly being promoted to corporal. After an earlier skirmish at James Island, where forty-two men of the regiment lost, the 54th was involved in the siege of Fort Wagner, portrayed in the 1987 movie *Glory*. James was then promoted to sergeant after one of the company's previous sergeants, also from Xenia, was missing in action and was presumed dead. Within two weeks Thomas was also promoted from private to corporal. Although both brothers escaped the siege unscathed, their luck changed early the following year.

The Battle of Olustee was the only major battle fought in Florida and also had the second highest casualty rate for the Union in any clash, ending with 34 percent of their troops dead, wounded, captured, or missing in action. The Union forces wound up retreating from the field, with the 54th covering the rear. A train carrying the wounded away from the battlefield broke down after the collapse of its smokestack. Among those on board this train were the Hewett brothers, both of whom had been severely wounded.

Capture of Black troops was especially dangerous since the Confederates had begun a killing them and their white officers under a policy that held they were fomenting "servile insurrection."[5] Rather than leave their wounded comrades to this fate, other members of the 54th tied ropes to the engine and pulled the train three miles. Horses were requisitioned and added to the task, which eventually took forty-two hours before the wounded reached safety ten miles away. The Hewetts eventually spent over six months recovering in the Union hospital in Beaufort, South

Carolina.

Four months after the surrender of the Confederacy at Appomattox, the Hewetts were mustered out of the service in Charleston, South Carolina. By 1867 they had both returned to Washington County. In 1870 James married America Webb, a woman ten years his junior. They were living with their four-month-old child outside of Burton, along with a sixty-eight-year-old white farmer named William Hewett. No documentation clearly indicates a relationship between the two before the war, although it was not uncommon for slaves to take the surname of someone who previously held title which leads to certain suspicions. This sort of speculation is further deepened by several legal documents filed following William Hewett's death in the mid-1870s. James had the land surveyed and in 1876 he and Thomas bought adjacent tracts of land along Indian Creek west of Brenham from the executors of the will, each for a promissory note of $2,029.50 and a percentage of the crops raised. Two years later James appointed a Burton merchant named Knittel to serve as his power of attorney, and to "receive from the executors of Wm. Hewett all moneys due me by reason of said will and to receipt said executors for same."[6]

Thomas and James lived next to each other on these farms for several years, mostly raising cotton and some Indian corn, probably for the few cattle and chickens they also raised. In October 1877 the younger brother married Maria Matson; they named their first child William. The two brothers became involved in local politics, with Thomas running unsuccessfully for precinct constable in 1876. James served as secretary for the Republican County convention in Watrousville in 1878 and was elected to the office of district clerk in 1882. He was defeated in the following two elections for the same position; when nominated again in 1888, his name was withdrawn. While he never held another elected office, he remained a respected member of the community, serving on the county grand jury and as a jury commissioner selecting jury members. These experiences were called on when he delivered presentations on civics to the Washington County Colored Teachers Institute in 1905.

African American Union veterans, including James Hewett, met at the Little Zion Baptist Church in the Camptown area of Brenham in September 1893. They organized the first reunion of colored veterans in Texas in response to recent developments in the Grand Army of the Republic, an organization of men who had served in the Civil War as Union soldiers and sailors. They had been gathering at "Grand Encampments" since 1866, but white members in the South were beginning to segregate their local groups to exclude Blacks, fearing their posts would be overwhelmed by them in numbers. The drawing of these color lines had been a growing concern for several years, with the Texas encampment in 1892 resolving not to affiliate with African American veterans. At the twenty-fifth annual encampment in Detroit, the topic of segregation was coming to a head. "It is peculiar that after the organization has been in existence for a quarter of a century it should be threatened with disruption by the ever living 'color question,' but such is the fact. Men in the southern states who were loyal to the Union in the dark days of '61 are the ones who insist that the negro has no place in the social gathering of the Grand Army of the Republic."[7] Quoting Colonel George T. Hedges, the commander of the GAR department of Louisiana and Mississippi said that "unless this thing is straightened out during this encampment…there won't be a white member of the GAR south of the Ohio or Potomac a year hence. They are outnumbering us in the posts, thus putting us directly under them. That we will not stand. Now, we want to rule ourselves and have the colored people go by themselves."[8]

Colonel James Lewis, the Black administrator of police and administrator of public works of New Orleans was championing the colored side":

> We were regularly enlisted, we fought as history tells you and then we were honorably discharged. With these things to our credit, we had all the rights to form G.A.R. posts. We did this and we were recognized…when the fight was made on us…We have nine posts with a membership of over 1000, yet we are not recognized by the commander of our department. We get no representation…The department commander thinks we want social recognition. I claim the order is not a social one, but a historic and fraternal one.[9]

Two days later the subject came up again, with W. S. Decker, a Colorado veteran writing the minority report for a committee dealing with the "vexed race problem," defending the segregation. "There are representatives on the floor today that went there (to the Southern States) …and established the Grand Army of the Republic in the midst of rebels. As there is a difficulty existing down there we may say to the colored comrades: 'You have your own colored churches, you have your colored orders of the masonic fraternity, you have your colored associations in other respects.'"[10] His speech was met with hisses, and William Warner, an ex-congressman and "special champion of the negro cause," spoke up in opposition:

> "When these black or white men or whatever color or nationality they may have been shouldered muskets in defense of the union, it was not a question of etiquette or of sociability, but it was a question of patriotism and

loyalty. (Applause.) The black men fought for the flag that never up to that time had protected him in anything but bondage. (Applause.) This organization had better bury the old flag, comrades had better tear the buttons from their breasts, than now as our heads are silvering o'er with the frost of years to go back on the principles for which we bled. (Applause)"[11]

The state encampment of the GAR the following year passed its own resolution not to affiliate with the Black veterans. In response, five months later "the first reunion of colored veterans ever held in the United States" took place in Fort Worth, complete "with baseball, foot and wheelbarrow races, climbing greasy poles, etc." a parade headed by bands and speeches by N. W. Cuney, the head of the Texas Republican party, and other prominent Black orators.[12] Soon organizations of Black Union veterans were cropping up throughout Texas and the first "grand re-union of all the colored soldiers in the late war residing in the State of Texas" was being organized. It was to be held in Brenham during its Emancipation celebration in 1894, and second in command among the eight Washington County veterans serving as "staff officers" was Rev. J.C. Hewett." Brenham became the "the headquarters of the colored veterans and sons of veterans organization, and the company here is known as Company A." Companies were required to have fifty members. There were four in Washington County, as two from Bexar County, and one each from Travis, Bastrop, Burleson, and Fayette counties, as well as other counties making application to join the Grand Re-union.[13]

James Hewett continued to live out on the farm he had bought from William Hewett. He and his wife, America, eventually had ten surviving children, at least three of whom went on to become schoolteachers. The fate of his brother, Thomas, is less clear. The brothers seem to have had a falling out of some sort, with a lawsuit between the two of them in 1888 resulting in a judgment by default. An 1890 census record that enumerates veterans lists him with a Brenham post office address. After James died in September 1929, he was buried in the Hewett Cemetery on Mill Creek outside of Burton. His grave was considered unmarked in that it had no "private stone, monument or other permanent marker," so his daughter Lorena filed for the permanent headstone from the federal government he was entitled to as a veteran. It now marks the final resting place of a man who had proudly "fought for the flag that never up to that time had protected him in anything but bondage."[14]

Not all former Washington County slaves who fought for the Union and came home fared as well as the Hewett brothers. Richard Wright had been born there around 1848, with very few other details about his early life available. As a young man he was about five feet, eleven inches tall, with brown eyes, black hair, and a dark complexion. On November 4, 1864, he joined the Union Army in New Orleans. How and when he arrived in New Orleans from Texas is not clear from military records, aside from mentioning that his occupation was listed as "laborer" and he received a $100 enlistment bounty for his year in Company A of the 1st Regiment of the United States Colored Troops, also known as the Corps D'Afrique. He was mustered in on November 22, 1864, and in April 1865 was transferred into the 96th Regiment at Stark's Landing, Alabama.[15]

Wright's year in the Army was uneventful, and he was mustered out in New Orleans in November 1865. After being "discharged with a good character," he returned to Texas, where his family still lived outside the town of Independence. He also took on another name, Richard Porter, for reasons unknown. Emancipation meant a new reality greeted him – freedom from being considered property but still bound by the necessity of economic survival in a world where so many of the old rules had changed. He was able to survive for a while on his sign-on bounty, but he eventually took on a contract to work on the farm of W. J. Williams for the growing season of 1867. Such a contract would reimburse him with either a set amount of cash for the season's work or a portion of the crop he helped raise.

Life back in his old home had changed after returning from the army, but Wright still faced problems after his return. He had "evidently incurred the ill will of the blacks [sic] by his attentions to some of their wives." At the same time, he was despised "by the whites by his having served in the army of the U.S.,"[16] not only because he was now a free Black man, but also because he had been on the other side in a conflict which had wrecked the entrenched slave economy and left behind an unwelcome occupying force. In the final days of February 1867 Wright would find out just how little had really changed.

Around nine in the evening of the 27th Wright had been out hunting and found himself out on property belonging to Albert Haines. Haines had been a wealthy planter and merchant in Independence before the war, owning thirty-three slaves by 1850. A decade later, he had amassed a personal estate of over $50,000, most of it in his increasing number of slaves, which stood at thirty-nine. The war had been hard on the fortunes of slave owners like Haines; after Emancipation the value of his family's personal estate had dropped to less than $500 by 1870.

While Wright was on the Haines place, he was attacked by a dog, which he then shot with his shotgun before heading back to his home on the Williams plantation. On the road home he was confronted by Albert Haines' son, Harry, and another individual. The three got into some sort of altercation that resulted in Harry shooting Wright. Wright lived long enough to make his way home and tell his father what had happened before succumbing to his gunshot wound.

Haines turned himself in after the shooting and was released on $5,000 bail but was never convicted of the murder. Wright's father was all too aware of the poor chances of his son's murderer coming to any sort of meaningful trial in a county still dominated by the planter class that had ruled it before the war, so he went to Captain Edward Collins to appeal for justice.[17]

Collins was the Sub-assistant Commissioner of the Freedmen's Bureau for Brenham and Washington County. The Bureau of Refugees, Freedmen and Abandoned Lands was established as a branch of the United States Army to supervise the peaceful transition of the South back into the Union. Its three primary purposes, as indicated in its title, included resettlement of Black and white refugees and administration of lands that had been abandoned during the war. These functions had little relevance in Texas, which had suffered relatively little from these devastating disruptions, especially in comparison with the rest of the South. It was the even larger chore of transitioning the vast new population of freedmen that occupied most of the attentions of the bureau in Texas, which its commissioner, General O. O. Howard, judged from the beginning "seemed…to be the post of greatest peril."[18] Although General Robert E. Lee had surrendered the Army of North Virginia to General Grant at Appomattox on April 9, 1865, the Army of the Trans-Mississippi in Texas didn't. Senior confederate leaders there urged them to fight on, until on June 2, 1865, the army in Texas officially surrendered, and it was only after the arrival of 2,000 Union troops led by Major General Granger in Galveston on June 19 that the state was occupied and measures were taken to assure the newly established freedom and civil rights of slaves.

Collins was all too aware of those perils General Howard had spoken of. When he referred the Wright case to his superiors, he described it as "one of those cases common to the country and called in Texas 'justifiable homicide in self-defense' and anywhere else '<u>willful murder</u>.'"[19] A year later in another letter he addressed the level of lawlessness faced by Union soldiers attempting to restore order in Washington County. Two companies of Union troops had been sent to Brenham in July 1865 under the command of a Captain Post. Their encampment consisted of a collection of tents east of town in an area still known as Camptown. One of their primary purposes was to restore a degree of law and order that the local civil authorities were unable or unwilling to maintain in the chaotic period following the war, especially where it involved the newly established class of citizens known collectively as freedmen.

Although the War Between the States had come to an end, the war within the states still simmered, its violence continuing for many years. Within a month of their arrival the troops from the Post of Brenham attempted to arrest a man named Boyd, who had been accused of murder. When the soldier arrived at Boyd's family's home, shots were fired from the house, killing one soldier and wounding another. Another soldier was murdered in front of the courthouse, shot from the doorway of a saloon by two gamblers. Two other soldiers were wounded when attempting to arrest his killers. A mustered-out Union officer who was taking up farming in the county also was murdered. None of these cases were brought to justice by the local authorities.

By far the greatest amount of violence following the war was suffered by freedmen, often at the hands of those who had previously held them in bondage. One such victim was Leonard Gee, who was found on a road four miles outside of Brenham, tied up and murdered. The apparent murderer was the man who had formerly held him as a slave and who had been trying to "compel him to action."[20] The murderer was probably the same John Gee who, along with Alfred Gee and another man, had recently broken up a church meeting, driving the worshipers out of the building and beating some of them with pistols.

Near the community of Long Point, a freedman named Ben was shot in the abdomen by William Plaugh, his former slaveholder. Near Independence a former slave held by Dr. Erwin Randle asked if he was free. When he was told he was not, he stated he didn't believe it since the other Blacks he knew were free. Randle shot him in the arm, which he later lost to amputation. Henry Davis was murdered in Mill Creek by Dock Davis, the man who formerly had claimed to be his owner, when he attempted to leave him and seek employment elsewhere. Near the town of Washington, a freedman named Isaac Heddick was shot to death by Cook Jones, who was captured and held shortly for the murder but escaped. An eighty-five-year-old ex-slave named Thomas Long was murdered "by party or party unknown." A "white desperado" named Williams who had previously murdered five men and one woman in Alabama killed the freedman Parker Thompson "without the slightest provocation," escaping with the help of friends. In the midst of a home robbery at night, a Black man named Washington was murdered when he tried to escape. Numerous other murders occurred with frightening frequency, of Black men as well as white, whose names were never learned by the authorities.

Often the violence was at the hands of former Confederate soldiers. One of the worst was Jim Holt, who was born in Texas, the son of James Hines Holt and Mary Watson. After his father's death, his mother was remarried to J. G. Berlin, a wealthy farmer living around Brenham, who moved in with young Jim and five other brothers and sisters. Berlin owned 1,050 acres of land, growing corn, wheat, and cotton. He also held seven slaves, according to the 1860 slave schedule, with an overseer living on the farm to work them as well. As an adherent of the Confederacy Berlin joined its army, eventually holding the rank of lieutenant in the State Reserve when he was paroled after the end of the war. As a teenager, with war fever and hopes of a ready victory for the South running high after the first Battle of Bull Run, young Jim Holt enlisted in the Fifth Regiment of the Texas cavalry, supplying his own horse and tack.

A year after his enlistment he came down with measles and was laid up for two weeks in a hospital in Franklin, Texas. In February 1864 he was transferred to Captain Leander McNelly's scouts. McNelly had been born in Virginia but had moved with his family to Washington County, where he tended sheep with the Burton family. He had enlisted in the same unit as Holt on the very same day, though ultimately serving in different companies. Due to his outstanding gallantry during the Battle of Galveston, McNelly was promoted to captain of a troop of scouts with Holt serving under him as a private. Engaging in guerrilla warfare against Union forces in Louisiana they operated in the swamps and backwaters to harass their foes with crafty effectiveness: at one time their band of fifteen to twenty captured 380 soldiers by a skillful use of trickery, marching back and forth over a nearby bridge in the dark while shouting out to imaginary officers. They then marched into the Union camp under a flag of truce and demanded surrender, which was readily given under the impression of being surrounded by a superior number of troops. McNelly and Holt eventually were assigned to fight jayhawkers in East Texas; toward the final months of the war to hunt down deserters in Washington County, their unit was one of the last ones to disband. After the war, both Holt and McNelly returned to their homes. McNelly became a legendary—and controversial—Texas Ranger, while Holt joined a band of desperadoes acting against what many in Texas considered an occupying foreign government, as well as former slaves whose freedom they had just fought against for five years.

In March 1866 $300 was stolen from a white man in Union Hill, and Alex Green and A. Whitener decided to avenge the theft. A freedman by the name of Jake was in his cabin one evening shortly afterward, along with Green Taylor, his father-in-law James Mayfield and wife, Maria Mayfield, unaware that Jake was suspected of the theft. When Alex Green and Whitener burst into the cabin and held the four at gunpoint, Jake took up an ax in defense, killing Green. Whitener began firing and wounded Taylor as he fled the cabin. Knowing all too well the terrible consequences of killing a white man, whatever the situation, the freedmen (and freedwoman) escaped as soon as possible to seek the protection of Craig and the Freedmen's Bureau in Brenham. Although newspaper accounts[21] mentioned that it was expected they would be turned over to the civil authorities, it was clear to Craig that the local government probably wouldn't be looking out for their best interests as witnesses to the murder of a white man, releasing Taylor and the Mayfields afterward.

This is where Holt and his gang of desperadoes come into the story. Seeking out their twisted version of vigilante justice, Holt and at least four others descended on the cabin where the witnesses lived, dragging them out of their home, first hanging and then shooting them. The local authorities did nothing in the way of tracking down Holt and his gang, who continued to operate openly in Washington County. A month later two Union cavalrymen from Austin were passing through Union Hill and "engaged socially" (a euphemism for gambling) with Holt and his gang. When they got into a dispute, Lieutenant Tupper was pistol whipped, breaking his cheekbone and cutting open the back of his head. The sergeant with him was shot at when he attempted to come to Tupper's aid before riding off to Brenham for assistance.

The case came to the attention of Captain Samuel A. Craig, the Sub-Assistant Supervisor of the Freedmen's Bureau for Washington County and Collin's predecessor. He began to investigate, "dressed in citizen's clothes, visiting the huts of the colored witnesses, making the proper notes and returning."[22] He wrote to his superiors in the bureau seeking permission to round up the gang:

> The civil authorities have done nothing in the murder case and I believe will do nothing. Are these things to pass unnoticed and with impunity? Such is the fear of all who know anything about this affair in that neighborhood, and so intently and carefully do these men operate that it will be difficult to obtain evidence; but I think evidence sufficient can be obtained against at least two of the party. I have the names of nearly all (I am speaking of the murderers of the freedmen.) And I wish to ask what is my duty in the premises? I think we ought to do something, without delay.[23]

In early June permission was granted to arrest Holt and, accompanied by Captain Smith and seventeen soldiers from the Union Camp at Brenham, Craig rode out to capture him:

> We went on horseback, by devious ways, so as to arrive near the place where the accused was stopping, about a little before daylight. I knew Holt was a desperate man, had escaped before, was said to have "killed his man" and through his daring, succeeded in escaping. We arrived near our quarry before daylight and consequently

rested near, and at the first peep of day, were in our agreed positions. Capt. Smith was to take about half of the men and take charge of the road and front. I was to have the other half and approach at the same time from back cornfields and close in upon the back of the house. As I came close to the back of the house, I saw a young black [sic] girl at an upper raised window. Instantly I made motion indicating silence and as low as I thought my voice would carry, asked to point me to where Jim Holt slept. She pointed down to a window in a one-story ell to my right. It wasn't fifteen feet from where I stood and I was on a block and raised myself till my arms were at the sill, my head looking in, and my right hand with a cocked Colt's Navy revolver in it, pointing in the face of two men lying just close inside the window. One, Jim Holt, was not five feet from me, as I covered him with the revolver and said—"Not a motion, or I fire!' "He looked at me and said, "Well, that's a damn cold thing to look into before breakfast," but he did not move."[24]

Holt was the only suspect apprehended that day. They rode back to Brenham with him on horseback, surrounded by three soldiers on every side. Craig followed behind, "with a ready cocked six shooter in my hand, ready always with my eye watching for any effort to glide right or left from his horse at any place where chapparal bushes were thick and close beside the road."[25]

Three of Holt's henchmen were later arrested, but the "excitement and danger consequent" among the citizens of the town was so high that Craig accompanied them personally to Houston to await trail.[26] But collecting evidence from witnesses was more difficult, with "the witnesses already examined…so alarmed that it is next to impossible to satisfy them of their safety.

And those who know anything of the case refuse to testify."[27] Jackson and Henley were soon released because evidence for their conviction could not be obtained, although Craig was "by no means convinced or satisfied" of evidence, because of "the great difficulty we labor under in ferreting out the truth of this matter."[28] Burton and Holt were tried in August before a military commission, and a contemporary news account states that both were "declared not guilty, and discharged," although in his memoirs Craig states that "Holt was convicted and sentenced, but how or why or at whose instance I never knew, President Johnson reprieved or pardoned him!"

Chapter 13

# BLACK LAWMEN IN POST-EMANCIPATION BRENHAM AND WASHINGTON COUNTY

One of the challenges in post-emancipation Brenham and Washington counties was policing the Black community in a way befitting their new roles as citizens rather than chattel. This was a dangerous period of casual violence and volatile shifts in social and cultural expectations. The white community, and especially the previous slave owners, were used to a system of systematic oppression and clearly defined restrictions on Black behavior. The Black community already was intimately familiar with the previously existing control structure but suddenly was exposed to an unaccustomed degree of freedom. The boundaries of these freedoms often were tested because of economic necessity, misplaced expectation, pent-up frustrations over vastly unbalanced opportunities, or due to the frailties of the human condition. The white community also encountered some of the same disruptions, though its response often focused on restoring a semblance of the previous power balance while at least nominally accommodating the strictures imposed by the federal government in enforcing the Fourteenth and Fifteenth amendments.

The reestablishment of a workable system of law and order

was important to both the white and Black communities. In Brenham a segment of the Black population already was aware of the prevailing legal framework Emancipation cast them into and was able to function within it. Bringing Black citizens into law enforcement roles became an important element in not only stabilizing the Black community but also incorporating it into the larger population. A surprising amount of information is available from contemporary news sources to begin to understand the degree to which Black law-enforcement officers were used and the difficulties they faced. Although one must be cautious in using these sources since they often reflect deep-seated prejudices and, at times, blatant racism, they do allow a window into this rarely considered aspect of Black history.

The pages of contemporary newspapers reveal the names of at least twenty Black men who served, in one capacity or another, as lawmen in Brenham and Washington County in the post-Emancipation era. Several of these are known to have been buried in Camptown Cemetery. At least one of these, Robert Sloan, has been the subject of a lengthy chapter in this book about his life. Others are less known other than mentioned in a law enforcement role or in contemporary new articles.

Lawlessness in Texas had reached epic proportions after the Civil War, leading the nation in the number of homicides and with 2,790 known criminals reported at large. One of the responses was the establishment of the state police and state militias to help bring about a degree of civil order, with a mix of white and Black officers.[1] One such state policeman from Washington County was Jack Lands who, according to his obituary, was "appointed captain of a negro state police company here."[2] This was likely the 8th Regiment of the State Guard, Company B, although he is listed there as Capt. John Lands.[3] However, in 1870 he received a receipt for "services as Private of State Police, Third District, from

July 19 to Aug. 3, 1870, being 15 days, at Sixty dollars per month."[4] In most press accounts his previous service is acknowledged, usually referred with an honorific such "Capt. Jack Lands," although at least once he was referred to as "Captain(?)" in what seemed an attempt to question his previous status. An absence of local press accounts during the periods when he was most active in the state police makes much information on his service there largely unknown.

Although Jack Lands is not found in census records, he seems to have had at least two least children. His son, Jack Jr., is mentioned in 1877 as a brother-in-law to Dick Houston and "son to freedman Jack Lands, Sr."[5] He died in October 1880, and his burial procession consisted of "a large number friends, headed by the Brenham brass band, colored. The mournful strains of the tune 'Flee as a Bird,' attracted the attention of many as the procession passed through town."[6] Although it is not noted where he was buried, there is a hint of where he lived: "John Lands, son of captain Jack Lands, and Henry Sands [sic]," died in early October of 1880. His mother's name is confusing, perhaps compounded by a typographic error and a contraction of a name such Henrietta. No clear candidate appears in the census data, although one account from 1885 does mention his wife, though only as "Mrs. Lands," and that they lived in "the west end," most likely Watrousville[7]

A frequent early reason for Lands' later appearances in the press was his role in Black Republican politics of the time. His obituary mentions that "just after the war he took a more prominent part in local politics than any other colored man in the county."[8] As early as 1877 he was the chairman of the Executive Committee of the Republican Party in Washington County, a post he held, though tenuously, as late as 1886.[9] In this capacity he was present at many of what came to be known as "Owl Meetings," at least in part because of their tendency to run late into the night and often until the next morning. These meetings of Radical Republicans, both white and Black, often were held at the Black schoolhouse in Camptown. Drinking and fights were common, which the local Democratic-owned paper was quite pleased to report on:

> Owlisms—On last Saturday the Owls, or Radicals, had a meeting of their county executive committee. The chairman, Captain Jack Lands, a colored gentleman, had the greatest difficulty in maintaining order, and, it is said, did not succeed. The meeting was very boisterous; every Owl present, black [sic] and white, had something to say. The result of the very stormy session was that they could not agree upon any definite plan of action. On Saturday night and lasting until daylight Sunday morning, there was an informal meeting of the office-seeking owls and their strikers held at a "wet grocery." This meeting was much more disorderly than that held in the afternoon. Tarantula juice, bug juice and snake medicine was [sic] dispensed with a lavish hand and numerous fights were indulged in: several heads were more or less bruised, and one negro had to take his head to a doctor for repairs, it having been damaged by a blow from a stick. A number of the white owls were at the night meeting, and it is said, several Democrats were looking on as spectators. The informal meeting was worse than the regular one.[10]

After the state police was dissolved, Lands continued as a lawman, serving as a deputy sheriff in Washington County. This required posting a bond and taking an oath of office and gave him the right to carry arms and make arrests. The presence of Black men serving as deputy sheriffs seemed to have been the source of concern. "The county is crowded with quasi deputy-sheriffs, mostly of the colored persuasion. People from the country say that big and little negroes, some of them mere boys, are in the habit of riding about with gigantic revolvers; when asked what they are doing with a pistol, they reply, "I is a deputy sheriff," and show a slip of paper signed by the sheriff, Mr. Hutchinson, stating that ___ is a deputy sheriff."[11]

Another indication of the difficulties encountered by deputy sheriffs comes from an 1879 article. The newspaper clipping is torn and all details are not present, though there is enough to make out that a city policeman attempted to arrest a man named Silas on a charge of being drunk and disorderly, resulting in a pistol being pulled at one point. Sheriff Hub Hutchinson and Jack Lands bonded Silas out of the city jail and stated that he was a deputy sheriff and his carrying of a pistol was lawful, a claim that the city attorney agreed to during a jury trial.[12]

The arresting officer in that case, William P. Doran, had previously served as city marshal and was seeking re-election the day after he shot an unarmed Black man on the crowded streets of downtown Brenham in an incident where Jack Lands was present:

> In April 1879, Jim Gibson, a Black man who was out on bond while appealing a ten-year sentence, "...was in front of Bill Brown's, colored, [sic] saloon, in the basement of the Cotton Exchange building, raising a disturbance by boisterous language. Marshal Doran attempted to quiet him and left him with some other colored men. Upon his return from supper about 7 o'clock Gibson was still

making a fuss. Doran blew his whistle and summoned several colored men to assist in arresting Gibson. Doran knocked Gibson down, he got up and at the same time picked up a rock to strike Doran. The coon was very threatening when Doran drew his pistol and firing, shot Gibson through the breast inflicting a wound from which in all probability Gibson has died before this morning."[13]

Gibson did die, and at the coroner's inquest Lands, who'd been summoned by from the jail by Doran's whistle, gave his testimony. "Capt. Jack Lands, colored, corroborated the evidence as to bad language and drunkenness, but says Gibson was under arrest and that Doran shot him as he was rising after being knocked down; he also says that Doran struck Gibson after he was down and that while in the act of striking him again he, Lands, pulled him off."[14]

Doran surrendered himself to the sheriff and lost his bid for election the next day. There is no evidence that Doran ever went to trial for Gibson's death, with the coroner's inquest finding it occurred "by the hand of W.P. Doran while in the discharge of his duty." He did manage to carry on as a city policeman, and two weeks after the shooting he was presented a gold badge by "a committee of leading citizens…as a token of honor."[15] Interestingly enough, according to the 1880 census, his occupation was listed as "editor + policeman," and in 1900 as "Newspaper Reporter" and his son as a "printer."[16]

Among his other duties, Lands also served as jailer at the county jail and later at the city jail. An 1878 account in the *Banner* speculated that there might be some conflict between his political activities and his jailhouse responsibilities:

> Terrible Fuss—On Saturday morning between ten

and eleven o'clock the prisoners in jail set up a shout that fairly made the welkin ring. This they continued for some time drawing quite a crowd. The noise is accounted for in two ways; one is that the prisoners had not been given breakfast, and other that they had not been let out of their cages. Major General Jack Lands, colored, jailer and politician, had in all probability been out all night attending an owl meeting and feeling weary had not got out of bed. This, however, is simply a hypothesis to account for the bellowing.[17]

Jack Lands' work as a jailer also came under fire in 1880 during the investigation of what the *Banner* described as the first lynching in Washington County "since the war."[18] On August 16, 1880, Rube Carothers was taken from the county jail for a hearing in the court of Justice of the Peace C.G. Campbell of Precinct 6 in Greenvine, on the charge of cattle rustling. Carothers requested the deputy sheriff, Ben Ligon, transporting him to let him get a small bottle of whiskey to drink along the way on the six-mile journey, saying that "Jack Lands gave him as much whiskey as he wanted all the time."[19] Surprisingly enough, Ligon did allow him to get the whiskey and drink some of it, though taking it away from him before turning him over to other guards when they arrived. Following is an account of the trial:

> ...the prisoner conducted himself badly; he showed no respect for the court, and insulted the witnesses, cursing and swearing. The court bore the insults for it was manifest that the prisoner was intoxicated. On inquiry as to how he got the spirits I was informed that on leaving Brenham, deputy sheriff Jack Lands, at the request of the

prisoner, furnished him with a half pint flask of whiskey. The court adjourned till 8 o'clock next morning and Wm. Brandt deputized to take charge of the prisoner, bring him to court next morning. From their report about a quarter to 11 o'clock in the night, about 50 masked men suddenly charged on them, taking the prisoner by force and carried him away; his body was found about 9 o'clock next morning hanging to a cottonwood tree in La Bahia prairie.[20]

This incident of lynching created considerable condemnation in the press at the time. The *Banner* referred to it as "Mob Law," "an exceedingly bad precedent," and stating that "it is to be hoped that the lynchers will be brought to justice."[21] The *Galveston Daily News* ran a two-column editorial against the lynching, stating that the perpetrators "are far greater sinners against the laws of God and man, and far worse enemies to society and civil order than the lynched negro was."[22]

With this sort of public pressure, both Justice of the Peace Campbell and Deputy Sheriff Ligon published lengthy accounts of their own to distance themselves from the lynching. Although Lands was not directly implicated in this lynching, his name still was bandied about in the papers regarding Carothers and the whiskey, and he attempted to clear his name as well, though with far different results:

> Jack Lands, deputy sheriff of Washington county, called at the *Banner* office yesterday morning with a document in relation to the recent lynching, and in reply to the charge made by justice Campbell that Lands furnished Carothers with a half pint bottle of whiskey.

The *Banner* offered to publish Lands' denial of having furnished the whiskey and his assertion that he gave Carothers $1.25 of his own money. Considering the other matter as irrelevant the *Banner* refused to publish it unless it was paid for.[23]

Lands continued as a deputy jailer for the county for another four years, although he still suffered problems with the press regarding his image as a jailer, as one account of an attempted escape from 1883 shows:

> Dick McKinney, a negro who is frequently in trouble, is now serving out a fine in the county jail. He was allowed the run of the yard and a day or two ago he refused to return to the jail when ordered. He stood off the jailer, Jack Lands, with a spade and when Jack went to get his artillery Dick took a walk. Mr. John Davis, the keeper of the jail, followed Dick and rounded him up in a deep gully in the northern part of town. Dick, when halted, objected to returning to the jail. Dr. Davis told him he would convert his body into a lead min if he didn't. Dick did not wish to become a cold and clammy corpse containing only an ounce or two of lead. He quietly marched back to jail.[24]

By September 1884 Lands had "either resigned or been removed" from his position as a county turnkey.[25] This did not necessarily improve security at the county jail, but at least it kept him from being involved in its most notorious jail break. In December 1886 three Black witnesses to theft of a ballot box were taken from the jail by a masked mob and lynched a mile north of town. Lands was soon serving as city jailer again.

But not all the news stories about Lands were about his law enforcement or political duties. An article from 1885 entitled "KuKluxed" described "a white man named Stamps ..who has been in a habit of gambling and associating with negroes" who went to Lands' house one Saturday night. Lands gave the man a blanket and allowed him to sleep on the porch of his house; the next morning Stamps was confronted by masked men and forced to a railway trestle where he was badly beaten.[26] In 1888 a Black man named Andrew Hosea went to Lands' house and "'cussed' him out," for which Hosea was fined "$1 and costs."[27] And in 1886, Lands himself was fined $5 for fighting in mayor's court, with no details given.[28]

Lands enjoyed a good horse race as well. On June 8, 1883, he entered Brown Dick, a brown gelding, at the races, although he only finished third out of four on a muddy track. Two days later he won a $25 dollar purse, though not in the usual way. He entered Maud S., a sorrel mule, in the half-mile dash for mules, in which the judges chose the riders, and the slowest mule won. Much to the amusement of the cheering men and women in the crowd, Maud S. took the prize, coming in with a time of five minutes and fifty-seven seconds for the half mile.[29]

Like many other prominent Black citizens in post-Emancipation Brenham, Lands belonged to a Black fraternal order. In June 1884 he was elected to the rank of "L.S. To N.G." in the Band of Progress Lodge No. 1934 of the Grand United Order of Odd Fellows, which held meetings in their hall on Kerr Street a block from the Mount Rose Baptist Church. The public installation of these officers was to be held the following month at the Emancipation Day celebrations at the Fair Ground, south of Camptown.[30]

In the winter of 1889-1890, an influenza epidemic known as the

Russian Flu began to spread throughout the northern hemisphere, eventually claiming a million lives. Lands contracted one of the first cases in Brenham, and the local paper, which had frequently reported on the recurring epidemics of yellow fever and other deadly diseases that periodically ravaged the town, noted Lands might not recover.[31] He didn't, and within a week he was dead. His obituary was printed the day after his funeral:

> Jack Lands Dead—There is one fatal case of the Russian influenza or "la grippe" in Brenham to report. Jack Lands, the colored man, whose serious sickness from the malady had been noted, died on Sunday at 7 o'clock at his house west of town and was buried at 3 o'clock on Monday afternoon. The funeral was largely attended by the colored people. The attending physician announced it a genuine case of Russian influenza and pronounced that it would result fatally nearly two weeks ago. Jack Lands was quite a noted Brenham darkey. Just after the war he took a more prominent part in local politics than any other colored man in the county. He was appointed captain of a negro state police company here; was for seven years deputy sheriff and jailor under Hub Hutchinson, who attended his funeral Monday and says that he was a good, honest, faithful, trustworthy and reliable man. Of late years the deceased had not taken any active part in local politics, but died respected by all of his race in Brenham and in the enjoyment of the confidence of the white people."[32]

It is not known where "west of town" Jack Lands was buried, or even how old he was, but he was one of the Black citizens who played a significant law enforcement role in post-Emancipation Brenham.

Another Black lawman in Brenham with a military title was Tom Day, often referred to as Colonel Thomas Day. The title leads one to speculate whether he also served in the state police, perhaps with Captain Jack Lands. Day also had been a deputy sheriff when the previous, unnamed Black policeman was dismissed, with Day "to take the place of the discharged African. Tom will make a good officer."[33] He also was elected by the city council as a policeman for Camptown in April 1878 for a short time. For an unstated reason, a complaint was filed against him by Sheriff Doran, and Day was dismissed. He did serve, at least temporarily, to "wear the star and wield the baton"[34] while Ed Inge, who was serving as policeman in Camptown, was on a leave of absence.

Articles referring to Day's policing activities are scant, and include shooting a mad dog, catching an ox thief, and chasing down a female escapee "...over more fences than he could count and through kitchens finally proving to be the best man of the two."[35] The only gunplay he was reported to have been involved in was when he accidentally shot himself in the ankle when he reached for his gun on a mantle and it discharged when he dropped it.[36] He also served as a bailiff in at least one district court grand jury session, with two other Black men, Logan Jones and P.K. Allen, serving as grand jurors.[37]

Day's obituary is unusual for its mention of his former enslaver, more information about his life before Emancipation than most Blacks were ever afforded in their published death notice:

> Notable Darkey Dead—Tom Day, a well-known colored man of this city, aged about 60 years, died at his residence

in Camptown at 7 o'clock on Thursday morning from dropsy of the heart. He will be buried at 10 o'clock this morning by the colored Masonic fraternity, of which he was a member in high standing. Tom was one of the oldest landmarks and one of the most notable darkeys in the city. In the days of slavery, he was owned by John H. Day and was his constant and faithful body-servant. Just after the war he took a prominent part in local politics and served as deputy sheriff and jailor under Dr. Lyd Smith. He used to be crier of the court and was familiar to all of the older members of the bar. For the past few years prior to his death he ceased to take any part in running county politics and lived quietly and inoffensively. He was extremely polite and was liked by white and black [sic].[38]

The role of law officer is never safe for those who chose to undertake it, as one finds in the case of Anderson Helms. Little is known about Helms except for his death in the line of duty as a policeman in the Camptown suburb of Brenham (or "Yankee Camps," as it is referred to in one article.)[39] He was on foot patrol one evening in late July 1876 when someone rode up and killed him with a shotgun blast. The only evidence reported at the time was a hat that the murderer dropped while making his escape.[40]

The case was pursued by Sheriff Hutchinson of Washington County, who tracked down the suspect for months before arresting Elijah Jones at Round Rock in late November 1878. The suspect, who when arrested was reported to have had "the appearance and garb of a 'cow boy,'"[41] was held without bail (likely under the care of county jailer Capt. Jack Lands) until September of the following year. His trial lasted two days, with the court instructing the jury to that a finding of guilty would subject Jones to a sentence of either death or life in prison. After thirty minutes of deliberation, a verdict of not guilty was returned.

Helms was not the only Black Camptown policeman to be shot in the line of duty. Candy Garland was named "special policeman" for the eastern suburb in July 1878, an appointment which the newspaper reported in this way:

> Armed—Candy Garland, an ancient colored gentleman has been appointed special policeman for the classic locality of Camptown. On Saturday he was up in the city with a star on his chest and the largest kind of a revolver strapped to his waist. He looked as proud as Lucifer or a peacock in full feather.[42]

Garland did not last long in this role. Several weeks later he arrested fellow Camptown resident Adam Sanders for being drunk and disorderly. On their way to the jail Sanders changed his mind about going to jail, pulling a pistol on Garland. The special policeman went back to the jail, returning with two other officers to arrest Sanders at his house. Sanders finally agreed to surrender and sent his wife back into the house for his coat. When she returned, he again drew his pistol and shot Garland in the neck, then escaped past a crowd of onlookers to avoid being shot himself by one of the other arresting officers.

Sanders turned himself in later that same evening, but his disposition regarding Garland didn't seem to change much. The day after he'd turned himself in, he was walked downstairs with the other prisoners for breakfast and "remarked he wished he had killed Garland." One of his fellow prisoners, who had already been "on bad terms before they were trapped," attacked him at this point and "gave him a very sound drubbing, nearly putting out one of his eyes." That fellow prisoner was Jim Gibson, who himself was to be gunned down in the streets the next year by Marshal Doran, as witnessed by the jailer who brought them down to breakfast, Capt. Jack Lands.[43]

Garland eventually recovered from his wounds, and Sanders was sentenced to three years for the shooting. No further record exists of his serving in law enforcement, though he is later mentioned as "an old negro peddler" of tamales frightened by children "placing a snake in his basket."[44] Sadly, after he suffered a stroke from which he was not expected to recover, a news article on "Uncle Candy" neglected to mention his previous service as a law officer, mentioning only that he had "been peddling tamales on the streets of Brenham from a time when the memory of the average man runneth not to the contrary."[45]

In another case, Shed Hazely, a Black deputy sheriff living in Chappell Hill, was shot fatally by a white ex-constable of Brenham, John Traylor, though reports indicate that it may not have happened in the line of duty. One account mentions that the two "had for a long time been in the habit of drinking and gambling, which may have been the cause of the difficulty."[46] Another account states that "Hazely had been around town armed with a shotgun making threats to kill Traylor on sight. Traylor happened to get the first sight."[47] Traylor was bonded out and found not guilty of Hazely's death, though he eventually murdered another gambler and denizen of Brenham's Hell's Half Acre, Bill Allen. While on bail awaiting trial for murdering Allen, Traylor began publicly threatening Henry Hancock, the proprietor of a more successful (and well heeled) gambling house than his and which it competed against. Hancock, who also had been a constable in Brenham before losing an election to Traylor, felt threatened enough to shoot Traylor from a second story window; Traylor died in the same street where he had gunned down Allen a few months earlier.[48]

Some of the other Black men who served in law enforcement roles in post-Emancipation Brenham rarely made the news, and relatively little is known about them. Harry Key was appointed a policeman in Watrousville in April 1879 by the city council after having lost a council election for the same post in 1878.[49] He escorted paupers to the poor farm, was charged of firing a pistol by a local black restaurateur who later dropped the charges, and served on a coroner's jury for a dead woman found in a field and for a dead cigar maker[50] His last reported appointment as a city policeman was in 1881,[51] and is mentioned in his father's obituary:

> Died in his home in West Brenham last Monday at 1:15 p.m., Harry Key, an old and industrious colored citizen of Brenham, at the claimed age of 107 years and 8 months. The writer has known deceased since 1853 and he was a middle-aged man then. He was a servant of the late Dr. John P. Key, and says he was born in Nashville, Tennessee in August 1800 and came to Texas when a young man – was here when the battle of San Jacinto was fought in 1836. He was the father of Harry Key, Jr., one of the employees of the city street force.[52]

Law enforcement in Brenham did not pay well, and Black law enforcement officers were paid even less than whites. The city council proceedings for April of 1902 reported that two white policemen were paid $45 each, while Ed Inge and Austin B. Burkhead, colored policemen for Camptown and Watrousville, respectively, received only $5 each. That was less than the $10 they had received six years earlier.[53] However, Inge (and possibly Burkhead) was also making an additional $1 per arrest resulting in conviction,[54] and there was also the possibility of collecting rewards for arrests. In 1900 Burkhead and a local constable, R.H. Burch, were to receive two rewards, $300 from the governor and $50 from the sheriff of Waller County, for their arrest of a murderer, contingent on his conviction.[55] On the other hand, Burkhead did not receive the $25 reward for Will Parker when he arrived with him in Lavaca County, since the sheriff informed him this was not the right man, whereupon Parker was returned to Washington County to be held on a theft charge.

Burkhead also found other ways to supplement his salary. He operated a barbershop in the rear of the White Elephant Saloon called the Lone Star Tonsorial Parlor, advertising in the *Brenham Daily Banner* his services for "colored people only at 15 cents a shave and 25 cents for hair cutting."[56] His occupation in the 1900 census was given as "grocer" as well, though in the 1910 census it is given as "policeman," and in the same residence at the county jail as Sheriff Teague and his wife.

Burkhead also supplied Black contract labor throughout Texas and other states, filling positions as cooks, porters, sawmill workers, railway workers, and cotton pickers. Some contracts were for as few as ten workers, others for as many as 150. The cotton-picking contracts tended to be the largest behind railway workers; he would have the laborers gather at the railway station, accompanying them and the employer to their location. This was a booming business, filling requests for as many as a thousand in 1900, and supplying 652 contract workers in the first ten months of 1903 alone.[57] This was an important source of local income for Black laborers in 1902, when the cotton crop in the Brazos Valley was hit first by an overflow of the Brazos River and then by boll weevils, with the cotton crop processed in Brenham little more than half of what it had been the year before.

Burkhead served as a policeman in Brenham for two decades, and early in his career he peripherally involved in a "lead lynching."

He was sitting in the Santa Fe saloon with Jim Mike Watkins one rainy Sunday afternoon when Bob Carter came running by him, a shotgun in his hand. Watkins said to Burkhead, "I'll bet that nigger had done something or is going to do something," and chased after him. When Watkins caught up to him, Carter told him "I have just killed Jim Burch." Watkins returned to Burkhead and told him what he'd just been told, and they went to the Casino saloon where Jim Burch lay dying in the street, a shotgun blast having taken off most of the right side of his face, a pistol with a single discharged chamber in his hand.[58]

Jim Burch had been a guard at the county farm north of town when Carter had been a convict; the two apparently had bad blood between them. Jim Burch was also the brother of Robert L. Burch, a Brenham constable. Soon a mob gathered and "it was apparent that Judge Lynch would hold court as soon as the prisoner could be arraigned for trial."[59] Carter fled on foot to Watrousville, where he left the gun with Harry Key, confessing to the ex-policeman there and surrendering to Mr. R.S. Farmer with an understanding that he could be safely brought to the jail to be held for his crime.

Carter and Farmer had nearly made it as far as the back of the jail when the mob found them, overpowering and disarming Farmer. Carter died in a hail of at thirty bullets, with over a dozen bullets in his body, some fired from such a close range that his clothes were caught on fire. The mob then produced a rope and were attempting to hang the corpse from a telephone pole until they were stopped by Sheriff Teague and other officers, possibly including Burkhead.[60] Constable Burch, the victim's brother, was arrested and held on $1,000 bond. At Burch's trial for the murder, where a number of the state's witnesses refused to take the stand on grounds of self-incrimination and Farmer testified he saw Burch shoot Carter, the verdict was found to be not guilty.[61] Although Burkhead was not called upon to testify at the trial, there are numerous accounts of his working together with Constable Burch afterward, including the case which could have led to splitting reward money mentioned earlier.

Burch also encountered Burkhead on the evening of July 18, 1907, at the Magnolia saloon when Burkhead was shot at (and missed) five times. The Magnolia was, according to one account,

> a double-header, with one section of it devoted to negroes, the other to whites. Burkhead was sitting on a beer keg in front of the saloon when Mr. Helf came along and asked him if he got the papers that he left at the saloon for him. He replied in the negative and started in the saloon to get them when John Wood, the negro bartender, came from behind the bar and commenced shooting at him. He (Burkhead) hastily retreated and was met coming back with a shotgun. Officers Sallis and Burch, and Constable Guyton with County Attorney W.R. Ewing, disarmed him and found that his six-shooter had not been fired, the mould of time showing in the barrel and cylinder, and all the cartridges being loaded. Finding John Wood, he secured his pistol, which was a 30-40, and found that five shots had been fired out of it. He was placed under arrest, but subsequently gave bond. Mr. Helf, the white man whom Burkhead referred to, corroborated the statement made by Burkhead. Many of the other occupants of the saloon say that not a word was spoken between the two. Neither of the participants in the difficulty was hit. Burkhead says that he does not know or have any idea why Wood wanted to shoot him.[62]

Ed Inge was the most controversial of Black lawmen in post-Emancipation Brenham, at least judging from contemporary accounts. In 1872 he was a state policeman who shot and killed two men in January 1872, with no other information except a possibly politically motivated insinuation in a newspaper account that "(a)t the last election he was very energetic in hunting up Clark voters and forcing them to the polls."[63] Inge was confirmed as a policeman for the Camptown region of Brenham by the city council on June 19, 1878, but was discharged from the police force less than two weeks later after he arrested John Collins, a Black barber, on a charge of being drunk and disorderly. Inge later decided that Collins was "...not doing anything. The city marshal, having a conviction that Collins had put a 'spell' upon Inge requested His Honor to discharge Mr. Inge upon the ground of not doing his duty and allowing himself to be bulldozed by Collins' friends."[64]

The residents of Camptown petitioned the city council for Inge's reappointment as their local law enforcement officer in April 1879, although the request was tabled at least once.[65] By January 1880 he was once again serving as the area's policeman, with a salary of $15 a month. However, in May of that year he petitioned the council for pay equal to that of other policemen in Brenham, a petition which was "read and laid on the table."[66] Although the pay may not have always matched that of his white peers, he did receive a uniform along with the job:

> In Uniform—Ed Inge, colored, the Camptown policeman, made his appearance on the street yesterday in full uniform, navy blue sack coat and trousers. The coat is elegantly mounted with gold buttons, each button with a talismanic "P" on it; the buttons are so bright that they can be seen by daylight as far as a locomotive headlight at night. Ed is a good officer, and looks really nobby in his new uniform.[67]

Much of Inge's routine day-to-day work involved breaking up fights, arresting drunks, guarding prisoners, and dealing with complaints against him by local citizens. If guns were involved, the situation could become anything but routine. Although Texas had laws in place since the 1870s against public carry of handguns, an unsettling amount of gunplay and dangerous violence involving firearms still existed. It was the job of policemen to step into these often-volatile situations, one in which Inge found himself in on a Sunday morning in late September 1881.

Willis McIntyre was a young Black man who figures often in the Brenham papers as a "bad negro," involved in crimes, convicted of them, sent to the penitentiary, or escaping from incarceration. Around two in the morning he came across three other Black men involved in a fight where a pistol was drawn and one of the participants shot. McIntyre stepped in, stating "Well! You shot him, and I'll shoot you," and true to his word he shot the shooter in the forehead. Fortunately, the ball flattened and passed around the skull, lodging in the temple. Although the three others were arrested and jailed, McIntyre managed to escape. A warrant was sworn out for his arrest and Inge sent to arrest him. Although McIntyre was readily found in Camptown, he was determined not to be arrested and pulled his pistol on Inge.

> ...Inge knocked it out of his hand with a stick, and Willis reached for it again when Inge fired, the ball taking effect about eight inches above the knee joint and ranging downward breaking the thigh bone; Willis then gave up, a hack was procured and he was conveyed to the county jail. On Monday the doctors thought he would recover without losing his leg. Inge is as cool as a refrigerator and deserves credit for arresting McIntyre, who is regarded as a dangerous character. Inge says he could have killed

him as easy as not, but thought he would let him live and make a man of himself.[68]

Inge's reputation for putting down the hammer won him not only credit as a lawman capable of dealing with the black criminal element in Brenham, but also animosity from the criminal element. In February 1887 Inge, who was not serving as a policeman at the time, was described as "a black negro about 45 or 50 years old and during his official career has killed several negroes, in every case the law has fully justified him," and with "a good many enemies among his own color."[69] Because of his fearless reputation, Inge was specially deputized by the city marshal to arrest Jim Smith, who was terrorizing prostitutes in the red-light section of town known as Hell's Half Acre and threatening to kill anyone who tried to arrest him. Smith was sighted and eventually tracked down to an area known as Coon Flat, "a twin sister of the half acre [sic] and only a few blocks distant."[70] During the pursuit, a shot was heard, and Smith was found dead, leaning against a cabin with a gunshot wound. Two witnesses stated Inge had shot him in the chest, and Inge was arrested an hour later at his home in Camptown, denying the charge of murder. An examination of his pistol showed it had not been fired recently, and although the body was already in a coffin and at the graveyard, a postmortem examination was ordered that proved that Smith had been shot from behind, rather than in front as the witnesses had testified. Inge eventually was cleared of the murder charges.[71]

While the city government felt comfortable with a Black man policing the Black populace, Inge frequently found himself in trouble when he began to exercise the power of the badge over whites. During Maifest in 1882, W.I. McMahon, a white Bell County deputy sheriff, was in town Friday morning for the weekend's celebration. He ran into Lucius Lomax, with whom McMahon had had a previous run-in while serving as a Washington County constable. In July 1880, McMahon had been walking in front of Tammany, a "colored barroom" on Ant Street and kicked a beer keg on the sidewalk. Lomax, a barkeeper at the Tammany,

> ...came out and commenced cursing McMahon and using language that was, to say the least, calculated to provoke a breach of the peace. At this McMahon drew his revolver, a full grown and remarkably healthy one, and blazed away at Lucius, missing him by, it is supposed, about a couple of inches. In less time than it takes to read this an immense crowd gathered in the vicinity, and for some time the excitement ran quite high. McMahon crossed over the street to Mark's store, where he was arrested by the police officers.[72]

This previous encounter must have still weighed heavily on McMahon's mind when he met Lomax on Ant Street once again, since this time he proceeded to pistol whip Lomax. Inge arrived on the scene and arrested McMahon, then took him to the jail and locked him up, probably in part for his own safety since "...a crowd of negroes, some it is said with pistols, gathered and...for a few minutes things looked quite squally."[73] But when City Marshal Doran returned to the city jail from the Maifest fairgrounds, he "...at once released McMahon on bond. Doran had given Inge special instructions not to arrest or attempt to arrest a white man under any circumstances, and his arrest of McMahon was a disobedience of orders."[74] Inge was suspended from duty but reinstated at a special meeting of the city council several days later, although the city marshal "again instructed Inge not to arrest any white men. The arrest by negro officers almost invariably results in trouble, whether this is right or wrong the fact remains, all the same."[75]

Inge was suspended from duty, but this did not ease the racial unrest that was building in Brenham. The next night another Black man, Bill Payne, was shot in the streets while in the same vicinity Lomax had been assaulted. It was not certain if he would die from his wounds, and he gave a statement that he had been shot by McMahon. By the next night "a rumor that the negroes contemplated burning the town spread like wild-fire. It was but a little while till many men were on the alert."[76] As if to feed the flames of these rumors, a "severe windstorm" was sweeping through town over the same night, uprooting trees, blowing some homes off their foundations, flattening some buildings completely and damaging many others, including the Mount Rose Baptist Church in Camptown. The tension had grown to such a volatile point that one of Brenham's leading Black citizens, C.P. Hicks, took out a "card" in the *Brenham Banner* to address the issue:

> On the night of the 6th inst. a colored man named Bill Payne was shot, which caused considerable excitement among the colored people. A rumor was started that the colored people intended to burn the town in retaliation for the attack on Payne. Now, Messrs. Editors, we as colored citizens, desire to say that we would not take any measures that would be contrary to law; we desire to see that the law takes its course, and will do all in our power to assist the officers in the execution of the same. It is true there are some lawless characters who come into towns and cities, who do not care for law and order, and it behooves us as good citizens to see that they do abide by the law. There is no disposition on the part of the colored citizens of this town to encourage or even

tolerate a violation of the law, and they hope that the entire community, white and black [sic], will sustain them." It was signed by "C.P. Hicks. In behalf of many colored citizens."

By Monday, Inge once again was reinstated as a policeman. "Inge explained that when the shindy began on Friday the marshal was at the fairgrounds and he did not know that any white officer was on duty in town. The marshal has again instructed Inge not to arrest any white men. The arrest of white men by negro officers almost invariably results in trouble, whether this is right or wrong the fact remains, all the same."

McMahon initially was released on bond for the charge of carrying the pistol, "as no complaint has been preferred against him, as it was further shown he was a deputy sheriff from another county." He was soon charged with assault with intent to murder in the case, but seems to have avoided conviction, since he is noted the following year to have resigned from the position of city marshal.

Although the storm had passed for a while, it was not long before Inge once again found himself in a whirlwind of bad press for his enforcement of the law, regardless of race. On August 9, 1882, he again arrested a white man for "using bad language on the street," a surprisingly common charge at the time. This sparked a concerned editorial piece in the press:

>...Inge is a very good officer, but the plan of keeping a colored policeman on duty up town is liable to provoke a serious breach of the peace any day and any time that he may attempt to arrest a white man. With the rights and duties of a colored officer we have nothing to do and it

has no bearing on the point at issue, viz: The liability to create a disturbance. The mayor and council should be aware of this fact if they are not. If a day policeman is needed up town let a reliable white man be put on and Inge can attend to his duties as a policeman at Camptown, where the population is colored.

This pressure from the press for a selective enforcement of the law, based on race, as well as a perceived racial favoritism on Inge's behalf, was brought up in the report of his suspension five days later:

Yesterday afternoon Mayor Reichardt suspended Ed Inge, colored policeman from further duty, until the next regular meeting of the city council. Inge came near precipitating a row on Saturday last by arresting a white man. Monday evening, he was after considerable talking finally induced to arrest a colored man who was raising a disturbance on Ant Street, and after making the arrest he, without any authority, released the man on a verbal bond. The mayor upon being informed of the circumstances, very promptly and is thought very justly, suspended Ed.

This was not the end of Inge's troubles, or his increasingly bad press. Two days after his suspension, he was arrested and came near to being shot in the process by the same trigger-happy city marshal who had killed a Black suspect in front of Jack Lands a few years before:

Ed Inge Again—Ed Inge, colored, suspended policeman

is just at this season coming in for a good deal of cheap notoriety. About 10 o'clock Wednesday morning it was reported by several parties to the marshal that Ed was on the street with a pistol fresh belt of cartridges (45 calibre) [sic] and when warned by others that he had no right to carry his pistol he replied that Doran couldn't arrest him. Doran found Ed near Schramm's corner and told him that it was reported that he had a pistol. Ed replied that he had. Marshal Doran told him he had no right to carry a pistol and that he would arrest him. Ed wanted to go to Mr. Hackworth, Doran then put his hand on Ed's shoulder and arrested him. Ed threw his hand near his pistol and Doran seeing the motion did the same and struck Ed who returned the blow. They then grappled; Doran threw Ed who was trying to draw his pistol. Doran got his pistol off his belt and was about to fire when Capt. Upshaw took Ed's pistol. Ed Lockett then appeared and said that Inge had papers to show that he was a deputy sheriff. Sheriff Hutchinson who was on the ground said that Inge was not a deputy sheriff. Ed produced a warrant signed by Hackworth, J.P. Dated December 7, 1881, whereby he was empowered to execute same. With the assistance of sheriff Hutchinson Doran took Ed to the bastille and locked him up, followed by about 150 negroes. Ed afterward deposited $50 cash with officer Neblett as a collateral security and was released.

His case was heard the next day, and Inge defended himself against the charge of unlawfully carrying a pistol on the grounds that he "was an officer with a warrant to serve; also that his life had been threatened, etc., etc." Inge was found guilty and appealed to the county court, and he was officially dismissed from the police force, again, the following Monday.

The next year Inge "orated" at an owl meeting before the April elections against Doran, who lost. By May the Black citizens of Camptown were once again campaigning for policemen for their communities, and Inge was once again serving as a special policeman without pay. But the *Banner* was not so quick to forget its underlying concerns about an armed Black policeman willing to arrest whites when reporting on his new appointment:

> Ed Inge is the man who figured so extremely before the public some months ago, and he is also the man who was dismissed from the police force for disobedience of orders. He is the colored police officer that had the big pistol in town and came near precipitating a riot. Since he has been off the force he has been behaving himself very well; he has quietly and peaceably attended to his business and interfering with no one. As a citizen Ed Inge is exceptionally well behaved and he certainly should have been allowed to pursue the even tenor of his way. The appointment of special policemen, either white or black, means simply a license to 'pack' a pistol which varies in size according to the taste of the 'packer' and it is just as likely – figuratively speaking – to be four, six or eight feet long as it is to be four, six or eight inches. Now to see a special policeman parading round, even though he gets no pay, with a pistol six or eight feet long stuck in his belt is calculated to disturb the equanimity of the most even-tempered person in the world, or for that matter in the city of Brenham.

It is difficult to track the seemingly on-again, off-again nature of Inge's employment as a policeman, but it remained controversial.

In October 1884 a city alderman doubted Inge's legal authority, leading to another article two days later questioned allowing an armed Black man on the street who might attempt to arrest a white man:

> Ed Inge, colored, says that he was sworn in as a special policeman by the mayor several weeks ago. His name is not on the city's pay roll. He gets fees, $1 for an arrest, and $1.50 per day. Making a colored man a policeman is something like throwing a fire brand into a powder house. If he attempts to arrest a white man it is liable to provoke a riot almost at any time. A year or two ago we narrowly escaped a serious riot on account of this same man. Inge is a very good colored man, but his presence on the streets armed with six-shooter – Columbiad pattern – is not agreeable to those who love law and order, and is not calculated to preserve the peace.

In November 1888, Inge was serving as a policeman again, judging from a newspaper account that he was being once again suspended, this time for "shooting off his mouth too freely and for transgressing his duties as an officer." He eventually found himself a policeman in November 1900, once again in the precarious position of arresting of arresting Mr. Baptist, a white man, leading the paper to lament, "White citizens what are we coming to!" The next morning Baptist was "discharged...without any fine" and Inge "also very properly discharged from the services of the city."

Along with the role of policing the community, Inge also often found himself the jailer of prisoners in the county bastille, a role for which his pugnacious character seemed well fitted, as when he foiled an attempted jail break in 1893. "About 7 o'clock Wednesday evening the prisoners in the county jail, about twenty in number, made an attempt to break jail by running over the colored jailer, Ed Inge, but failed to succeed. The plot was well arranged, but some of the prisoners seemed to have held back...Inge is a very plucky colored officer and had they not stopped when ordered, some of them would undoubtedly have been shot."

Inge's pluck also rubbed many people the wrong way, and he developed quite a few enemies. In 1892 he had to take a peace bond out on Henry Riley, a prisoner he had been guarding, for "threatening his life when he regained his liberty." While picking cotton in Burleson County in the fall of 1896 Inge was hit in the face with a brickbat by a fellow cotton picker in a dispute over who should weigh their load first. He had to bring charges twice against a loose-tongued woman by the name of Mary Felder, once for "cursing and abusing him," the second time when "she paid her respects...in very vigorous language" to him and a constable in court.

In 1896 Inge was even involved in a court battle over a reported assault on him by a deacon of the Little Zion Baptist Church in Brenham. A dispute between two members of the church's board of deacons (both named Smith) had been brewing for several months and had grown to the point where one of the deacons nailed the doors shut. Inge was seen as somehow responsible when he showed up on the scene, and as he got in earshot of what they were saying Elder Smith remarked to Deacon Smith: "There goes that old black [sic] devil you've got watching this church. First thing he knows I'll have him behind the jail bars." Inge then asked Elder Smith what he said, and the elder repeated the language. Inge then informed the elder that he was an officer and intended to have satisfaction, whereupon the elder "whaled" him over the head with a walking stick and struck him about ten times with his fist. Inge's testimony, however, was not corroborated by the cloud of witnesses summoned to appear in the case. Their testimony completely exonerated the elder and placed the blame for the entire transaction on the shoulders of Policeman Inge and the Deacon Jake Smith.

The press kept the story up for several days, largely due to a rumored mob bent on taking over the church and one of the deacons breaking in with an axe to attempt to retake control of the church. Inge's poor showing in the affair also was brought up again, with the *Brenham Banner* commenting that "...in the encounter...the Camptown policeman took a hand, and contrary to his previous record, came out second best." The article also mentions that charges were filed against one of the deacons and Inge, and no further account of the case against Inge is found.

However, it seems that Inge's reputation as a man not to be toyed with was beginning to fade. The newspapers had reported earlier in the year on another fracas that hints at his age, commenting that he was "well advanced in years" in July 1896:

> "Fun At The Depot—Bill Giddings, a well-known colored character of this town, was arrested at the Santa Fe Saloon Friday morning by Ed Inge the Camptown officer. Bill had been drinking pretty freely and was engaged in a hot dispute with a Quarry hand when the colored guardian of the peace arrived on the scene. Inge told him he would have to stop that fuss or he would be pulled. Bill paid no attention to the officer's warning and continued trying to outdo his friend. Inge waited several minutes and then quietly walked up to Bill and collared him. Bill pulled back and attempted to argue the case with the officer but it was 'no use,' he had to go, and after

being snatched down the steps leading to the depot he concluded he had best move along and not attempt to hold back, at least not there any way [sic]. All went well until the officer and his charge reached the crossing near Haubelt Bros. Store where the big struggle for liberty took place. Inge is well advanced in years, but he froze onto Bill in a manner that proved beyond a doubt that he was old. Joe Armenian came to Inge's aide however, and the desperate prisoner was marched away without further trouble.

The following year he had to call upon a fellow officer while making an arrest and escorting the prisoner to jail. "In emulation of Bill Nye's dog, Entomologist, Ed Inge, the Camptown policeman, came near biting off more than he could chew Saturday evening when he undertook to convey John Johnston to the lockup. Johnston had tanked up on bug juice until he felt entirely too large to be arrested by a 'nigger' policeman, although himself of African descent. The assistance of Policeman Lockett was necessary in conveying him to the calaboose, and both officers had their hands full."

A year later another prisoner he had arrested, Dick Lewis, decided to take "leg bail" and "darted away from Inge before that functionary could recover his breath." Despite giving "chase with guns trained on his receding foe...Lewis had the go on the officer and maintained it with all ease."

Although his physical prowess as policeman may have weakened, Inge's commitment to the full exercise of the law had not diminished. This again landed him in hot water with the city council in June 1900. The *Brenham Daily Banner* initially reported that a motion was made that Inge "be severely reprimanded in open council for using disrespectful language toward a member of the board of aldermen." Several weeks later the reason for his censure became the focus for many more headlines and controversy over the actions of one Alderman William Lusk.

During Maifest celebrations the month before, Inge had arrested Lusk's driver, Dude Walker, for speeding, a charge to which Walker plead guilty and was fined $10.20. At the following meeting of the city council, Lusk was serving as mayor pro tem in the absence of Mayor James Wilkins and brought up the matter with the council, which then remitted the fine. Upon his return, Mayor Wilkins rejected the council's paying of Walker's fine, causing heated feelings among other members of the council who had approved paying it. Inge caught much of that heat as the arresting officer and the council once again brought up the subject of his reprimand, with Alderman Burch calling for him to be dismissed because he "thought the city was paying too much during the dull season for the police." Lusk eventually began to feel the pressure as well, especially since "the papers of the city have contained the statement that Policeman Ed Inge was reprimanded for using disrespectful language toward Alderman Lusk." In response, Lusk had the following printed in a letter to the paper to attempt to present his side:

> I have been asked quite a number of times how it was that I had to have the city council reprove a negro policeman for "abusing me." It does look bad in print, and has grated on my nerves every time I have seen it in the papers, which has been on numerous occasions. I don't believe the papers meant any disrespect to me in placing it in that manner: "For abusive language to one of the aldermen." Then again "abusive language to Wm. Lusk," etc. I will state that Inge did not use abusive

language to me, but did not respect my orders in several ways. And that is why he was ordered by the full council to be reprimanded, and not for abusive language...

Although it is never made clear what orders Inge did not respect, it seems likely they were his arrest of Walker, and likely a request by the alderman not to arrest his driver for reckless driving during the town's most prestigious celebration. It also seems that this clarification was more for easing some of the onus Lusk was feeling for attempting to illegally have Walker's fine lifted than as any sort of apology to Inge for enforcing the law even in the face of political pressure.

Inge managed again to avoid serious repercussions to his career from his run-ins with white politicians on the city council. In April 1902 a newspaper account of council proceedings mentions he and A.B. Burkhead were reelected as "colored policemen," although their compensation at $5 each was still considerably lower than that of two white policemen reelected at the same time, who were making $45 each. But his days as one of early Brenham's most colorful law officers were rapidly coming to a close. That August Inge "had an attack of nervous prostration," collapsing to the sidewalk and brought to his house "in a wagon." Making matters worse for him, late one night in September his home in Camptown was found "in a state of hopeless conflagration." It was thought to be a case of arson, which would not be unreasonable considering the number of enemies he had made in his many decades as a policeman. Extinguishing the fire was made was even more difficult because "there was a box of cartridges in the building and ever and anon overheated cartridges would burst and frighten the crowd."

Two weeks later Inge was "found dead in his bed" at his home, though it's unclear if this was the same house that had just burned, or merely that "he was living alone." His three-sentence long obituary made mention of his many years of service protecting the citizens of Camptown and Brenham by simply referring to him as "the well-known colored policeman in Camptown…a good and faithful old darkey" who "had many friends among the white people of this city."

Chapter 14

# "THE PLOWS ARE STILL IN THE FIELDS..."

# AN INTRODUCTION TO BRENHAM'S EMANCIPATION CELEBRATIONS: 1878-1923

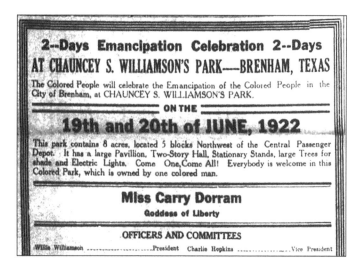

*Courtesy of Brenham Daily Banner-Press, June 18, 1922*

In a distant corner of Camptown Cemetery the tombstone of Josephine Yancy lies collapsing in a gully next to a railway line. It was covered in a canebrake while the cemetery was being cleared in 2014, and was next to the graves of her parents, Ben and Fannie, who had had to bear the terrible burden of burying their only child. Josephine was far too young when she died in August 1903, not yet twenty-nine years old. Little is known about her, but three things are clear from Brenham newspaper accounts in 1896. In March she gave a vocal duet at the Canton Excelsior Club at Lou Clark's Hall in Camptown. A few months later she presented a paper for the Union Program at the Mount Rose Baptist Church, a few hundred yards or so from her final resting place. And in June of that year, at the same church, Miss Josephine Yancy was nominated to become a Goddess of Liberty.

Josephine wasn't elected the Goddess of Liberty for the Emancipation celebration that year. She also isn't the only person buried in Camptown Cemetery whose life can be connected to these yearly observances. Her father, Ben Yancy, as well as Robert S. "Ketchum" Sloan, had been sworn in among the nine men specially selected as policemen for the two-day celebration two years earlier. Asa Rippetoe was an assistant grand marshal of the Emancipation Celebration parade in 1878. Mattie Bynum, daughter of Waterman Bynum, a Black alderman buried in 1886 at the cemetery, was also a candidate for Goddess of Liberty in 1885. In 1884 Felix Whittaker's father had a float in the parade decorated as "a complete blacksmith shop in full working order, decorated with the mottoes, 'We live by honest toil' and 'Patronize home industries.'"[1] Wylie Hubert entered a horse in a race at the Fairgrounds during the celebrations in 1894.[2] Frank Hubert served as treasurer for a widely advertised commemoration held at Chauncey Williamson's Park in 1922.[3]

As the predecessor of what came to be known as Juneteenth, Emancipation celebrations played an equally important role in the Black community in the late nineteenth and early twentieth centuries. They not only commemorated the freeing of slaves but also represented a chance for family and friends from around the state to gather, socialize, and relax for a two-day holiday free from their daily labors and full of entertainments. A study of contemporary newspaper accounts drawn from the Portal to Texas History digital archives presents not only a surprisingly broad understanding of how this holiday was celebrated, but also insight into the Black community in Brenham and Washington County. The articles, which cover the years 1878 to 1923, offer a useful tool for understanding local Black history during this period.

The earliest records of these Emancipation celebrations are difficult to come across, such as one from an 1865 Galveston newspaper ad. This "Emancipation Celebration by Colored Persons" was held at 10 a.m. in the town square "to celebrate the abolition of slavery," with speeches by Alex Pearce, Howard Cavenaugh, and Rev. Donald Gregory. It was advertised as open to "all colored people, and their friends," with the federal officers "especially desired to be present."[4]

Another can be found in the records of the Freedmen's Bureau. James Butler, the bureau agent in Huntsville, wrote to his superior officer in Galveston about a gathering of Blacks there "on the 19th of this month to celebrate their emancipation." They had printed up and posted handbills around town to advertise the event, but "complained that a man by the name of William Bowen went around town tearing down their bills and saying that 'niggers will not be allowed to have anything of the kind.'"[5] Butler brought him in to question him about it, which led Bowen to "answer me in a contemptible manner, making threats to shoot the party who told me. I informed him that I did not allow any man to make threats in my office. He very insolently answered me that he would say what he pleased, swearing and using very abusive language."[6] Butler told him that he would fine him $25 for "contempt in my office. Bowen refused to pay, but since "he had a number of other vagabonds waiting to rescue him" Butler, who had no troops to back his arrest up, released him. Butler recommended "the mayor have sufficient police force to arrest and imprison" the "twenty young men here of a disreputable character who have evinced a desire to mar the proceedings and create a riot. According to Butler's estimation, there would "be at least three or four thousand freed people here on the 19th to attend the celebration" and anticipated no problem from them."[7]

Unfortunately, newspaper archives covering Washington County are sparse to non-existent covering the period before the mid-1870s. After that, a surprising amount of detailed reporting on Emancipation celebrations exists. They were usually two days long, ideally on the nineteenth and twentieth. If one or of these days fell on a Sunday, the dates for the festivities could be moved either forward or backward to avoid conflicting with church services. One Emancipation celebration, however, was held by the Washington County Ex-Slaves Association at Stockbridge's pasture on October 1, 1896. It is not clear from the news article why the date was chosen, aside from being originally planned as a two-day affair before being reduced to a single day due to "a conflict in dates with another colored celebration."[8] It was commented in the press that whites would have to arrange for their own meals and many forms of work was halted, as it was expected that during the celebrations Blacks were to be free of their daily labors. "The plows are still in the fields. Cooks have abandoned the kitchens. Industries that are handled by colored labor are silent for the two days, having realized the futility of trying to run, have generously closed up and granted them the two days holiday."[9]

The earliest reports of an Emancipation Celebration in Brenham was held in 1878 "in the grove at the head of Hog Branch,"[10] and was attended by a crowd estimated to be between twelve and 1,500.[11] The Brenham celebrations often were held at

VOICES OF CAMPTOWN | 243

the "old fairgrounds" south of Camptown and the site of a large circular racetrack. Later they were held at a park in Wilkins' Addition owned by Camptown's Hook and Ladder No. 2 fire department known as the "Colored Firemen's Park." It later was sold to Chauncey Williamson, who continued to maintain it as a park. In the 1920s, celebrations were held at Williamson's Park and advertised as having "...a large Pavilion, Two-Story Hall, Stationary Stands, large Trees for shade and Electric Lights. Come one, Come all! Everyone is welcome in this Colored Park, which is owned by one colored man."[12] Often two celebrations were going on in Brenham, as well as smaller celebrations in other freedom colonies throughout Washington County. In 1905 there were three separate celebrations, "one at Oak Grove Park, one mile east of Brenham on the Independence Road (a commonly used location), one near Mrs. Dawson's Sanitarium, given by ex-slaves," as well as one at "Hyde Park by the colored Hook and Ladder Company"[13] (the same Wilkins' Addition park formerly operated by Robert Sloan and later by Chauncey Williamson.) Some of the celebrations were free, while others charged admission from ten cents to twenty-five cents.

The celebrations in Brenham were well attended by other communities, including Chappell Hill, Hempstead, Navasota, Austin, Independence, William Penn, Gay Hill, Whitman, Kenney, Caldwell, Burton, Carmine, Somerville, Temple, Bellville, Giddings, Orange, and Houston.[14] As early as the 1880s the events attracted crowds of two to three thousand, and by 1914 the crowd at the celebrations were estimated to be as high as six thousand. The influx of visitors from distant communities was encouraged by reduced railway rates offered for the celebrations; the beneficial effects of such large crowds on the local economy was not lost on either white or Black businessmen.

Preparations for the celebrations began months beforehand.

The nomination and elections of a Goddess of Liberty were an important element of these preparations, with tickets sold for the various candidates to raise money for the organizing committees. The candidates were elected to serve as a feminine figurehead of the liberty recently won, much as the Goddess of Liberty had served as a symbol of freedom since the early days of the Texas Republic. She also was to deliver speeches at the Emancipation celebrations' opening ceremonies. These elections were often quite lengthy and elaborate affairs themselves, with friendly rivalries between various communities nominating their candidates.

> The colored people closed the polls for the election of a goddess of liberty for their emancipation celebration at 11 o'clock on Saturday night at the Mount Rose Baptist church. Miss Esther Johnson, daughter of Rev. Moses Johnson, was declared elected, after which 300 guests, headed by Randle's brass band went to Henry McAdoo's residence to partake of refreshments prepared by the committee. They then went to the residence of the goddess of liberty about 12:30 a.m., and tendered her a serenade. An address was delivered by J.H. Clinton, which was responded to.[15]

The celebrations' opening day usually began with a parade through downtown Brenham, or two parades if separate celebrations were being held. The parades were typically led by a grand marshal "wreathed in gorgeous silk sashes of emerald and crimson,"[16] followed by a brass band. Next would be that year's elected Goddess of Liberty in a carriage covered in lace and led by six white horses, accompanied by her maids of honor and flower girls, and followed by the various orators who were delivering speeches at the opening ceremony.

Then came the floats, which ranged from the mundane to the elaborate. Aside from Felix Whitaker's working blacksmith shop, which had a float that showed his craft, these covered a wide range of themes and topics. They included "a children's float decorated in the National colors, with swings suspended from the canopy, in which little children were swinging,"[17] "a choir singing sacred songs," various community groups, "a representation of Ransom's tonsorial parlor,"[18] "a juvenile fire company with a boat on a truck," and "an ox wagon load of imitation cotton." In 1897 there was even a float representing raccoon hunting, on which "a good-sized tree had been transplanted, and amid its spreading branches a festive coon disported in apparent satisfaction, despite the fact that he had been shackled in freedom's name. At the root of the tree a veteran coon dog bayed deep mouthed defiance to the treed coon and a lot of small boys with sticks and horns and other implements of noisy warfare added their full quota to the din."[19] The parades, stretching on for up to two hundred yards, also would be accompanied to the grounds where the celebrations were held by, at various times, a colored militia unit known as the Brenham Blues, Camptown's own fire department, the Hook and Ladder Company No.2, local uniformed baseball teams such as the Famous Nine, bicyclists, men, women and children on horseback, and various other hangers-on.

The local lodges and societies were well represented, including the Camptown Mutual Aid Benevolent Society, the Masons, the Lady's General Missionary Society, Ladies Aid Society, Missionary Building society, the Draymen's Club No. 1, the Band of Progress, the Grand United Order of Odd Fellows, the order of the Seven Stars of Consolidation, the Sons and Daughters of Zion, and the Peculiar Sevens. Many of these social groups also played an important role in organizing the celebrations in addition to marching in the parades.

After the parade's arrival at the fairgrounds, the celebrations were opened by speeches, sometimes with responses by that year's Goddess of Liberty. Speeches also were given by white politicians as well as Black community leaders, with the more accomplished Black speakers in demand at other ceremonies. Although there is no record of the content of these speeches, there does exist portions of another speech delivered by J.D. Bushell, the orator of the day at the 1917 Emancipation celebration at Chauncey Williamson's Park. Bushell was not only the principal of the Brenham Normal and Industrial college, but also a veteran of the Spanish American War and had charged up San Juan Hill with the Rough Riders. Delivered at Williamson's Park two months earlier, just as the United States was entering the Great War, parts of that speech also touched upon Emancipation. Following are some quotes from that speech, which might give some sense of the power of the speeches delivered by the principal orators at the Emancipation celebrations:

> ...These ties are ties of blood, and may be seen upon battlefields, on southern plantations, in the home and in the forest. We made the crops, tilled the fields, felled the forests and did the primary, the fundamental, the strenuous labor for a period of more than two hundred years.
>
> Our hands have not grown weary. The same arms of iron, and fingers of steel that tilled the fields when we were not citizens, are doubly ready to do now that we are part and parcel of this great nation. The man who walks behind the plow, who sits upon the reaper, who begins

at early dawn and labors till the purple twilight deepens into night, is as much a soldier as the man who stands by his guns. While our brethren are in the field, be they white or be they black [sic], let the rest of us be making it possible for them to stay in the field until they shall have wrested from the crown of autocracy the incubus of human authority.

There was never a war in the United States to free slaves. The North has never had any more love for negroes than the South. Slavery was not a Southern institution, but an American institution. The Emancipation Proclamation was not issued to free the slaves, but it was issued as a fit and necessary war measure for suppressing rebellion and was used as a military necessity. Mr. Lincoln clearly and distinctly stated in his first inaugural address delivered March 4, 1861, "I have no purpose, directly or indirectly, to interfere with the institution of slavery in the States where it exists. I believe I have no lawful right to do so, and have no inclination to do so. While the North and the South were engaged in a war between themselves, making determined efforts for good government the gates flew open and the negro slave walked out and he has been walking ever since. It is in the South where he was held as a slave that the negro is given a man's chance in the commercial world. The South has never desired to re-enslave the negro, but it has helped, like the North, to Christianize and educate him."

Our emancipation was not an accident, but a result. It was the culmination of the working out by the mighty forces of faith and prayer through two hundred and fifty years of the proposition that "All men are created equal, and are of right and ought to be free." It was not the triumph of a system, nor of the North over the South. When freedom tore the azure robe of night and set the stars in glory over the camps of four million slaves, it was the result of the well-defined and determined efforts of men and women North and South, many of whom were the descendants of Puritans and Huguenots, who, themselves had felt the fires of persecution and were wedded to liberty.

Negro blood forms a part of the red in every stripe in "Old Glory." We have rendered valuable services in the nineteen wars of the United States, from the Revolution in 1775 to Carrizal where negro troopers went singing to their death. If anywhere their bravery and valor are questioned, when they have been called upon to defend their country, go to San Juan Hill. Ask the bleeding earth that drank their blood! And if the rocks could find a tongue, they would tell you that negro troopers saved the day for America, by marching to the old Block House midst shot and shell, "while horse and hero fell." They routed the Spaniards with victory perched upon their banners and while the band played, "There'll be a Hot Time in the Old Town Tonight," negro soldiers seized the artillery, turned it upon the fleeing Spaniards, and through their brave and heroic deeds, wrote their names in blood upon the records of military triumphs and scored a decisive victory for America.

Every member of the race stands ready now to serve the country's needs. Let it be remembered that the man with the hoe is as much a factor in this contest as the man with the sword. Everyone is not fitted for service at the front. Let everyone serve where he is best fitted, and in this we serve not only our country, but we serve humanity and God.

This is no time for quibbling or shuffling. The constitution [sic] of the United States is the expression, the highest expression of the organic law of our land. That law gave us the elective franchise and we are citizens.[20]

In addition to the speeches, various amusements were available at the ceremonies, including horse races, goat roping contests, shooting contests, military company drills, fiddler's contests, mule riding, tournaments, and stock shows. Children could "join in a potato race, and egg race, running and hopping abstracts and many other such contests."[21] There might be Ferris wheels and merry-go-rounds. Contests were held, such as one for "the lady that proves herself to be the most talkative and entertaining,"[22] prettiest woman and ugliest man, best needlework, neatest dressed woman, best quilt, best oil painting, best recitation, best essay, best jubilee singing, best lady rifle shot, best milk cow, best bicycle rider, best cotton, best corn, fastest trotting horse and best decorated float. Prizes included cash, hats, scarves, rockers, paintings, items of jewelry, vases, boxes of candy or cigars, and even sacks of flour.

Baseball was a big event during the celebrations. Local teams, such as the Lee, the Famous, the Strikers of Camptown, and the Lone Star of Watrousville played matches not only with each other, but also with teams from Navasota, Hempstead, Beaumont, Galveston, Bryan, Bellville, and Austin.

Concessions were available at stands that had been leased to the highest bidder before the celebrations for categories such as saloon, chili, tamales, ice cream, confectionery, restaurant, shooting gallery, bootblack, barbecue pit, wienerwurst, lemonade, milk shake, "blue rock" (rock candy), dancing, "cane stand and doll baby," and hobby horses. Barbecue dinners were common at some of the smaller celebrations and usually were provided free. Alcohol was generally present, especially at the larger gatherings.

Music played a large part in the celebrations, starting with the parades all the way through the grand balls held at night. One or more local bands usually provided entertainment, such as Prof. Foss's Brass Band, Manuel Taylor's Lone Star Band (which earned $90 for the celebrations in 1900), Jerry Randle's Cottonpatch Band, the Zobo Band (directed by Mrs. Estella Lindsey), the Twentieth Century Quartette, and Gus Hopkin's Band. The Brenham Brass Band, under the leadership of Prof. C.P. Hicks, even composed special music for the occasion, such as the "Emancipation Quadrille" and "Out of Bondage Waltz." Out-of-town bands included the Seaport Band of Galveston and the W.H. Hawkins Band of San Antonio, with Sid C. Isles' Ragtime Band from Houston being especially favored in later years, with music playing until the early morning hours. An account of a musical contest between the Hawkins and Isles bands was published in a 1938 edition of *Down Beat Magazine*:

> Here's an invitation to a carving contest that took place way back in the 'teens on the 19th of June in Brenham, Tex. The occasion was the yearly celebration of the Emancipation Proclamation, which freed the slaves, and every mother's son was really ready to hear a battle of the music between the two best Colored bands in Texas. (A vote of thanks to Ray R. Hone, Jr., the well-known record collector, for digging this dope.)
>
> The line-up was as follows: W.H. Hawkin's Brass Band, the pride of San Antonio, was bucking Sid Isles' Ragtime Band from Houston. And this man Sid Isles blew

a hot horn that had echoed all over Texas. The boys from Houston were sold on Sid, and packed the excursion train to the roof on the trip to Brenham. Excursion trains were puffing in everywhere, but they calculated that there were over a thousand Sid Isles fans from Houston alone. The Hawkins Brass Band was unafraid. They played strictly legit usually, the regulation stuff, for clubs, lodges, and city functions. Besides Hawkins himself had composed that "March Tanforn." But they did have a solid cornetist, who could get off if he had the chance, named George Washington Smith.

Well, the final decision was one of those things. The newspaper men had organized the battle, and they voted for the Hawkins Brass Band, because they played a legit overture. But the crowd went the other way. And the most disappointed cat was George Washington Smith, not because he wasn't allowed to get off, but because he wished he was playing with the Sid Isles band, that didn't "pay no mind" to music reading. George knew the real thing when he heard it and lost no time starting a real band of his own.[22]

Despite the differences in music venues and otherwise, the similarities between Brenham's annual Maifest and the Emancipation celebrations were often noted. "(T)he colored people pattern their celebration a good deal after the manner of the white have their Maifest, save that a Goddess of Liberty takes the place of a May Queen"[23] even though it was recognized that best special railway fares for Maifest were not as good as those the Emancipation committees arranged for their celebration and at times drew a much larger crowd. Just as the Maifest is held at the Firemen's Park, the Emancipation celebrations were at one time held at the Colored Firemen's Park, and many of the floats that had been used in the Maifest procession were later used in the Juneteenth parades. Eventually, as the designation Emancipation Celebration" gave way in the early twentieth century to "Juneteenth," the festivities in Brenham found a home at Ed Henderson's park.

However, there is one ironic note about Emancipation Day. On June 19, 1891, the Texas separate coach law was to go into effect, a seemingly odd choice for any law to come into effect, but especially this one. The fuller segregation that led toward growing inequities were being backed by the full force of new legislation passed by the State of Texas.

> Today is the last day our colored friends can claim the social privilege of occupying the same coach or even the same seat with their white friends on the railway lines of Texas. The separate coach law goes into effect tomorrow, and as the colored people are rushing about to the most accessible points to celebrate the 26th anniversary of their emancipation the change will be particularly noticeable and as the *Banner* has previously remarked will seem like the irony of fate that it should have gone into effect on this particular day. But this is best, and while there may be some recalcitrant colored individuals who oppose the law and will perhaps not accept it with good grace, it will be enforced. The colored people will be furnished equal accommodation with the whites but they will ride in the same coach no more.[24]

The Black citizens of Brenham were reminded that the special rates offered by the railroads for transportation to other cities for celebrating their Emancipation would also be affected. "The colored people almost throughout the state are preparing for a grand emancipation celebration. The Brenham colored people have done nothing so far, and if they don't hurry up will have on that day to enter the 'separate coach' and go elsewhere to celebrate."[25] In the same issue of the *Brenham Weekly Banner*, the irony of this situation was more directed toward whites who would see it as their own reason for celebrating. "It is a coincidence worth of note that on the day when the colored people of Texas will all be celebrating the anniversary of their emancipation, going on excursions and etc., they will be quietly ordered out of the coach with white people into coaches prepared for them, for the separate coach law goes into effect on that day. There is no doubt that this law was one of the best for all the people of Texas that was enacted by the last Legislature."[26]

This was one of the many separate coach laws that were proliferating throughout the country at the time, leading ultimately to the U.S. Supreme Court's "separate but equal" ruling in the Plessy v. Ferguson decision of 1896. It was one of the legal precedents that helped solidify Jim Crow laws throughout the next sixty years, which were separate even if rarely equal. As surely as the directive issued by General Gordon Granger in Galveston on June 19 in 1865, this separate coach law issued by the Texas Legislature and taking effect on June 19 in 1891 was to have a long-lasting effect on Black citizens in Brenham, Washington County, and throughout Texas for many years to come.

Chapter 15

# BRENHAM'S FORGOTTEN FIRE DEPARTMENT:

# THE PROTECTIVE HOOK AND LADDER COMPANY NO. 2

Fires have played a significant role in Brenham history, with none more infamous than the Burning of Brenham in 1866. In a town primarily built of flammable wooden structures, an entire block of downtown was consumed on September 7, with more than $130,000 in damage. One of the most recent books on the town's history focuses on this conflagration, despite the unfortunate mistake of stating the Union soldiers implicated in starting the fire were Black, which they were not since there were no Black soldiers serving there. But the military Post of Brenham to the east of town, viewed by defeated citizens who had aligned with the Confederacy as an occupying force, was besieged by outraged members of the local population for days. An indelible animosity against the federal troops was established before the confrontation resolved to an uneasy truce.

Five months later, on the night of February 21, 1867, another major fire swept through downtown Brenham. Three buildings were destroyed with $50,000 in damage, but this time the soldiers posted in Brenham were pointed out in the press "for their good behavior. They were promptly on the ground, labored faithfully

VOICES OF CAMPTOWN | 255

to suppress the flames, and voluntarily stood guard all the night over the goods which were thrown from burning buildings into the street."[1] Although the *Brenham Banner*, which had suffered so much in the earlier conflagration, gave this good report of the soldiers' assistance at this second fire, some forty-eight years later it shifted the blame. In an article on the ongoing pursuit of "war claims" from the earlier fire, the *Banner* changed the tone to cite a report that "another section of Brenham was burned by the federal soldiers in January [sic], 1867."[2] Among the losses was the office housing the Brenham office of the Freedmen's Bureau, which "was consumed by fire and all books and papers pertaining thereto were destroyed."[3]

After these two major fires had devastated much of downtown Brenham, leaders in the still-occupied town established the Brenham Volunteer Fire Department on May 28, 1867. Comprised of twenty-two men, it was organized into two companies, the Hook and Ladder and the Brenham Fire Protection company, with D.C. Giddings serving as the foreman. Their stated goal was firefighting, but as a 1917 article commemorating their 50th anniversary states, they functioned "in reality as military companies. They protected the lives and property of the citizens against the indignities offered by the Federal soldiers encamped at Camptown, during reconstruction days." The article goes on to state that while freedmen "made many complaints against the white people," M.A. Healy, charter member of the department and sheriff at the time, "refused to put the citizens in jail."[4]

But fires remained a problem, even after the soldiers left. The issue not only consumed the white businessmen of downtown, but also the less influential freedom colony of Camptown, which had sprung up to the east of town around the Union camp where many of the freedmen of Brenham and Washington County had settled for protection.

Although the Black community of Camptown was still located largely outside of the business center of Brenham surrounding the courthouse, it suffered not only from its highly flammable wooden structures, but also from its location a mile outside of town. That placed them outside the cistern system that had been developed in the downtown area for fire protection. In response to this need several citizens decided to organize their own hook and ladder company, as was noted in the newspaper. "This part of the city is quite thickly settled and being nearly a mile from the courthouse an ordinary frame house burns down before the firemen from the business part of town can reach it. This enterprise is commendable and should be encouraged."[5]

At this meeting a slate of nine officers was elected, with W.R. Van Buren, a schoolteacher, serving as president and Hughes McAdoo as vice-president. They submitted paperwork to the Texas Secretary of State for a charter for the Brenham Protective Hook and Ladder Company No. 2 as a Domestic Nonprofit Corporation and was acknowledged by certified letter on June 28, 1886. The following month the city council passed a motion, by a vote of three to one, "That Hook and Ladder company No. 2, composed of citizens of Camptown, be admitted into the fire department as a special fire company to extinguish fires and protect property in the immediate vicinity of Camptown; the said special Hook and Ladder company are not to have any voice in the election of chiefs of the Brenham fire department."[6]

The following decade recorded little about the Hook and Ladder Company No.2, though there are mentions in the local paper about fires in Camptown. In September 1893 the home of Harvey Hubert was fully ablaze. The family awakened around 2:30 a.m. as the roof was beginning to cave in. They barely escaped alive but safely as the fire consumed their home.[7] Another fire broke out at the "one story frame shanty belonging to Rachael Johnson, colored, just across the Hog branch in Camptown." Johnson was out of town picking cotton, but the house and contents, estimated to be valued at $300, were a total loss. This story also mentions that "the alarm was sounded from the courthouse," signaling to members of the fire department to gather up their water buckets and any other firefighting apparatus they could gather. In this case, the paper also mentioned that at the sounding of the alarm bell in the nearby courthouse, the Opera House was giving a performance to a full audience which panicked and almost caused a stampede, thinking the fire might be in the theatre.[8]

In 1897 a meeting was held to reorganize Protective Hook and Ladder Company No. 2 at Lou Clark's Hall. A slate of new officers was elected. Arthur Day, who worked at the Houston and Texas Central Railway freight depot, was elected president. Ben Bradly, a cook at A. Woehlers saloon, became vice-president, while James H. Swain, a drayman, was chosen as the secretary. Albert H. Milton, a driver for a local carpenter, was elected assistant secretary and would continue to play a prominent role in Hook and Ladder No. 2 over the coming decades, while A. Ayers, a well digger, became treasurer. Foreman was John Tanner, laborer and accomplished local musician who boarded with Swain, with R.M. Mackey, a schoolteacher, as the first assistant foreman and J. Tom Hill, a barber, as the second assistant foreman. Wesley Jackson was elected steward.

One of the problems Hook and Ladder No.2 encountered in its early days was the lack of a firetruck dedicated to transporting the equipment needed to effectively deal with fires. In June 1900 the fire company petitioned the city council for "an allowance of $25 to assist in the purchase of a truck."[9] No action was taken at that time, but this resourceful group of volunteers turned to another source of fundraising, organizing its own Emancipation celebration at the old fairgrounds southeast of the city, complete with baseball games and prizes for contests. Financially it was a success, and several days later Milton and Swain published, in a front-page letter in the newspaper, a "statement of expenses and profits of recent emancipation [sic] celebration held under its auspices." Among the total expenses of $181.90, $90 was paid for the services of Manuel Taylor's Lone Star Band and $30 for rental of the fairgrounds, which left a balance of $55.65 in the treasury after additional expenses. In the letter, "the Colored Fire Department of Brenham...beg leave to extend to the white and colored citizens our thanks and gratitude," with a "special thanks to the Honorable Chief and members of the Brenham Fire Department for the loan of their reel for the two days celebration."[10]

Later that month Milton was re-elected as president of the Hook and Ladder No.2, with A.F. Riggins as vice-president. Swain won the position of secretary again, and barber A.D. Patterson was selected treasurer. And with the funds now in their treasury, a fire truck was commissioned to be manufactured by "Messrs. Hartmann and Schaefer," who operated a blacksmith and wheelwright shop on Ant Street. Perhaps they finally could be fully integrated with the rest of the Brenham fire department.

But this was not to be. The first intimation of opposition appeared the following year in a short piece in the *Banner*, which noted that the fire department was made up of "patriotic, energetic white men...and it is not to be desired that their efficiency should in any manner be impaired, but that it should be kept up to its former standard of excellence. The proposed admission of the Colored Hook and Ladder Company, of Camptown, to membership in the department is bitterly opposed; in fact, such action would result in the immediate disbandment of the department. Be cautious, city fathers! Don't act hastily in this matter."[11]

When the matter of admitting the Hook and Ladder Company

No. 2 was referred to the department chief, the department's board of chiefs reported to the city council in a letter dated May 25, 1901. The report, which was adopted by the city council, made the position quite clear:

> After consulting many of the firemen individually and separately, and ascertaining their views on the proposed organization being admitted to the department, we believe such action on your part will make it necessary to change the complexion of the entire department, as none of them want to belong to a mixed department, and believe it impossible to admit this organization and define a line of demarcation that will separate them so effectually as to make it agreeable to all concerned, hence we recommend that no action be taken that will impair the efficiency of the present department, who have never yet failed to respond to the call of duty or halted in their efforts at its performance. Believing this to be the only course that will satisfy the fire department, we leave it to you to say this day whom you will have to serve you.[12]

This rejection did not deter the Hook and Ladder No. 2 from moving forward, especially since the company already was making plans for that year's Emancipation celebration at the fairgrounds, which was going to be bigger and better than before. In addition to baseball matches, a baby show, and singing and dancing, the circular track around it would be used for running, trotting, fat men foot races and bicycle races. Concession stands were rented for chili, ice cream, confectionery, restaurant, a shooting gallery, a dancing platform, bootblack, hobby horse and a saloon, which raised $122.75. Before the celebration tickets were sold at the Methodist church in Camptown to elect the Goddess of Liberty, during which "quite a spirited rivalry was waged between the supporters of the various candidates and voting was brisk for a while." At five cents a ticket and a total of 1,180 tickets sold, an additional $59 was raised.[13]

The funds collected for the Hook and Ladder No. 2 were quickly put to use. A firetruck was finally completed by Hartmann and Schaeffer. Constructed of ash and hickory, it measured sixteen feet long and was light but still appearing "almost unbreakable."[14] The truck was outfitted with "fifty feet of extension ladders, fifteen buckets, two hooks with poles, draw hooks, axes and all the other necessary appliances found on modern fire trucks." It was painted in the traditional red with black trim and the ladders in a vibrant blue. The truck would soon be put to use in a meeting "to practice for the sham fire on Emancipation Day," with the department having "a good time learning the maneuvers of a fire company."[15]

That year two Emancipation Day celebrations were held, one at in the northern part of town and the Hook and Ladder No. 2 again holding its event at the old fairgrounds south of town. That celebration started with a parade headed by three grand marshals, followed by the Lone Star Band and a white carriage bearing Miss Malinda Matthews, that year's Goddess of Liberty. These were followed by floats decorated in colored flowers, including one bearing a May Pole complete with dancers and tournament riders. Next in line were the uniformed members of the Hook and Ladder Co.2, proudly accompanied by the new fire truck. The rear was brought up by a Shetland pony drawing a cart and a boy riding an ox. The parade headed south to the fairgrounds for the coronation of the goddess and a general commencement of the ceremonies. These included a demonstration of firefighting and wound up that evening with a shooting match and speeches, including one by J.C. McCoy, the principal of the Camptown school and son-in-law of Wiley Hubert.[16]

The next election of officers for the Hook and Ladder No. 2 took place a week later at the barbershop run by the group's treasurer, with plans underway for a more permanent meeting place, as well as for storage of the new firetruck. By September construction had begun on a one-story building built on a lot in central Camptown owned by Albert Milton, the organization's president and a practicing carpenter by that time. The structure also would serve as a meeting place for further meetings of the fire company. Fundraising continued later that year, with a circular that advertised "an entertainment and afternoon luncheon on Ant Street on Nov. 16$^{th}$ to be given by the Hook and Ladder No2." Lest anyone worry that it might get rowdy, it also noted that "Good order will be maintained by Officer Burkhead, who will keep a vigilant eye on the assembly."[17] Burkhead was not only a city policeman at the time but also had served as a grand marshal at the last Emancipation Day parade and operated the Lone Star Tonsorial Parlor, a barbershop in the back of the White Elephant Saloon advertising its services for "colored people only."[18]

Planning for what was now being referred to in the press as a Juneteenth celebration began as early as mid-April the following year and included flyers promoting the fire company's third year of staging the event. The parade would include "the colored militia company, of Houston, under command of Captain J.H. Henderson" and a Zobo band, which "deserves special mention as it was probably the best feature of the parade." During the turn of the century Zobo bands were all the rage, relying on what was essentially an elevated form of kazoo, dependent on a vibrating membrane usually housed in brass instruments resembling trumpets, coronets, saxophones, or even simple horns. Being inexpensive and simple enough that anyone who could hum a tune could use them, they made participation in a marching band open to almost anyone who could afford one, which must have quite an auditory and visual experience for parade goers.[19]

But life for the Hook and Ladder No.2 was not all fighting fires and marching in parades. They also turned out to provide support for family, friends and members of the company who had died. They turned out for seventeen-year-old Frank Hubert, who had died while working out of town in the boomtown oil field of Beaumont and returned for interment in Camptown Cemetery. When the company's foreman, Ed Day, died at age thirty-three, he also was buried in Camptown Cemetery under the auspices of the Hook and Ladder Co. 2 and also United Brothers of Friendship, a fraternal organization Day belonged to. Another huge loss came with the brutal murder of Manuel Taylor in front of the Taylor Saloon, which he operated on Quitman Street. Taylor was a man of many skills, including leading the Lone Star Band, which had played a prominent role in many of the Emancipation Celebrations and parades organized by the Hook and Ladder No. 2. His funeral procession was headed by the Lone Star Band, "the local lodge of the Seven Stars of Consolidation and the colored fire department," and "many beautiful floral tributes, some from white people, bedecked the dead man's coffin."[20]

The Protective Hook and Ladder No. 2 finally had its new fire truck and a new fire house to place it in. They were on a roll, and their next big acquisition would be land for a park of their own to serve as the "Colored People's Park,"[21] as well as a dedicated place to celebrate Juneteenth. On September 21, 1904, a deed agreement was signed with M.W. Becker and the Brenham Protective Hook and Ladder Co. No.2 Camptown, for eight adjacent lots in the Lewis addition north of the Higgins Branch. The price was $1,400, to be paid out over twelve years in annual payments, the first due on July 1, 1905. An addendum filed two years later clarified that A.F. Riggins, Mat Foote, John Fisher, Robert Davis, A.H. Milton,

Louis Brown, and E.H.R. Graves were trustees for the Hook and Ladder No. 2.

Although in 1905 Brenham still held two Emancipation Celebrations, the news accounts saw fit to focus primarily on the one organized by the Camptown fire department, "held in their pretty little Park, northwest of the city." It had been "put in good shape to accommodate the crowds expected," including a dance platform that was being laid down and refreshment stands "at convenient points in charge of persons experienced in conducting them." Special railway excursion rates had been obtained for participants from Orange and Beaumont, "who are coming here with some fine concert attractions for the entertainment and amusement of its patrons."[22]

The day of the inaugural celebration at the park was bright and clear. Although the train from Orange was delayed and didn't arrive until one that afternoon, the town was still crowded with people attending the celebrations from Hempstead, Chappell Hill, Independence, Whitman, William Penn, Gay Hill, Somerville, Temple, Giddings, Burton, Carmine, Bellville, Kenney, Beaumont, Orange, Houston and Navasota. Recovered from the death of Manuel Taylor, the Lone Star Band headed up the parade, followed by a stream of participants:

> ...the Goddess of Liberty's trap, decorated in white and drawn by four prancing steeds; followed by a boy in a small wagon drawn by a goat; next a tandem trap of green and yellow; this was followed by a dozen girls, dressed in white, on horseback; the Hook and Ladder Company, in full uniform and their truck decorated, upon which was seated a little girl in a rocking chair; a large float decorated in the National colors, filled with children, followed; next

speakers in carriages; then the Beaumont queen, a Miss Blanchette, in a richly decorated trap...this was followed by another trap in yellow and black, the Zobo band in a decorated float was next, followed by a girl in a chariot; a white and green trap; a carriage containing prominent Beaumont visitors; this was followed by another float in red, white and blue filled with children.[23]

When they arrived at the park, the celebrants found "a portion of Parkers Carnival attractions to amuse and entertain their patrons." A week later, "the Colored Hook and Ladder Company No.2 gave an additional "entertainment at their new park in Wilkin's Addition."[24]

The Hook and Ladder No. 2 continued to hold Juneteenth celebrations at its park for close to a decade, at times while competing celebrations were still being held at the old fairgrounds. The gatherings there were large, with an estimated 1,200 to 1,500 celebrants expected in 1906, and were bringing in bands such as Sid Ilsie's from Houston and carnival companies to entertain the guests. The final mention of a celebration put on by the company is found in 1913, likely because of the financial difficulties being encountered.[25]

In July 1911 the trustees of the Protective Hook and Ladder Company No. 2 met because they were no longer able to pay the remaining notes and interest on the park property. It was agreed then to reconvey the property to M.W. Becker, who had issued the deed to them and agreed to cancel all further debts on it in exchange. On June 30, 1915, a full warranty deed for the property was issued to Becker in consideration of the exchange of the cancelation of the remaining $400 in lien notes. But this was not to be the end of the park.[26]

VOICES OF CAMPTOWN | 265

Chapter 16

# "THE COLORED PEOPLE'S PARK"

In 1893 Brenham's newspaper reported on the opening of Hyde Park, with a small crowd drawn by free admission, a musical program in the evening, and a baseball game that failed to materialize when a visiting team failed to show. It also noted that "no city can have too many resorts of this kind where her people can congregate, rest and recreate," and that it was "used exclusively by colored people."[1] An association of six Black directors, including Robert Sloan, had been formed to operate the five-acre site. Despite the initial welcome by the paper, within weeks the park was described as the source of crowds that were making "the nights hideous for the people of that entire section of the city," with "discordant vulgar tunes" keeping people awake until after midnight, cursing, and a general disruption. It eventually settled down after the appointment of several of the managers as "special police to keep the order."[2]

The park wasn't mentioned in the press for over a decade until 1904, when it was erroneously still being referred to as Hyde Park. But this site was no longer under management by the Hyde Park Association, having been sold to "the Brenham Protective Hook and Ladder Co. No. 2, Camptown, a corporation,"[3] for the price of $1,400, to be paid out in annual payments over twelve years. The first payment was due on July 1, 1905, less than two weeks after the compay held its first Emancipation celebration there, which would help fund the note due. Two other celebrations were going on around Brenham that year, but the one held at what came to be known as the Colored People's Park was the most successful, drawing in a crowd not only from the town, but also from surrounding communities as far away as Houston and Beaumont making use of special railroad rates. The following event was even more successful, bringing in an estimated 1,200 to 1,500 celebrants. The annual two-day events continued at the park for at least another eight years. The park was also used for other events as well, such as baseball matches between local teams.[4]

Despite the success of the Emancipation celebrations held there, the trustees of the Protective Hook and Ladder Co. No. 2 met in July 1911 because they could no longer meet payments on the annual notes and their interest. They agreed to reconvey the property to M.W. Becker, who then agreed to cancel all further debts on the property in exchange. On June 30, 1915, a full warranty deed was then issued to Becker. But even though the Hook and Ladder Co. No. 2 no longer owned the property, it would continue to be a location for celebrations by the Black citizens of Brenham.

Chauncey Williamson was born in Texas on February 18, 1859, to a mother from Missouri and a father born in Virginia. Although he eventually became a merchant, grocer and dealt extensively in real estate, little information is available on him before 1892,when press accounts began to report on his involvement in the Republican Party, which continued until at least two years before his death. He ran for tax assessor in 1896, notable not so much for losing but for pot shots being taken at him when campaigning in the small community of William Penn, apparently by some boys who were "offended at his remarks about the village" and "wanted to give him a good scare."[5] But other than this and a small note about his five-month journey in Mexico[6] and political activity, little was remarkable about him until he began to purchase the parkland that would later bear his name.

In 1914 Williamson bought a half-acre of the property the Hook and Ladder Company No. 2 had reconveyed to Becker. By 1915 he also purchased the rest of the property, which was described in the deed as "what is known as the Colored People's Park."[7] The following year he purchased the rest of the property, which continued as a place of rest and recreation for the Black community for decades to come.[8]

Under its new name, Chauncey S. Williamson's Park began appearing in press accounts as early as the spring of 1917, when it began a long-standing tradition as the site of the annual spring "field days." Segregated schools on the east and west side of town gathered for athletic and literary contests, with races for the younger students and the Brenham Normal and Industrial College joining in as well while it was still in existence. These would usually start off in the early morning, gathering at East End High School (later renamed after its most famous principal, A. R. Pickard) before leading a parade to the park, located on the east end of town, with music provided by the school's band and, at times, the band from Prairie View College.

With the entrance of the United States into World War I, the surge of patriotic fervor that seized the country found over "300 men, representing the negroes from all parts of the county" gathering at East End High School to plan a "monster patriotic demonstration at the Chauncey S. Williamson park." A crowd estimated at 2,000 showed up, as well as "all the pupils in the colored schools and the Brenham Normal and Industrial College" to hear J. D. Bushell. He was not only president of that college but also was a veteran of the Spanish American War, serving at San Juan Hill. Bushell gave a "ringing appeal to 'Black Americans'" in support of America's coming sacrifices in the coming conflict. The newspaper carried a significant portion of his speech, reminding his audience that "negro blood forms a part of the red in every stripe in 'Old Glory'" and proclaiming that "every member of the race stands ready now to serve the country's needs."[9]

After he had purchased the property, Williamson continued to improve the park with a new pavilion and holding patriotic gatherings and fund drives for the Black community during World War I. He also continued the use of what was now his park as a site for Emancipation celebrations, contributing twenty-six dollars of the proceeds in 1918 to the Red Cross in a further show of support for the war effort. That year also marked the first time these gatherings in his park were advertised in a Brenham newspaper in oversized font proclaiming "Big Celebration! 'Are you going or going to get Left?'—Be There," a "Celebration of the Emancipation of the Colored Americans" with "fine music— Celebrated Speakers—Dancing, and all forms of high class entertainment."[10]

This was not the only year a paid announcement of the event can be found in the press. In 1922 the ad covered almost a quarter of page four and contained a wealth of information about the various activities that went on over those two days, including music brought in from Houston by Sid Isles and his band, boxing matches ("6 preliminaries and 2 main bouts"), baseball games with visiting teams "and other amusements," as well as the reading of the Emancipation Proclamation and a main speaker. There is also a description of "this Colored Park, which is owned by one colored man" as covering "8 acres, located 5 blocks Northwest of the Central Passenger Depot. It has a large Pavilion, Two-

Story Hall, Stationary Stands, large Trees for shade, and Electric Lights." Another article on the Emancipation celebration that year indicated that admission to the park was a quarter and that "white people are especially invited as spectators. Reserved seats at 25 cents each have been reserved for spectators, who must also pay 25 cents to get in the park."[11]

It may be that Williamson felt ads were an important enticement for these gatherings because of "rival factions" engaged in "two very creditable celebrations of Emancipation Day" with separate parades on the same day, seeking "to outdo each other, but they should show a spirit of friendliness and cooperation, and get together next year."[12] But this problem persisted through at least the following year, with the *Brenham Banner* again noting that "if the two factions would get together and hold one celebration, then white friends would help them and the affair could be made a big success. But Brenham is not large enough for two successful celebrations held in opposition to each other," also noting once again "that attendance was smaller than in former years."[13]

Scattered reports of later Emancipation celebrations at the park can be found in local papers, the latest being from 1929, although accounts disappear after the onset of the Great Depression that year. Intermittent reports of the field days continued, one in 1961 held for "Negro schools" at "old Chauncey Williamson Park" as late as 1961, with a reporter citing that they started "during the World War II Period," although "for several years, during the period of recession, the celebration was discontinued." Williamson himself continued as a well-to-do grocer in Brenham, as well as owning several rental properties and continuing to lock horns with members of the Washington County Republicans. He succumbed to kidney and heart disease and a fatal heart attack on March 13, 1934, at age seventy-five. He is listed as single on his death certificate, with no hard evidence of marriage or children;

a Wille Williamson is frequently listed as president or manager of various events at the park, but it is uncertain that they were related. To further complicate matters, Chauncey Williamson died without leaving a legal will and well over a dozen heirs noted in the partition deed, making it difficult to track ownership of the property on which Chauncey Williamson's Park sat.[14]

Hattie Mae Flowers, Brenham's first Black principal, had most likely attended at least one field day at the park while attending school. She came into possession of some of the property after Williamson's passing, selling it to the city of Brenham in December, 1971, and it was dedicated in 1977 as Hattie May Flowers Park. Though none of the history about the Chauncey Williamson Park that preceded it is on the city's website for the park, the site does recognize Flowers' contribution in making sure that this same land has remained a park for the people of all races for a century-and-a-half now.

Chapter 17

# ED HENDERSON'S PARK

by Tina B. Henderson, Ph.D., and Charles Swenson

The story of North End Park and its transformation into Ed Henderson Park is integral to understanding the Black community in Brenham during the heart of the Jim Crow era. It is a story with many parts, and one of the best places to start is to understand the man whose name and legacy is indelibly connected to it.

The exact date of Henderson's birth is unclear, with various dates found in an oral history, census data, and death certificate. The most accurate and believable information is from a WWII draft registration certificate, which gives a birth date of February 15, 1879. Henderson was born in Chapell Hill to Joseph and Sydny Henderson, with three older siblings.[1] He wedded Christiana Keener in March 1896, with one child, Walter, from this marriage.[2] The ultimate outcome of the marriage is unclear, but in the next federal census in which Henderson appears, in 1930, he is listed as being married to a woman by the first name of Lena. In a 1950 affidavit, Lena Ransom was the same person as Lena Henderson, his wife, who died in 1935.[3] He then married Zerline Williams in July 1938, though this marriage was short lived since he is listed in the 1940 census as being widowed. In the 1950 deed of North

End Park to the City of Brenham, Henderson testified he was a single man.[4] He died on September 24, 1961, of liver cancer, living out the last days of his life in a house on the south side of the park that bore his name.

This data from various records presents the bare bones of Henderson's life. But he left behind other traces that present a much richer picture, primarily in various news accounts. The details of his earlier life aren't clear, although it seems that he spent some time in Austin since that is where he married Christiana, the daughter of a farmer there. The marriage was not to last because by 1920 he was single again and living in Brenham while working as a salaried club manager and boarding in a home owned by Lena Ransom. That relationship blossomed into a marriage between the two five years later. By 1930 he was the proprietor of City Cafe and owned the home where the two of them lived, valued at the time at $1,000.

Managing a club or running his cafe weren't Henderson's only business dealings. According to a press account, he was "one of Brenham's well known negroes, a leader in activities among the negroes." Unfortunately, in 1925 he also went on trial for "running a gambling house," with "other similar cases, including charges of selling whiskey" pending against him as well.[5] Although it was the early years of Prohibition and gambling had long been illegal in Brenham, both seemed to have been tolerated. This did not stop the jury from convicting Henderson of the charges and sentencing him to two years in the penitentiary. A front-page column in the *Brenham Banner-Press* opined that "we see so many people gambling and so many buying whiskey and making it that we do feel it is right to send one negro to the pen for a violation when so many white people are doing the same." Perhaps this is why, the column continued, "in less than an hour these self-same jurymen (as far as we have been able to ascertain, every one of them) signed a petition to parole the self-same Ed Henderson."[6] The petition seemed to have been effective, since after only spending a month in Huntsville, Henderson was out on parole.[7]

As soon as it was clear that Prohibition was doomed and the sale of beer was to be legalized in Texas, Henderson applied for a permit to sell it.[8] His clubs gained some notoriety in the press afterward. A teenager was charged with throwing a bomb in his club on Commerce Street in 1936; a year later, a state liquor inspector found a craps game being operated upstairs at his club on South Park Street. And in 1940 his nephew Orange accidentally shot a customer in the face at the Henderson Cafe, leading to a charge of murder.[9]

But it was another business for which Ed Henderson was much more well known, even now over sixty years since his death. It has gone by many names, but the earliest was North End Park. In the later portion of the nineteenth and early twentieth centuries, Chauncey Williamson's Park was the primary gathering place for various events in the Black community, including Emancipation Day celebrations.[10] In 1924 there were three separate locations for the Emancipation Day celebrations, which were reported by the *Brenham Banner* to hurt its observance.[11] Although there is no mention of North End Park in the local paper until an article in 1925 reporting on baseball games held there,[12] from 1926 on it was the primary gathering place for what was to become known as Juneteenth. These celebrations were organized by the Brenham Laboring Men's Club, with Ed Henderson serving as manager, and were advertised as "bigger, better than ever, our motto."[13] In addition, there were baseball and football games, boxing matches, carnivals, musical concerts, the "colored county fair," training sessions, bond drives during the war, annual field days for the schools, and numerous other events that most likely never made it into print.

The earliest mentions of North End Park deal with baseball games being played there by the Brenham Black Tigers. Although Blacks may have been segregated from most white activities at the time, whites were always welcome at the games with special seating reserved for them. This bonding over sports between the races could be quite tenuous at times though, as it was in June 1925. Three months earlier a white shoe salesman had slapped a Black girl he thought was showing him "impudence and disrespect." The incident was reported in a local "negro paper 'the Comet'" run by the wife of J. C. Arwine, a local "astro-psychologist" in an article calling for a boycott of the store, urging instead the use of mail-order houses that "would be glad to have the negroes' money." Several local Black citizens, including a doctor and a local preacher, joined in the call. The city's chamber of commerce finally met with several of the "leading negroes of the city" to resolve the issue, noting that "unless this incident was settled...it could lead to serious trouble."[14]

By late June there was still unease in town over the incident. A "notice" contributed to the *Brenham Daily Banner-Press*, possibly by Henderson himself, addressed the issue and the importance to "the colored baseball team." On June 28, the club canceled its game at North End Park "to show as much respect as possible" over the death of seventeen-year-old Billy Teague, the son of a local white lawyer, even though "this resulted in a great loss for the club financially." The notice went on to mention the *Comet* turmoil, stating that "the colored people do not approve of such things that will sow the seed of discord among the races...The colored ball club cannot survive unless it gets the patronage of the white people. The white people helped buy the uniforms we are now wearing...we extend hearty thanks to all that helped us and we wish you would help us by coming out to our ball games." The previous game "only had 4 white persons" attending, and that "we know you are going to see this in the right light by turning out Sunday...Special seats for white people."[15]

This last phrase, "special seats for white people," in one form or another, appears in almost every newspaper account of games at North End Park, as well as in the numerous ads for sporting or musical events at the park. In addition, both local and out-of-town white baseball clubs would occasionally play their games at North End when Fireman's Park was not available. It isn't clear from newspaper accounts whether these games were segregated, but there is no mention of "special seats for colored people" or something similar.

In press coverage of baseball games at North End Park, the number of teams mentioned is over thirty, although it isn't always clear whether this is because of a rebranding of some of the teams. Some names frequently were used by city teams, such as the Tigers (Brenham, East End, La Grange, Smithville, Eagle Lake, Bellville, Texas City), Bears (Taylor, Wharton, Somerville, Bryan – also known as the Dr. Pepper Bears), and Black Cats (Giddings, Caldwell, Navasota, Clay). Others were more unique, such as the Taylor Grand Prize, Southern Steamshippers, Galveston Sandcrabs, Houston Black Buffs, and the Luling Gushers. Some were simply descriptive, such as the Southern Pacific Shop team. A 1934 ad proudly noted that North End Park would host two days of the Negro World Series, played between the Austin Black Senators and Van Dyke's House of David Team from Sioux City, Iowa.[16]

The park was used for other sporting events as well, such as basketball, football (especially local high school teams), boxing, and the occasional rodeo. Gatherings for out-of-town groups, brought in on trains offering special rates for the events, were common and described as "excellent park facilities for colored folks, a drawing card in having this place selected for the picnic."[17] A thousand Southern Pacific employees from Houston were estimated to have come in August 1932, while a picnic for the Southern Line dock workers tallied 432 arriving by train.[18] The local Pickard High School also used the park for its annual end of school field days, with parades from the school to there for ball games.

Juneteenth celebrations were, of course, annual events coordinated by the Laboring Men's Club and later the Business Man's Club, and if rained out would be rescheduled. They would be preceded by a parade through the business district with colorful floats and bands arriving at the park grounds for the baseball games, BBQ dinners, sometimes a carnival, and always a band with dances. In the twenties and early thirties, the tradition of electing a Goddess of Liberty, who rode in the parade in a float decorated by flowers and accompanied by an attendant during the parade, continued. By 1939 the Goddess of Liberty role had evolved into the coronation of a Queen of Springtime.[19]

In early October a "Colored County Fair" was held at the park. Such fairs also were preceded by a parade and accompanied by rodeos, ball games, bands, and dances. An advertisement for the fair from 1930 boasted the rodeo and carnival, which went on for a week, was "bigger and better than ever...featuring 7 Shows, 4 Rides, 200 People and 25 Novelty Concessions," with a "Saturday afternoon matinee for all school children."[20] In 1934 county schools participated for best school exhibits, stunts and character impersonations, and there also was a baby show. Home and livestock prizes were awarded for best jelly, thrift exhibit, quilt, bed spread, sewing, artwork, furniture, model house, poultry, turkeys, hogs and horses.[21]

Musical events were big, with a long string of performances appearing at North End Park, usually well-advertised ahead of time. These included not only bands, but also a whole show that traveled along with them. A partial list would include the Carolina Cotton Pickers, Sister Rosa Thorpe, Dandy Dixie All Colored Revue, Troy Floyd's Band, the 15-person Red Hot Minstrel featuring Sugar Foot Green, Don Albert and His Ten Pals, Jack Ransom and His 10-Piece Orchestra, Ida Cox with a Company of Twenty, Chester Boone and His Greater Orchestra from Houston, Boots and His Buddies from San Antonio, the Rhapsody in Tan All Colored Musical Comedy with 40 singers, dancers and comedians, as well as "16 Fast Stepping Girls." Coming from out of state was a plus, drawing in L.C. Toland's Chocolate Rhythm, "that Hot Black and Tan Revue direct from Harlem," Willie Crisp, "his piano and his recording orchestra," Leo Davis and His Orchestra, 11 Colored Musicians, The Toast of Hollywood, Direct from the Famous Club Montmarte, Radio Artist NBC and CBS," and "Gertrude Calloway and her Twelve Blue Devils, see her truck-hear her sing-watch her direct!"[22]

As with sporting and other events, whites were invited to attend and did. Ernie Fields played several times and was clearly popular with both audiences. When he performed at the 1939 Juneteenth celebration, it was reported that his band "featured a singer who made a distinct hit with the large crowd of white spectators who overflowed the section reserved for them. In fact, most of the socially prominent younger set were present to look on. The gyrations of the sepia jitter-bugs was something to behold, and seemed to be enjoyed equally by the participants and the lookers-on."[23]

This is not to say there were no incidents occurring at the park. In 1933 a woman was stabbed to death at a dance, with Ed Henderson himself intervening to take the knife away from the assailant.[24] During a baseball game in 1936 between Southern Pacific employees and the Morgan Line Dock Workers, the grandstands collapsed, injuring ten spectators. Although some were treated at the hospital, no one was seriously injured, and the ball game continued.[25] Later that year a two-story structure at the park known as Ed Henderson's Club House burned to the ground. Fortunately, it was insured.[26]

The advent of World War II affected the park's activities. Although in his fifties, Henderson registered with the draft board, but was never called up. He did do his part for the war effort, coordinating activities among the Black business community for the Red Cross[27] and contributing funds for War Bond sales,[28] including fundraising held at the park itself. At one event in 1944, a total of $4,000 of bonds were sold there by auction with accompanying items contributed by Black-owned stores.[29] Following the war he also worked on collecting Victory Loan Bonds.[30] As soldiers began returning, a barrack was erected at North End Park in 1946 to supply housing for four families of Black war veterans who were mustered out of service.[31] During the Juneteenth celebrations in 1948, Black veterans who had served in the war were presented the World War II Victory Medal.[32]

After a quarter of a century as Brenham's premier gathering park for its Black citizens, the city recognized North End Park's significance. Mayor C.D. Dallmyer of Brenham was sure to mention the addition of playground equipment to the park during his administration.[33] In August 1950 the city announced it had negotiated with Henderson "to turn over North End Park as a negro recreation ground." The press proclaimed that "the move makes Henderson the first important negro benefactor in Brenham. He was paid a nominal sum for the 9-acre park and its facilities."[34] Mayor Dallmyer announced that "the park deal...will provide negro recreation facilities and afford first class athletic fields for the schools' athletic programs."[35]

The deed transferring the property described the park as having "been a meeting and gathering place for the colored race, for celebrations, games, and festivities originated by them" and that Henderson, "as a benefactor of the colored race, is desirous of turning over this property."[36] The city, on its part, agreed to "relieve the property of lien debts, and to make the same a public park for the Colored Race of this community, and maintain, and improve the lands, and provide facilities, for the use and enjoyment of the colored people."[37] Henderson had certain conditions stipulated in the deed. One was that a portion of the park was to be retained for his "use, occupancy and possession… for and during his natural life." He would also "have the prior right to all concession, such as food and drink allowed on the Athletic Field, during public games." But the first condition was that "the said Property shall always be known in name as the 'Henderson Park.'"[38]

Ed Henderson continued to live on this tract on the south end of his beloved park at 313 Riggs Street, dying there at his home there at the age of eighty-one. He was buried in Chapell Hill.

# ACKNOWLEDGEMENTS

There are so many people involved in the writing of this book that it's hard to know where to begin, so let me start with the late Eddie Harrison. I speak of him in the introduction, giving just a scant few of his many accomplishments but wore none of these on his sleeve. One of my earliest memories of him involves a local from Brenham addressing him as 'Judge;' afterward he said he hated it when people called him that, despite it being one of many titles, such as Deacon and Mr. Harrison and so many others which he surely was entitled to. I was proud to simply know him as Eddie, which was fine with him and whenever I referred to him as such everyone knew just who I was talking about. He was the go-to person on Washington County history, a sure font of comprehensive knowledge, early on I came across an academic archaeology paper which listed him in a footnote as the source of an obscure bit of information on a farm in a long-forgotten corner of the county. Much of his encyclopedic knowledge of Washington County history came from years of travelling throughout the county as a farm extension agent among a rural black population willing to share long-standing oral traditions and histories with him. Unfortunately, much of that information was lost with his passing. When I was researching Wiley Hubert, one of the leading citizens in post-emancipation Camptown he would tell me stories about him that he had heard directly from the grandchildren of Wiley that were shared with him while on their fishing and hunting trips along Yegua Creek. When I told him about the extraordinary story we had put together about Mary Marks and her husband, Eddie told me that one of the earliest things he'd been told when he started looking into the black history of the county was that he needed to look into the story of Uncle John Marks. Heck, Eddie was even the person who first told Bob and I about Camptown Cemetery, where he'd been already been working to rehabilitate for over a decade prior to our meeting. His ease in dealing with the white communities was extensive as well, and it was his hope was to integrate the importance of the mutual relationship between the Black community with the German immigrant community in understanding the county's history. As he so often told me, there is no white history and Black history, there is only history.

Shortly after efforts in clearing Camptown began to bear fruit, Eddie also helped organize serve as the first chairman of the non-profit Texas Ten Historical Explorers (Tx10.org) with the mission "to inform, promote, and connect historical and cultural contributions of minorities that have impacted the communities from the ten original counties, thereby filling in the historical gaps of Washington County, Texas, and American history." Although I've benefited from everyone who has participated in this organization, I'd especially like to recognize Cheryl DaBera and Tina Henderson for their continuing devotion toward meeting the goals of the "Tx10" and helping to see this manuscript through so many phases of its rocky inception. Between the two of them the group has continued its mission beyond anything we'd ever expected in its early days, Cheryl facilitating the fine details and Tina stepping up as chairman when Eddie, knowing his time among us was limited, appointed her and she accepted, filling his shoes as no one else could.

When Rob Bubb contacted Eddie about the research he'd conducted on his great-great-grandmother, it provided an outstanding exploration of the fluidity of what it meant to be considered Black in the post-Emancipation period, serving less as a potential barrier due to ability than as an artificial construct based on pre-existing prejudices. He remains integrally connected with preservation of the cemetery, and although his telling of the story of Louisa Mangrum didn't quite make into this volume, her spirit continues to live on through him.

I also can't thank Bob Wishoff enough for getting me involved in the first place and helping organize the year-long effort it took to eventually clear the cemetery grounds. Bob and I have been friends a long time, and his encouragement led me to believe that I can write and helped me develop what few skills I do have along those lines. He led me to appreciate the value of avocational archaeologists and to take on the role of avocational historian, and although no longer involved there his encouragement remains invaluable.

Ray Mildren was one of the very first volunteers in clearing the cemetery continuing to maintain it, even after he suffered a heart attack there while doing so at one point. Doug Price, as the Executive Director of the Brenham Historical Museum, drew Bob and I to Brenham in the first place to explore potential archaeological sites and helped coordinate the clean-up efforts, as well as his delightful assistant Cynthia Eben, who also taught me the meaning of "who are you from home" as a Brenham way of asking about where one's family is from.

The inimitable Reggie Brown played a key part in getting historical markers not only for the cemetery but for the Brenham Normal Industrial College but also for numerous other sites as well. He was one of the early intermittent members of the Tx10. Amy Erhardt, Associate Professor of English at Texas A&M helped us organize one of our early meetings and understanding the importance of engaging with the academic community in furthering our ends.

Bill Page, Library Associate II working for the Ask Us Services at Texas A&M University helped shaped my early research methods, whether he knows it or not, and was always eager to help out in answering questions, marveling at serendipitous shelf elves which show up while delving through musty digital aisles of in search of yellowing articles in online newspaper archives.

Stephanie Klemm, Curator of Collections and Exhibits at the Star of the Republic Museum in Washington on the Brazos, provided access to the Hoxey papers that opened insights into Wiley Hubert's pre-Emancipation life, as well as an enduring curiosity as to whatever gems await the intrepid researcher there.

Jan Kelm and her associates with the Washington County Genealogical Society helped provide material in developing the initial census of the cemetery and understanding some of the vast complexities that can arise in doing genealogy work, as well as an opportunity to share some my research at one of their meetings.

Nick Cimino pointed out my oversight of Robert Sloan in an early attempt of a census of the cemetery, and in turn provided some very valuable information about him that his research had uncovered. He also put me in touch with Gesenia Sloan, his great-great-great granddaughter, who also kindly offered the photo of her ancestor for publication here.

Mike Vance, provided much encouragement at various stages in the development of this book, including the Mary Marks story, while his wife, the lovely Anne Shelton Vance, helped put me in touch with Jenny McWilliams, Cemetery Preservation Program Coordinator for the Texas Historical Commission, who was so helpful in helping Eddie in gaining Texas Historic Cemetery status for Camptown Cemetery.

James Pharaon, of James Pharaon Creative, not only provided the wonderful photograph of the Isaacs grave on the cover but also assisted in the recordings used for the SoundWalk project with the Museums on Main Street project and the associated SoundBoard installed at Camptown Cemetery.

Don Nieman's article 1989 article on Black politics and criminal justice in Washington County, was a tremendous influence on me early on, and Bill Richter helped in understanding more broadly the 1866 fire which held such a stranglehold on Brenham history for far too long.

Melodey M. Hauch, editor of the Bay Area Genealogical Society Journal, published the Hiram Williams story in its March 2016 issue, an early encouragement that helped spur my research along the lines of telling the story of individuals as a means of understanding the historical backdrop in which they were enveloped.

Mark Everett, Professor of Geology and Geophysics at Texas A&M University helped in providing the knowledge base and students to do a sub-surface survey of the cemetery, while his lovely daughter Laura Evertt followed in his steps and helped provide a detailed maps of the surface of the cemetery and it's features.

Various BiBs and BoBs (a local distinction between those born torn inside and outside of Brenham) who have helped in this endeavor over the past decade, such as the proprietor of Glissman's Drug Store who let Bob and I wander through their attic, where uniforms and dress swords from the Knights of Pythias spurred an awareness of the importance of fraternal organizations in the late nineteenth and early twentieth century) or the staff at the Ant Street Hotel, who still send me birthday greetings every year. I was never good at remembering all their names, never forget the hospitality.

The City of Brenham is continuing to understand the importance of Camptown and freedom colonies as an important aspect of the city's previously overlooked history and featured them as a part in their 2024 Museum on Main Street exhibitions. They were also invaluable in helping haul off the brush during the initial phase of clearing the cemetery and provide what assistance they can in helping to maintain it in the face of nature's attempt to reclaim it.

Don Nieman's article 1989 article on Black politics and criminal justice in Washington County, was a tremendous influence on me early on, and Bill Richter helped in understanding more broadly the 1866 fire which held such a stranglehold on Brenham history for far too long.

I am absolutely sure that I am missing far too many people who deserve to be recognized for their help along the way, but please don't hold it against me. But above all, I have to acknowledge the love of my life, my late wife Jennifer. She encouraged me along the way not only in this research but throughout our life together as well. One of my biggest regrets is that she isn't around to see this book finally come to fruition, although as she taught me, all is forgiven and nothing else matters.

# ENDNOTES

**Introduction**

1. Thad Sitton and James H. Conrad, *Freedom Colonies – Independent Black Texans in the Time of Jim Crow* (Austin: University of Texas Press, 2005), 1.
2. The Texas Freedom Colonies Project maintains an atlas of freedom colonies throughout Texas, with those in Washington County including Sauney's Stand, Bluff, Graball, Flat Prairie, Lott, Mill Creek, Mount Fall, Pleasant Grove, Jerry's Grove, and Old Gay Hill.
3. General Order No. 3, from the holdings of the US National Archives and Records Administration. Citation: RG 393, Part II, Entry 5543, District of Texas, General Orders Issued.
4. Washington County Records, Deed Book Vol. X, pages 340-341.
5. Donald G. Nieman, "Black Political Power and Criminal Justice: Washington County, Texas, 1868-1884," *The Journal of Southern History* LV, no. 3 (August 1989): 395.
6. Annie Mae Hunt and Ruthe Winegarten, *"I Am Annie Mae": An Extraordinary Black Texas Woman in Her Own Words* (Austin: University of Texas Press, 1983), 49.

**Chapter 1**

1. The 1850 and 1860 figures come from federal censuses, while the 1864 figure is from county tax rolls, which likely are low since slaves were considered taxable items. The figure continued to grow during the later part of the Civil War, when many slaves were moved into Texas from other Southern

states. The Brenham figures are from R.E. Pennington's *The History of Brenham and Washington County* (Standard Printing & Lithographing, Houston 1915).
2. From records "Compiled and transcribed by Carolyn Wambles and Hugh Smith from Record at the cemetery, VA records, Obituaries and tombstones," found at http://files.usgwarchives.net/la/state/cemeteries/military/alex-cem.txt. The Post consisted primarily of tents, but one of the few wooden buildings there was a suttler's office, which was later to be used as one of the first schoolhouses in Camptown.
3. Washington County Records, Deed Volume X, p37-38
4. "City Council Proceedings." *The Daily Banner*, May 24, 1878.
5. "City Council Proceedings." *The Daily Banner*, June 19, 1878.
6. *Temple Weekly Times*, October 30, 1891.
7. *Brenham Daily Banner*, September 23, 1893.
8. Cynthia Eben, verbal interview, 2018
9. Memorandum from Sherri Koepnick on "Autumn NRT Project,"August 22, 2001.
10. Camptown Cemetery Project minutes, July 11, 2002.
11. Camptown Cemetery Project minutes, July 11, 2002.
12. Reggie Browne email to Eddie Harrison, October 26, 2007.
13. Texas Historical Commission, Declaration Of Dedication For Cemetery Purposes For The Camptown Cemetery, July 9, 2009
14. Texas Historical Commission" Undertold Markers," http://www.thc.texas.gov/preserve/projects-and-programs/state-historical-markers/undertold-markers, accessed May 23, 2018.
15. Texas Historic Sites Atlas, "Details for Camptown Cemetery (Atlas Number 5507017617)," https://atlas.thc.state.tx.us/Details/5507017617, accessed May 23, 2018.
16. Alan Tate, "Brenham hopes to uncover history with cemetery." *Houston Chronicle*, February 1, 2013, https://www.

houstonchronicle.com/news/houston-texas/houston/article/Brenham-hopes-to-uncover-history-with-cemetery-4244594.php#photo-4124911, accessed May 26, 2018.
17. Ibid.
18. Ray Mildren, e-mail correspondence to author, July 22, 2018.
19. Ibid.
20. "Death of Alderman Bynum." *Brenham Daily Banner*, June 29, 1881.
21. Rolling Thunder, http://www.rollingthundertx2.com/index.html, accessed May /27, 2018.
22. "Camptown Cemetery Heritage Ride flyer," Rolling Thunder, http://www.rollingthundertx2.com/Brenham%20flyer.pdf, accessed May 27, 2018.
23. Ray Mildren, e-mail correspondence, to author, July 22, 2018.
24. Texas 10 Historical Explorers, http://www.tx10.org/; accessed May 30, 2018.

**Chapter 2**
1. Washington County Records, Volume E, Pages 197-198.
2. Deed of Gift, Washington County Records, Volume E, Pages 258-259; Land Grant Number 326, Washington County Records, Volume LG 2, Page 241.
3. Washington County Records, Deed Volume O, page 462, and Deed Volume Q, Number 74.
4. Special thanks to Stephanie Klemm, Curator of Collections at the Star of the Republic Museum, for assistance in locating this document from its collection, Papers of Asa Hoxey Family, SRM 2012—10.0084.
5. "New Store, New Goods." *Brenham Enquirer*, July 16, 1858.
6. Works Projects Administration, *Slave Narratives: A Folk History of Slavery in the United States from Interviews with Former Slaves,* Volume XVI, Texas Narratives, Part 4; Interview with

Yach Stringfellow, Pages 60-61.
7. Ibid.
8. Washington County Records, Deed Volume Q Number 241, Deed Volume R Number 64, Deed Volume R Number 557, Deed Volume S Number 442.
9. Washington County Records, Deed Volume Q, Record 240, Pages 288-299.
10. Washington County Records, Deed Volume Q, Record 789, Pages 759-760
11. Washington County Records, Deed Volume Q Number 240, Deed Volume Q Number 789. Although the second of these documents was filed a year later, the dates within it are the same as in the first.
12. "Another Washington County Outrage." *Brenham Weekly Banner*, January 5, 1888.
13. Ibid..
14. Ibid.
15. "Obituary. Another Texas Hero Gone." *The Weekly Telegraph*, November 24, 1858.
16. Ibid.
17. Ibid.
18. Ibid.
19. Ibid.
20. Ibid.
21. Ibid..
22. According to records on the death certificate, Wesley Moore may have also been another son born to Wiley Hubert and Hannah Moore in 1861. There is a Hannah Moore who lived in the city of Washington, now Washington-on-the-Brazos, born in 1840, so that there is a very real possibility that Wesley Moore was a son born to Wiley while still a slave.
23. The Washington County Official Public Records website, www.

edoctecinc.com/, lists twenty-three different transactions between 1867 and 1876, one involving a promissory note for $200 "American gold" with property owned by Hubert as collateral. Numerous other transactions are found in the Brenham press, including the sale of the street, can be found in the *Brenham Daily Banner*, May 10, 1883.

24. *Brenham Daily Banner*, June 9, 1896. The building was reported to have been used "as a church, schoolhouse and public hall by the colored people" until it "blew down" after several years of not having been occupied in 1896.

25. Washington County Records, Deed Volume X, Pages 340-341.

26. The document is part of the Niles-Graham-Pease Papers provided by the Austin History Center of the Austin Public Library, described as "Expenditure of the $1000 currency advanced by EM Pease for the Freedmen's Hospital at Brenham." It was found on the Portal to Texas History website at texashistory.unt.edu/ark:/67531/metapth712482/citation/?q=brenham%20e%20m%20pease%20hospital#top.

27. National Archives Microfilm Publication, Microfilm Publication M822, Records of the Superintendent of Education for the State of Texas, Bureau of Refugees, Freedmen, and Abandoned Lands, 1865-1870, Roll 6, Image 0528.

28. National Archives Microfilm Publication, Microfilm Publication M822, Records of the Superintendent of Education for the State of Texas, Bureau of Refugees, Freedmen, and Abandoned Lands, 1865-1870, Roll 10, Image 1458.

29. National Archives Microfilm Publication, Microfilm Publication M822, Records of the Superintendent of Education for the State of Texas, Bureau of Refugees, Freedmen, and Abandoned Lands, 1865-1870, Roll 10, Image 1458; additional information from Federal Census Bureau records.

30. National Archives Microfilm Publication, Microfilm

Publication M822, Records of the Superintendent of Education for the State of Texas, Bureau of Refugees, Freedmen, and Abandoned Lands, 1865-1870, Roll 6, Image 0582.
31. National Archives Microfilm Publication, Microfilm Publication M822, Records of the Superintendent of Education for the State of Texas, Bureau of Refugees, Freedmen, and Abandoned Lands, 1865-1870, Roll 6, Image 1458.
32. "Council Proceedings." *Brenham Daily Banner*, February 22, 1881; "Commissioner's Court." February 15, 1883; "Council Proceedings." December 22, 1886. Numerous other payments by the city council and county commissioners to Hubert were also found in the *Brenham Daily Banner* but they are not always detailed as to what the payments were for.
33. "The Colored Churches." *Brenham Daily Banner*, January 8, 1901.
34. Ibid.
35. "The Big Gin House Moved." *Brenham Daily Banner*, May 5, 1893.
36. *Brenham Banner*, February 27, 1908.
37. *Brenham Daily Banner*, June 1, 1900.
38. Washington County Records, Deed Volume X, p37-38.
39. "Death of Alderman Bynum." *Brenham Daily Banner*, June 29, 1881.
40. "An Appeal to the Benevolent." *Daily Banner*, November 15, 1876.
41. Ibid.
42. Ibid.
43. "A Card to the Public." *The Daily Banner*, January 19, 1877.
44. "Council Proceedings." *Brenham Daily Banner*, July 15, 1885.
45. "Fashionable Wedding." *Brenham Daily Banner*, July 1, 1886. Hubert's relationship with the press seems to have been congenial and continued to be so throughout his life.

46. "Meeting of School Trustees." *Brenham Daily Banner,* February 22, 1887; *Brenham Daily Banner,* March 25, 1890.
47. Donald G. Nieman, "African Americans and Meaning of Freedom: Washington County, Texas as a Case Study, 1865-1886 – Freedom: Politics," *Chicago-Kent Law Review* 70, no. 2 (1994): 398[PAGE HUMBER?]]. This is a comprehensive study of politics in post-Emancipation Washington County. It specifically addresses the prevalence of Black political influence during this period in Hubert's far more extensively and eloquently than time, space, or skill allow here. The article is available free online at https://scholarship.kentlaw.iit.edu/cklawreview/vol70/iss2/6 .
48. "Personal." *Brenham Daily Banner*, February 2, 1897.
49. "Citizens Meeting." *Brenham Daily Banner*, March 27, 1881.
50. Ibid.
51. "Social Equality" *The Galveston Daily News,* August 20, 1905. Hackworth was deeply involved in post-Emancipation politics in Brenham, serving as a justice of the peace. He was also a real estate speculator involved in selling land to Black people in Fort Bend County, and was a prolific letter writer later in his life. Some of his letters offer interesting insights into post-Emancipation Brenham. Hackworth also was instrumental in bringing about the Senate investigation into the 1886 elections, blaming the Ku Klux Klan for instigating the lynching.
52. *Brenham Daily Banner*, May 22, 1900.
53. *Brenham Daily Banner*, December 9, 1893.
54. *Brenham Daily Banner*, November 4, 1893, and November 5, 1893.
55. "Nearly Suffocated." *Brenham Daily Banner,* August 23, 1883.
56. *Brenham Daily Banner*, April 10, 1894.
57. "Chronological History of Brenham." *Brenham Daily Press,*

September 1, 1913. According to Gloria Nix, a local historian, one set of fire alarm bells meant get to the fire, another meant get your guns.

58. "Council Proceedings." *Brenham Daily Banner*, July 21, 1886.
59. "Brenham Fire Department." *Brenham Daily Banner*, May 22, 1901.
60. "Neat Work." *Brenham Daily Banner,* June 13, 1901; *Brenham Daily Banner,* August 7, 1902.
61. "Wrapped in Flames." *Brenham Daily Banner*, February 6, 1898.
62. Ibid. The company's fire engine, when it finally was acquired, was also housed in a building on a lot owned by Albert Milton.
63. "Colored Normal Entertainment Tonight." *Brenham Daily Banner*, July 21, 1892.
64. "Cuney vs Pullman." *Galveston Daily News*, February 27, 1894.
65. "Colored Normal." *Brenham Daily Banner*, July 23, 1892.
66. *Brenham Daily Banner*, April 6, 1893.
67. "Pistol Practice." *Brenham Daily Banner*, September 16, 1893.
68. "Anti Cain Convention." *Brenham Daily Banner*, February 26, 1896.
69. Ibid.
70. *Brenham Daily Banner*, November 26, 1902.
71. "Found." *Brenham Evening Press*, July 7, 1908; "owner can recover by calling at the residence of Prof. S.C. McCoy, Camptown."
72. "Wiley Hubert . Well Known and Prominent Colored Man Dead." *Brenham Evening Press*, October 6, 1909; an abbreviated version appeared in the *Austin American- Statesman* on October 8. The information on his cause of death is from his death certificate.
73. "Card of thanks." *Brenham Evening Press*, October 8, 1909.
74. "District Court Discharges." *Brenham Evening Press*, September

21, 1909.
75. "School Matters." *Brenham Evening Press,* December 3, 1908.
76. *Brenham Evening Press,* July 6, 1910; "School Trustees Meeting." *Brenham Banner,* June 15, 1911.
77. "Commencement of East End School." *Brenham Daily Banner-Press,* June 4, 1915.
78. "Negro Assessed $50.95." *Brenham Daily Banner,* December 27, 1912; "County Court Meets Monday January 18." *Brenham Daily Banner-Press,* January 11, 1915.

**Chapter 3**
1. *Brenham Daily Banner*, September 19, 1889.
2. "United States, Freedmen's Bureau, Records of the Superintendent of Education and of the Division of Education, 1865-1872. NARA microfilm publications M822. Records of the Bureau of Refugees, Freemen, and Abandoned Lands, 1861-1880, RG 105; roll 15; FHL microfilm 1,695, 182, as found in familysearch.org.
3. Ibid.
4. "The Dead Alive." *Brenham Daily Banner,* May 23, 1889.
5. Hans Peter Mareus Neilsen Gammel, *The Laws of Texas, 1822-1897* (The Gammel Book Co., 1898) 7: 288.
6. "Radical Precinct Meeting." *Brenham Weekly Banner*, August 9, 1878.
7. "Caned." *Brenham Weekly Banner,* March 28, 1879.
8. "School Trustees." *Brenham Daily Banner,* August 3, 1881.
9. "A Self Made Colored Man." *Brenham Daily Banner*, September 16, 1881.
10. *Brenham Weekly Independent*, February 23, 1882.
11. "To the Board of School Trustees and Honorable Board of Aldermen." *Brenham Daily Banner*, August 29, 1882.
12. Testimony on the Alleged Election Outrages in Texas b United

States Senate Committee on Privileges and Elections, 1889, 286.

13. Robert W. Shook,,"The Texas "'Election Outrage" of 1886," *East Texas Historical Journal* 10, no. 1 (1972). Available at: http://scholarworks.sfasu.edu/ethj/vol10/iss1/7
14. Testimony on the Alleged Election Outrages in Texas, before the United States Senate Committee on Privileges and Elections, 1889, 231. Kirk was a major figure in this investigation, and many Republicans believed he must have been directly implicated in ballot improprieties.
15. "Real Estate Transfers." *Brenham Daily Banner*, September 16, 1886; *Brenham Daily Banner,* October 10, 1886.
16. "District Court." *Brenham Daily Banner,* April 8, 1887; "District Court." *Brenham Daily Banner,* April 15, 1887; "The Dead Alive." *Brenham Daily Banner,* May 23, 1889; "District Court." *Brenham Daily Banner,* October 24, 1889.
17. *The Standard* (Clarksville, Texas), July 7, 1887.
18. "Love Interviewed." *Brenham Daily Banner*, May 26, 1889.
19. "The Dead Alive." *Brenham Daily Banner,* May 23, 1889.
20. *Brenham Daily Banner*, May 25, 1889.
21. "District Court." *Brenham Daily Banner,* September 18; *Brenham Daily Banner,* September 19, 1889.
22. *Brenham Daily Banner,* October 5, 1889. Cunningham's plantation eventually became part of the Imperial Sugar Company, and portions of it eventually became the Central Prison Unit at Sugarland.
23. "Found His Man." *Brenham Daily Banner*, March 30, 1893.
24. Texas Convict and Conduct Register, 1875-1945, Huntsville, B004456-006375, 504.
25. *Brenham Daily Banner*, November 13, 1889.
26. Texas Convict and Conduct Register, 1875-1945, Huntsville, B004456-006375, 504.

27. "Personal Mention." *Brenham Daily Banner,* December 25, 1890.
28. *Brenham Daily Banner,* October 13, 1895.
29. "Teacher's Meeting." *Brenham Daily Banner,* December 3, 1893; "Colored Teachers' Meeting." *Brenham Daily Banner,* December 8, 1894; Teacher's Meeting. *Brenham Daily Banner,* October 20, 1895; "Teacher's Meeting." *Brenham Daily Banner,* September 29, 1895; *Brenham Daily Banner,* April 26, 1896.
30. "Colored Teachers' Institute." *Brenham Daily Banner,* February 16, 1896.
31. *Brenham Daily Banner,* July 12, 1898.

**Chapter 4**

1. Further complicating the names of his parents, his death certificate lists their names as Maria Jordan and Sam Jordan. This information was given by their son Ketchum during a time of great trauma and may not be correct itself.
2. "Commissioner's Court." *Brenham Daily Banner,* December 1, 1883; Commissioner's Court." *Brenham Daily Banner,* February 16, 1884; Commissioner's Court." *Brenham Daily Banner,* February 17, 1884.
3. "A Negro Killed." *Brenham Daily Banner,* August 24, 1884; "District Court." *Brenham Daily Banner,* October 14, 1884; "District Court." *Brenham Daily Banner,* April 5, 1887.
4. *Brenham Daily Banner,* April 10, 1883.
5. "The Owl Brotherhood." *Brenham Daily Banner,* August 6, 1886.
6. "Owl Festivities." *Brenham Weekly Banner,* October 27, 1886.
7. "The Owl Brotherhood." *Brenham Daily Banner,* August 12, 1886.
8. "Justice's Court." *Brenham Daily Banner,* August 27, 1886.
9. "County Court." *Brenham Daily Banner,* October 5, 1886.

10. John G. Browning and Chief Justice Carolyn Wright, "Unsung Heroes: The Earliest African-American Lawyers in Texas," *Texas Bar Journal* 77, no. 11 (December 2014): 960-963.
11. A Gross Outrage." *Brenham Daily Banner*, November 6, 1884.
12. U.S. Congress. Senate. Committee on Privileges and Elections. Alleged election outrages in Texas.50th Congress, 2nd Session. 1899, 199. (Testimony of Carl Schutze).
13. U.S. Congress, Senate Committee on Privileges and Elections. Alleged election outrages in Texas. 50th Congress, 2nd session,. 1899. 60-63 (Testimony of G. A. Mayo)
14. U.S. Congress. Senate. Committee on Privileges and Elections. Alleged election outrages in Texas. 50th Congress, 2nd Session. 1899, 38-50. (Testimony of Felix Kinlaw and Andy Hayes). Many variants on the events of this evening appeared in the press, but Kinlaw and Hayes were present that evening.
15. U.S. Congress. Senate. Committee on Privileges and Elections. Alleged election outrages in Texas. 50th Congress, 2nd Session 1899, 35. (Testimony of Felix Kinlaw); ibid.(Testimony of Lewis Pennington).
16. U.S. Congress. Senate. Committee on Privileges and Elections, "Proceedings of the Coroner's Inquest in Regard to the Killing of W.D. Boulton," Testimony on the alleged election outrages in Texas, 50th Congress, 2nd eession1889, 318.
17. U.S. Congress. Senate. Committee on Privileges and Elections. Alleged election outrages in Texas. 50th Congress, 2nd Session 1889, 138.
18. Robert W. Shook, "The Texas Election Outrage of 1886," *East Texas Historical Journal* 10, no. 1 (1972): 22.
19. U.S. Congress, Senate. Committee on Privileges and Elections. Alleged election outrages in Texas. 50th Congress, 2nd Session. 185 (Testimony of Florent D. Jodon)
20. U.S. Congress. Senate. Committee on Privileges and Elections.

Alleged election outrages in Texas, 1889; 224. (Testimony of Stephen A. Hackworth)

21. "Meeting of Citizens - Incendiary Speeches Denounced - Responsibility for the Recent Murder." *The Galveston Daily News*, November 6, 1886.
22. U.S. Congress. Senate. Committee on Privileges and Elections. Alleged election outrages in Texas, 1889; 225. (Testimony of Stephen A. Hackworth).
23. U.S. Congress. Senate. Committee on irivileges and Elections. Alleged election outrages in Texas. 50th Congress., 2nd Session; 158 (Testimony of Paul Fricke)
24. Ibid., 158. (Testimony of Paul Fricke).
25. "Editorial Correspondence." *Brenham Daily Banner*, February 20, 1887.
26. U.S. Congress. Senate. Committee on Privileges and Elections. Alleged election outrages in Texas. 50th Congress, 2nd Session; 665 (Testimony of Stephen A. Hackworth).
27. U.S. Congress. Senate. Committee on Privileges and Elections. Alleged election outrages in Texas. 50th Congress, 2nd Session; 650 (Testimony of Edward. D. Durfee).
28. U.S. Congress. Senate. Committee on Privileges and Elections. Alleged election outrages in Texas. 50th Congress, 2nd Session; 276 (Testimony of Lafayette Kirk).
29. Ibid.
30. U.S. Congress. Senate. Committee on Privileges and Elections. Alleged election outrages in Texas. 50th Congress, 2nd Session; 646 (Testimony of D.H. Hart).
31. "District Court." *Brenham Daily Banner,* April 5, 1887.
32. "County Republican Convention." *Brenham Daily Banner*, March 27, 1888.
33. *Brenham Daily Banner,* May 8, 1888.
34. *Brenham Daily Banner,* August 4, 1889; August 7, 1889; August

8, 1889.
35. "Trying to Escape Death." *The Galveston Daily News*, July 29, 1891.
36. "Black Elephant Saloon." *Brenham Daily Banner,* December 14, 1892; *Brenham Daily Banner,* January 3, 1893; *Brenham Daily Banner,* February 3, 1893; "Arrested." *Brenham Daily Banner,* March 26, 1893; "The Gaming Cases." *Brenham Daily Banner,* April 30, 1893; "County Court." *Brenham Daily Banner,* May 19, 1893.
37. "A New Park." *Brenham Daily Banner*, July 17,1893; "Park Association Organized." *Brenham Daily Banner,* July 19,1893; "The Cotton Picking Season." July 28, 1893; "About Those Unjust Charges." *Brenham Daily News,* July 29, 1893; *Brenham Daily Banner,* August 1, 1893; *Brenham Daily Banner,* August 6, 1893.
38. "Shooting at Bryan." *Brenham Daily Banner*, September 19, 1893; "Joe Jordan Shooting." September 23, 1893. Arch Gee, who had been the young man who shot Jordan, was acquitted two weeks after Jordan left Bryan.
39. "Died." *Brenham Daily Banner*, December 6, 1890. It is unclear exactly which Sloan family members were buried in the Sloan plot at Camptown Cemetery. The location of Robert Sloan's burial was enclosed by a fence in a plot easily large enough to contain several other burials, but no headstones exist within the plot except that for Robert Sloan.
40. Statement of Facts in Case No 7312, R.S. Sloan and wife vs. H. & T.C. R. R. Company, Testimony of Jim Rucker, September 12, 1894, page 4.
41. The best and by far the most extensive account of Sam's accident is from the Statement of Facts in Case No 7312, R.S. Sloan and wife vs. H. & T.C. R. R. Company, filed in District Circuit Court in Washington County, October 3,

1894. This and much more is found in the extensive articles and accompanying material Nick Cimino has posted in his articles on Robert Sloan on his AncestorPuzzles.com site.
42. "Sam Sloan Died of His Injuries." *Brenham Daily Banner*, October 3, 1893.
43. "Captures the Reward of $25." *Brenham Daily Banner*, December 20, 1893; "Matters at Brenham." *The Galveston Daily News*, December 21, 1893; "Got His Man." *Galveston Daily News*, December 25, 1893.
44. "Crime at Brenham." *The Galveston Daily News*, January 31, 1894.
45. "County Convicts Are Well Treated." *Brenham Daily Banner*, June 16, 1894.
46. "Willis McIntyre in Jail." *Brenham Daily Banner*, January 26, 1894.
47. "Escaped Convicts, Surrounded by Sheriff's Posse, Makes a Desperate Resistance." *Brenham Daily Banner*, March 28, 1894.
48. Burglars at Haubelft Bros." *Brenham Daily Banner*, July 20, 1894.
49. Ibid.
50. "Petition for a Policeman at Camptown." *Brenham Daily Banner*, April 15, 1894.
51. "City Council Proceedings." *Brenham Daily Banner*, April 17; *Brenham Daily Banner*, May 6, 1894.
52. *Brenham Daily Banner*, September 6, 1894; "Council Proceedings." *Brenham Daily Banner*, September 19, 1894.
53. "'Blue – Gum's' Bite." *The Galveston Daily News*, May 27, 1894; "Emancipation Celebration." *The Galveston Daily News*, June 19, 1894; "Brenham Negroes Organize." *The Galveston Daily News*, September 29, 1894.
54. "An Indignation Meeting." *Brenham Daily Banner*, February 4, 1896.

55. "Speaking Near Graball." *Brenham Daily Banner,* October 7, 1894; "Anti Cain Convention, *Brenham Daily Banner,* February 26, 1896; *Brenham Daily Banner,* January 8, 1895; "They Will Adjourn Today." *Fort Worth Gazette,* April 30, 1895; "The Senate." *The Galveston Daily News,* January 14, 1897.

56. *Brenham Daily Banner,* July 16, 1896; "B.Y.U.P. (sic)." *Brenham Daily Banner,* May 13, 1896; "B.Y.P.U." *Brenham Daily Banner,* May 27, 1896; "B.Y.P.U. Program." *Brenham Daily Banner,* June 10, 1896; "B.Y.P.U." *Brenham Daily Banner,* June 18, 1896; "Personal." *Brenham Daily Banner,* August 18, 1896; "Colored B.Y.P.U. Convention.": *Bryan Morning Eagle,* August 23, 1906; "B.Y.P.U. Convention." *Bryan Morning Eagle,* August 24, 1906; "Negroes in Convention." *Houston Post,* September 4, 1912; "Meeting at Brunner." *Houston Post,* August 8, 1915

57. "General Bowen Colored Baptist Association." *The Orange Leader,* September 11, 1903.

58. Ibid.; "Negro Convention." *Houston Post,* January 7, 1904; "Negro Education, A Study of the Private and Higher Education Schools for Colored People in the United States," Department of the Interior Publication, 1916; *Texas Almanac and State Industrial Guide for 1904,* 323; *The Democrat,* December 3, 1903; "Colored Academy At Waco." *Houston Daily Post,* December 9, 1902; "Corner Stone Laid." *Houston Post,* October 2, 1903

59. "Waco Convention." *Houston Post,* October 16, 1905.

60. Ibid.; "Colored Baptists Meet." *The Daily Express,* October 28, 1907; "Negroes in Convention." *Houston Post,* September 4, 1912.

61. "Negro Masons." *Houston Post,* July 20, 1904; "The Negro Masons." *Houston Post,* July 21, 1904; "The Negro Masons." *Houston Post,* July 22 1904

62. *The Galveston Daily News,* December 28, 1904; *The Redbook of Houston: A Compendium of Social, Professional, Religious,*

*Educational and Industrial Interests of Houston's Colored Population,* no. 1 (Houston: Soxtex Publishing Company, 1915), 132.

63. "Discrimination is Claimed." *Houston Post,* August 24, 1911.
64. Ibid.; "County Court." *Houston Post,* December 22, 1912; "Local Courts." *Houston Post,* April 18, 1913.
65. "History of Attentive Ear 350 Masonic Lodge," http://www.attentiveear350.org (accessed August 16, 2020).
66. "Old Negro Resident is Dead." *Brenham Daily Banner-Press,* October 23, 1916; "Negro Preacher Attending Dance is Assassinated." *San Antonio Express,* October 23, 1916; *The Rosenberg Herald,* October 27, 1916; "Was Given 45 Years." *Houston Post,* April 22, 1917.
67. "Old Negro Resident is Dead." *Brenham Daily Banner-Press,* October 23, 1916.
68. Most of this data comes from federal census records. The promissory note information is found in the Washington County Courthouse records Deed Book 75, page 415, the default from *Brenham Daily Banner,* September 5, 1921, and the information on the death benefits was from a search of the Prince Hall Grand Lodge of Texas records from 1902 to 1918 by its archivist, Don Gross.

**Chapter 5**

1. Hiram Williams, Death Certificate, March 1, 1943, File No. 15259, Texas Department of Health, Bureau of Vital Statistics.
2. 1870 U.S. Census, Washington County, Brenham, Precinct 3.
3. "Hiram Williams." *The Galveston Daily News,* June 6, 1894.
4. *Brenham Weekly Banner,* December 13, 1878.
5. 1880 U.S. Census, Washington County, Brenham, ED 145.
6. "Torchlight." *The Daily Banner,* August 1, 1880.
7. "Emancipation Day." *Brenham Daily Banner,* June 19, 1881;

"Austin." *The Galveston Daily News*, December 21, 1882: "Texas Volunteer Guard." *Austin Weekly Statesman*, February 25, 1886.

8. "Big Black Battle." *The Daily Banner,* June 16, 1880; *The Daily Banner,* October 5, 1880; "Mayor's Court." October 6, 1880; *Brenham Daily Banner* January 8, 1881; "Mayor's Court." *Brenham Daily Banner,* January 13, 1881; "Fight." *Brenham Daily Banner,* January 29, 1881; "County Court." *Brenham Daily Banner*, August 5, 1881.
9. "Policeman Waylaid." *The Galveston Daily News*, October 3, 1887.
10. *Brenham Daily Banner*, January 8, 1881.
11. "Local Brevities." *The Waco Daily Examiner*, April 8, 1882; "State News." *Brenham Daily Banner*, April 16, 1882.
12. "Waco." *The Galveston Daily News*, February 7, 1883.
13. "The Courts." *The Waco Daily Examiner*, June 8, 1884.
14. "Mayor's Court." *Brenham Daily Banner*, December 12, 1884.
15. "Mayor's Court." *Brenham Daily Banner*, July 21, 1886.
16. "Bounced." *Brenham Daily Banner,* November 23, 1884.
17. "Washington County." *The Galveston Daily News*, September 7, 1876.
18. Texas – Facts and Fancies." *Weekly Democratic Statesman,* October 19, 1876; "Texas – Facts and Fancies." *Weekly Democratic Statesman,* November 9, 1876; "Texas – Facts and Fancies." January 4, 1877.
19. *The Daily Brenham Banner*, January 20, 1877; "Hell's Half Acre." *The Daily Brenham Banner,* March 10, 1877; *The Daily Banner,* October 14, 1877.
20. "Robbery." *Brenham Daily Banner*, February 21, 1885.
21. "Brenham's Budget." *The Galveston Daily News*, February 5, 1887.
22. "Mysterious Murder." *Brenham Daily Banner*, February 2, 1887.

23. "A Murderous Assault on Policeman Lockett." *Brenham Daily Banner,* October 4, 1887.
24. "Policeman Waylaid." *The Galveston Daily News,* October 3, 1887.
25. "A Murderous Assault on Policeman Lockett." *Brenham Daily Banner*, October 4, 1887.
26. Robert W. Shook, "The Texas '"Election Outrage"' of 1886," *East Texas Historical Journal* 10, no. 1 (1972): 23.
27. "District Court." *Brenham Daily Banner*, October 21, 1887.
28. "District Court." *Brenham Daily Banner*, October 28, 1887; "District Court." *Brenham Daily Banner,* October 30, 1887.
29. 'District Court." *Brenham Daily Banner,* October 25, 1887.
30. "District Court." *Brenham Daily Banner,* October 30, 1887.
31. "Harris County." *The Galveston Daily News*, August 18, 1893; "Policeman Lockett's Assailant." *Brenham Daily Banner*, August 19, 1893.
32. *The Herald* (Los Angeles), May 26, 1894.
33. "Deputy Sheriff Sallis Returned." *Brenham Daily Banner,* June 6, 1894.
34. *The Herald* (Los Angeles), May 30, 1894.
35. "State News." *The Southern Mercury* (Dallas), May 24, 1894.
36. "Deputy Sheriff Sallis Returned." *Brenham Daily Banner,* June 6, 1894.
37. Ibid.
38. "Hiram Williams." *The Galveston Daily News*, June 6, 1894.
39. Ibid.; "Hiram Williams Talks." *The Galveston Daily News,* June 7, 1894.
40. "Hiram Williams Out on Bond." *Brenham Daily Banner*, June 24, 1894,
41. 1900 U.S. Census, Harris County, Houston Ward 3, District 0076.
42. "District Court." *Brenham Daily Banner,* September 21, 1894;

"Brenham Budget." *The Galveston Daily News*, September 23, 1894; "Hiram Williams Case Dismissed." *Brenham Daily Banner*, March 30, 1895.

43. 1898 Galveston City Directory.
44. The information on the Ninth Volunteers Infantry Regiment and Company G comes from Roger Cunningham, "'A Lot of Fine, Sturdy Black Warriors'; Texas's African American 'Immunes' in the Spanish-American War," in *Brothers to the Buffalo Soldiers; Perspectives on the African American Militia and Volunteers, 1865-1917*, edited by Bruce A. Glasrud (Columbia, MO: University of Missouri Press, 2011), 132.
45. Roger D. Cunningham, "'A Lot of Fine, Sturdy Black Warriors': Texas's African American 'Immunes' in the Spanish-American War,"*The Southwestern Historical Quarterly*, Vol. 108, No.3 (2005): 355.
46. W. Hilary Coston, *The Spanish-American War Volunteer; Ninth United States Volunteer Infantry Roster and Muster, Biographies, Cuban Sketches*, 2nd ed. (self-published, 1899), 217.
47. 1899 Galveston City Directory.
48. "Texas Marriages, 1837-1973," Database, FamilySearch, https://familysearch.org/ark:/61903/1:1:FXMX-9X2; accessed June 24, 2015).
49. Marriage Record, Washington County, Texas, No. 1689, page 351.
50. 1910 U.S. Census, Washington County, Brenham Ward 2, ED 0101; Jordan Johnson, Death Certificate, Texas State Board of Health, Bureau of Vital Statistics.
51. 1930 U.S. Census, Washington County, Brenham, ED 239-8; 1940 U.S. Census, Washington County, Brenham, ED 239-8.
52. 1880 U.S. Census, Washington County Enumeration District, Schedule of Defective, Dependent and Delinquent Classes.
53. Hiram Williams, Death Certificate, June 11, 1919, 20052,

Texas Department of Health, Bureau of Vital Statistics.
54. "Hiram Williams, Aged Colored Citizen Dies." *Brenham Banner-Press*, March 4, 1943.
55. Application For Headstone or Marker, War Department O.G.M.G. Form No. 623, for Hiram Williams.

**Chapter 6**
1. J. W. Yancy, M.A. *The Negro Blue Book of Washington County, Texas. A Centennial Edition.* No further publication information on this volume is given, although the page following the title page states it is "Dedicated to a Century of Negro Progress in Washington County, 1836-1936," indicating it was probably published around 1936. The author was probably the same James W. Yancy who was president of Paul Quinn College in 1940, and who, according to the 1940 census, was living in Brenham in 1935. The book was mentioned in the *Brenham Banner-Press,* November 30, 1936, titled "Book On Negro Life is Being Written. A book, Negro Life in Washington County, Texas," is being written by J.W. Yancy, colored extension school teacher. The theme of the book centers around the educational, economic, and religious activities of the colored people in the county. Names of the most outstanding colored people will be included in it also. This volume will have a wide circulation when completed. Copies will be placed in the libraries of every Negro College in the State, Negro Hall of Life at the Texas Centennial and the Negro Division in the State Department of Education. This book is a Texas Centennial Edition."
2. Wassermann, Lillie. The Common School Districts of Washington County, Texas, 1909-1967. A Sesquicentennial Project by the Brenham Louise Giddings Retired Teachers Association. First Edition, 1988. P217.

3. *The Southwestern Christian Advocate,* May 21, 1885. This reference was found at the extremely useful InformationWanted.org website, which "offers easy access to thousands of "Information Wanted" advertisements taken out by former slaves searching for long lost family members."
4. J.W. Yancy, *The Negro Blue-book of Washington County, Texas* (A Centennial Edition,1936), 75.
5. Anthony Flewellen. *Combined Cotton Chopper and Cultivator,* Patent 342,961, January 23, 1894; [United States Patent OfficeWashington D.C.].
6. "A Great Invention." *Brenham Daily Banner,* December 6, 1893.
7. Ibid.
8. *Brenham Daily Banner,* July 9, 1893. In this article we learn that Isaac had been teaching at Goodwill for sixteen years.
9. "Colored Teachers." *Brenham Daily Banner,* June 30, 1885; "Colored Teachers' Institute." *Brenham Dailer Banner,* June 3, 1894.
10. *Brenham Weekly Banner,* June 12, 1884. The Emancipation Celebration was a grander version of what came to be known in the twentieth century as Juneteenth.
11. "Installation of Officer." *Brenham Daily Banner,* February 12, 1893.
12. "Grand Church Rally." *Brenham Daily Banner,* November 20, 1898.
13. "Delegates to National Convention." *Brenham Daily Banner,* November 14, 1893.
14. "Colored Fair Association." *Brenham Daily Banner,* August 3, 1898.
15. "Republican Convention." *Brenham Daily Banner,* July 27; "A Lying Report." *Brenham Daily Banner,* July 28, 1894.
16. "County Court Judges." *Brenham Weekly Banner,* December 23, 1897; *Brenham Daily Banner,* August 5, 1900.

17. "Kugadt Placed on Trial" *The Galveston Daily News*, March 27, 1897. Kugadt was one of the first white men to be hanged for murder in Washington County, and the first hanging since Emancipation not held across the railroad track from Camptown Cemetery.
18. "Brenham News." *The Houston Post*. March 30, 1904: "John Yelderman's Trial." *Houston Post,* April 6, 1904.
19. "Real Estate Transfers." *Brenham Weekly Banner*, January 12, 1882; "Real Estate Transfers." *Brenham Daily Banner*, May 23, 1884; "Delinquent Tax List." *Brenham Daily Banner,* May 26, 1887.
20. Washington County Court Records. Suit for Divorce, George Isaacs vs Martha Isaacs, Case No. 9423, District Court of Washington County, September Term, 1901, Plaintiff's Statement.
21. The details of their divorce come from a copy of their divorce proceedings obtained from the Washington County Courthouse.
22. "In the District Court." *Brenham Daily Banner*, October 2; "Real Estate Transfers." *Brenham Daily Banner,* 9, 1901.
23. From their marriage certificate filed in Brenham, the marriage took place on the same day as it was signed, likely in a civil ceremony, and the bride's name was Sarah Jane rather than Mary Jane.
24. The date of her birth is from her 1982 death certificate. differing from later census data.
25. Henry Estelle later moved to Waco, becoming an agricultural extension agent and then a supervisor of the county's extension agency. He and Ruby remained married until his death in 1967 at age seventy-six; she died at age eighty-five in 1975.
26. This information leads one to believe that Estelle was possibly

the son of another J. L. Estelle from Waco, co-owner of Lone Star Undertaking, a large undertaking firm there according to the 1920 census. There are other connections to Waco as well with Henry Estelle, who along with his wife is buried in the Doris Miller Cemetery, and where he served as agricultural extension agent and supervisor after leaving Prairie View College.
27. Her ex-husband was back in Waco, remarried and operating a funeral home there.

**Chapter 7**

1. "Commencement Exercises of Colored School" *Brenham Daily Banner,* May 23, 1912.
2. *Brenham Daily Banner-Press,* October 25, 1934.
3. " Colored Citizens Patriotic Meeting." *Brenham Daily Banner-Press,* April 11, 1917.
4. Ibid.; "Negro Educator Sways Multitude in Outbursts of Firey Eloquence." *Brenham Daily Banner-Press,* April 16, 1917. Among the other members on the committee was James C. Hewitt, a veteran of the one of the first Black Union regiments to serve in the Civil War, who is covered more in a later chapter.
5. "Official List of Registrations With Serial Numbers and Address." *Brenham Daily Banner-Press,* July 11, 1917. The physical description comes from his registration card for the draft. This is also the source for his date of birth.
6. Jennifer Keene. "A Comparative Study of White and Black American Soldiers During the First World War," *Annales de Demographie Historique* 1, no. 103s (2002): 71-90. Keene's study found that draft boards had a "propensity to over-draft black soldiers," even though they tended to tended to be placed in non-combat roles. (Ibid. 3). Guy was an exception in that he

did perform in a combat role.
7. *Camp Funston: Illustrated—Cantonment Life, 1918*, (Baird Company Engravers, 1918, https://www.ggarchives.com/Military/WW1/Brochures/CampFunstonIllustrated.html and Wikipedia entry at https://en.wikipedia.org/wiki/Camp_Funston
8. "Handing 'em a Package." *The Mena Weekly Star*, October 25, 1917.
9. "To Campaign for Funds." *The Evening Missourian*, February 5, 1918; "K. of C. Farewell Party." *The Topeka State Journal*, April 24, 1918; "Army Officer Cashiered." *Evening Public Ledger*, December 24, 1918. Captain Sam Bucklew was found guilty of the embezzlement and forced to resign from the service as a result.
10. *Junction City Weekly Union*, November 15, 1917.
11. "Negroes Resent Camp Order." *The Kansas City Sun*, April 27, 1918.
12. *Application For Victory Medal*, filed by Australia Guy, received and approved Decemberr 6, 1920.
13. Lauren Elizabeth Neal, "Guarding Space and Place: Elite and Klan Counterbalance Communities in Jazz Age Dallas" (master's thesis, Texas State University, 2015), 41-42.
14. "Dallas Negro Branded With Ku Klux Symbol as Warning to Pals." *Topeka State Journal*, April 2, 1921.
15. Ibid.; "Whipped and Branded on Forhead." *The Fairfield Recorder,* April 8, 1921; Neal, 72.
16. Mark N. Morris, "Saving Society Through Politics: The Ku Klux Klan in Dallas, Texas, in the 1920s," PhD diss., (University of North Texas, 1997), 149.
17. Texas State Board of Health, Bureau of Vital Statistics, Standard Certificate of Death, A.W. Guy
18. "Body of Young Man Shipped to Brenham for Burial" and

"Card of Thanks." *Dallas Express*, December 16, 1922.

**Chapter 8**
1. Most of the details of the murder are found in a lengthy, three-column article in "'Crying Murder.'" *The Galveston Daily News,* October 31, 1891.
2. "Jail Delivery." *Brenham Weekly Banner,* July 30, 1891; *Brenham Weekly Banner,* July 2, 1891.
3. "Lee Hughes." *Brenham Weekly Banner*, July 16, 1891.
4. "Jail Delivery." *Brenham Weekly Banner*, July 30, 1891.
5. Ibid.
6. Ibid.
7. "Lee Hughes Sentenced." *Brenham Weekly Banner*, September 24, 1891.
8. Ibid.
9. *Brenham Weekly Banner*, October 22, 1891.
10. "Lee Hughes." *Brenham Weekly Banner*, October 8, 1891.
11. "Visitors to the Gallows" and "Lee Hughes Gallows." *Brenham Weekly Banner,* October 29, 1891.
12. "A Realistic Ghost Dance." *Brenham Weekly Banner,* October 1, 1891; "28th Year. Adam Forepaugh Shows." *Brenham Weekly Banner,* October 8, 1891.
13. "Ugly Words." *Temple Weekly Times*, October 30, 1891.
14. "Visitors to the Gallows" and "Lee Hughes Gallows." *Brenham Weekly Banner*, October 29, 1891.
15. Ibid.
16. Ibid.
17. Ibid.
18. "Hughes Hanged." *Brenham Weekly Banner*, November 5, 1891.
19. Ibid.
20. Ibid.
21. Ibid.

22. "'Cryin' Murder.'" *The Galveston Daily News*, October 31, 1891.
23. Ibid.
24. "Hughes Hanged." *Brenham Weekly Banner*, November 5, 1891.
25. Ibid.
26. "His Ghost on Hand." *The Galveston Daily News*, November 4, 1891.
27. "Brenham Triple Hanging." *Austin Weekly Standard*, May 28, 1896; Tyburn is a reference to the infamous London area gallows, notorious for its public executions.
28. "Three Negroes Hanged." T*he Conroe Courier*, May 29, 1896.
29. *Brenham Daily Banner*, May 12, 1896.

**Chapter 9**
1. "A Heavenly Visitor." *Brenham Daily Banner*, December 8, 1900.
2. " Marriage Licenses." *The Daily Banner*, March 28, 1879.
3. *Brenham Weekly Banner*, June 21, 1878.
4. "Train Ran Them Down." *Brenham Daily Banner*, January 5, 1900.
5. "County Commissioner's Court." *Brenham Daily Banner,* March 28, 1890.
6. "Team Ran Away." *Brenham Daily Banner,* June 21, 1912.
7. "A Rascally Treat." *Brenham Daily Banner*, August 31 1892.
8. *Brenham Daily Banner*, September 20, 1895.
9. "Another Runaway." *Brenham Daily Banner,* November 16, 1895.
10. "Train Ran Them Down." *Brenham Daily Banner,* January 5, 1900.
11. *Brenham Daily Banner*, January 24, 1900, 4: January 29, 1901.
12. "Wood Cheaper." *Brenham Weekly Press*, May 14, 1913. This series of ads ran for at least 5 weeks.
13. "Transfer Man." *Brenham Daily Banner-Press,* October 1,

1913. These ads ran until three months before his death the following year.
14. "Brenham Budget." *The Houston Daily Post*, December 27, 1893.
15. "Lost." *Brenham Daily Banner*, November 6, 1900.
16. "Important Notice." *Brenham Daily Banner*, May 2, 1913.
17. "Well Known Negro is Dead." *Brenham Daily Banner-Press*, June 16, 1914.

**Chapter 10**
1. "Eli Ross and the Inquiry." *The Galveston Daily News*, March 14, 1885.
2. "The Mystery Probably Cleared Up." *The Galveston Daily News*, March 13, 1885.
3. All the details in this section come from the lengthy coverage in *The Galveston Daily News*, March 13 and March 14, 1885.
4. All the details in this section come from the lengthy coverage in *The Galveston Daily News*, March 13 and March 14, 1885.
5. *The Daily Banner*, February 2, 1878.
6. "La Grange." *The Galveston Daily News*, December 2, 1884.
7. "He Works" and "Quashed." *Brenham Weekly Banner*, August 9, 1878.
8. *Brenham Weekly Banner*, August 19, 1880. The headline to this article is obliterated.
9. "A Colored Member." *Daily Banner*, September 6, 1879.
10. "District Court." *Brenham Weekly Banner*, October 10, 1879.
11. "From Burton." *Brenham Weekly Banner*, November 15, 1878.
12. "State News." *Brenham Daily Banner*, December 3, 1884.
13. "Court of Appeals – Galveston Term." *Norton's Union Intelligencer*, January 28, 1885; "State News." *Brenham Daily Banner*, January 23, 1885.
14. Texas Convict and Conduct Register, [DATE?} Convict No. 2830

15. Cited in "Hell-hole on the Brazos: Historic Resources Study of Central State Farm, Fort Bend County, Texas," by Amy E. Dase, (Prewitt and Associates, Inc., Cultural Resources Services, Austin Texas, 2004), 5. ("Technical Report, Number 70," submitted to Berg-Oliver Associates, Inc., Houston, Texas).

16. *Reports of the Superintendent and Financial Agent of the Texas State Penitentiaries, Embodying the Proceedings of the Penitentiary Board, and Statistical and Financial Exhibits*; also *Reports of Subordinate Officers of the Texas State Penitentiaries. For Two Years Ending October 31, 1892* (Austin: Ben C. Jones & Co., State Printers, 1892), 29.

## Chapter 11

1. "Fire Record." *The Galveston Daily News*, February 20, 1896; "Aunt Mary Marks." *The Galveston Daily News*, May 5, 1896. Additional quotes and details are from other sources cited throughout, especially "Born in Seventy-Six." *Londonerry Sifter* (Vermont), July 3, 1896; "Aged 119." *Houston Daily Post*, December 4, 1896; and Noah Smithwick, "San Felipe de Austin." *The Galveston Daily News*, November 29, 1896. The article from the San Antonio paper listed in Note 1, which also states the original correspondent, seems to have been from the "Globe-Democrat," but no further details are available.
2. "Born in Seventy-Six." *San Antonio Light*, June 29, 1896.
3. Ibid.
4. "The State Press." *The Galveston Daily News*, January 17, 1886.
5. Noah Smithwick, "San Felipe de Austin." *The Galveston Daily News*, November 19, 1896.
6. Ibid.
7. "Born in Seventy-Six." *San Antonio Daily Light*, June 29, 1896.
8. Ibid.
9. "Aunt Mary Marks." *The Galveston Daily News*, May 5, 1896.

10. Ibid.
11. Ibid.
12. Macum Phelan, *A History of Early Methodism in Texas* (Nashville: Cokesbury Press, 1924), 135. An additional line from Addison's manuscript, without further citation by Phelan, is from *The Life and Times of Dr. Joseph P. Sneed*, by Oscar M. Addison.
13. Johnnie Lockhart Wallis, *Sixty Years on the Brazos: the life and letters of Dr. John Washington Lockhart, 1824-1900* (Press of Dunn Brothers. 1930), 54.
14. Macum Phelan, *A History of Early Methodism in Texas*, Cokesbury Press, Nashville, 1924, 136.
15. W.P. Harrison, *The Gospel Among the Slaves: A Short History of Missionary Operations Among the African Slaves of the Southern States*, (Nashville, Tenn.: Publishing House of the Methodist Episcopal Church, 1893), 357
16. W. P. Harrison, *The Gospel Among the Slaves: A Short History of Missionary Operations Among the African Slaves of the Southern States*, 1893), 357
17. Washington County Public Records, Deed Book Z, 215-219, and Deed Book Z, 245-246.
18. "Independence Locals." *The Daily Banner*, December 2, 1879.
19. "Born in Seventy-Six." *Londonerry Sifter* (Vermont), July 3, 1896
20. "Aunt Mary Marks." *The Galveston Daily News*, May 5, 1896
21. Ibid.; also the source of many other quotes found throughout this article.
22. "Commissioner's Court." *Brenham Daily Banner*, November 17, 1895; "Commissioner's Court." *Brenham Daily Banner*, May 15, 1896.
23. *Brenham Daily Banner*, January 10, 1890.
24. "Reminiscences." *Brenham Daily Banner*, January 14, 1886;

January 10, 1890; "Brenham Budget." *Houston Daily Post*, December 5, 1896; *Brenham Daily Banner*, December 16, 1896.

25. "Cemetery at Independence is Sadly Neglected and Its Improvement Should Receive Attention of People of County." *Brenham Daily Banner-Press*, March 4, 1914.

26. Ibid.

27. *Massachusetts Ploughman and New England Journal of Agriculture*, February 16, 1876.

**Chapter 12**

1. *The Galveston Weekly News*, January 7, 1863; *Houston Tri-Weekly Telegraph*, April 17, 1863; Sir Arthur James Lyon Freemantle, *Three Months in the Southern States, April-June 1863* (Edinburg, London: William Blackwood and Sons, 1863), 69; *Houston Tri-Weekly Telegraph*, December 16, 1863.

2. "R.H. Boyd Publishing Corporation, *Bookstore Policy Manual*. (Nashville, Tenn.: 2016). 4.

3. *Brenham Daily Banner,* September 19, 1889.

4. The birthplace of the Hewetts can be found in the "Compiled Military Service Records of Volunteer Union Soldiers Who Served with the United States Colored Troops 54th Massachusetts Infantry Regiment Colored," as found at the Fold3.com website, as well as the particulars of their promotions and injuries. Although these records also state they were free men on or before April 1861, this was to satisfy requirements to assure they could collect a sign- on bonus. The information on Xenia enlistments and the Batttle of Olustee comes from Luis F. Emilio, *History of the Fifty-fourth Regiment of Massachusetts Volunteer Infantry, 1863-1865* (Boston: Boston Book Company, 1891), 385 Hewitt also is occasionally an alternative spelling of Hewett.

5. Ibid.7.
6. 1870 U.S. Census for the information on the living situation of the Hewetts; Washington County Public Records, Deed Book 5, Numbers 125 and 126, for the land indentures; Deed Book 7, page 417 for the power of attorney between Knittel and James Hewett.
7. "The Race Question in the G.A.R." *The Galveston Daily News*, August 5, 1891.
8. Ibid.
9. *Ibid.*
10. "The Blue and The Ray." *The Galveston Daily News*, August 7, 1891.
11. Ibid. Another article appeared in the same paper on August 6, 1891, on the racial issue, titled "A Nigger in the Woodpile," which seemed a blantantly racist editorial comment. Along the same lines of a headline editorializing on the article, a *Houston Daily Post* article, dated July 17, 1901, on the subject when it continued to be brought up in following years, was "Ohio Negroes Are Angry; Think They Are as Good as the White Veterans."
12. "Colored Veterans." *The Austin Weekly Statesman*, August 11, 1892.
13. "Colored Veterans." *Austin Weekly Statesman*, August 11, 1892; "Colored Veterans." Brenham Daily Banner, September 7, 1893; "Colored Veterans and Sons of Veterans." *Brenham Daily Banner*, February 25, 1894.
14. 1900, 1910, and 1920 U.S. Census; "The District Court." *Brenham Daily Banner*, March 10, 1888; Eleventh Census of the United States, Special Schedule. Surviving Soldiers, Sailors, and Marines, and Widows, etc., for Brenham; Application for Headstone, O. Q. M. G. Form No. 623, number 305426, filed 2-9-31.

15. Wright's military records from his service with the 1st and 96th Regiments of the United States Colored Troops are found at Fold3.com; they are the source of information about his birth in Washington County.
16. National Archives Microfilm Publication M821, Records of the Assistant Commissioner for the State of Texas, Bureau of Refugees, Freedmen, and Abandoned Lands, 1865-1869, Roll 4, Images 1004-1005.
17. National Archives Microfilm Publication M821, Records of the Assistant Commissioner for the State of Texas, Bureau of Refugees, Freedmen, and Abandoned Lands, 1865-1869, Roll 4, Images 1004-1005. Using the information on Wright from Collins' letter to Kirkman led to tracking down his military records, found at Fold3.com. The information on the Haines family comes from the 1860 and 1870 censuses, and their slave holdings from the 1850 and 1860 slave schedules for Washington County.
18. Barry A. Crouch, *The Freedmen's Bureau and Black Texans* (Austin: University of Texas Press,1992), 15
19. National Archives Microfilm Publication M821, Records of the Assistant Commissioner for the State of Texas, Bureau of Refugees, Freedmen, and Abandoned Lands, 1865-1869, Roll 4, Image 1004.
20. National Archives Microfilm Publication M821, Records of the Assistant Commissioner for the State of Texas, Bureau of Refugees, Freedmen, and Abandoned Lands, 1865-1869, Roll 32, target 4, Image 20.
21. "All Texas." *Southern Intelligencer*, April 12, 1866.
22. Samuel A. Craig, "Captain Samuel A. Craig's Memoirs of Civil War and Reconstruction (Part V – Conclusion)," *Western Pennsylvania Historical Magazine* (October 1931): 264.
23. National Archives Microfilm Publication M821, Records of

the Assistant Commissioner for the State of Texas, Bureau of Refugees, Freedmen, and Abandoned Lands, 1865-1869, Roll 4, Image 841.
24. Craig, 264-265.
25. Ibid, 265.
26. National Archives Microfilm Publication M821, Records of the Assistant Commissioner for the State of Texas, Bureau of Refugees, Freedmen, and Abandoned Lands, 1865-1869, Roll 4, Image 844.
27. Ibid., 907.
28. "Centennial Darkey", *Los Angeles Daily Herald*, February 11, 1876.

**Chapter 13**
1. Ann Patton Baenziger, "The Texas State Police During Reconstruction: A Reexamination," *The Southwestern Historical Quarterly* 72, no. 4 (April 1969): 470-491.
2. *Brenham Daily Banner,* January 14, 1890.
3. State Guard military rolls, Reconstruction military rolls, Military rolls, Texas Adjutant General's Department. Archives and Information Services Division, Texas State Library and Archives Commission, folder 401-728.
4. Found at https://tslarc.tsl.texas.gov/service/SP/l/la/lan12016.pdf, online collection of Texas State Library and Archives, Texas Adjutant General Service Records 1836-1935.
5. *The Daily Banner*, August 12, 1877.
6. *The Daily Banner*, October 12, 1880.
7. "KuKluxed." *Brenham Daily Banner*, August 17, 1885.
8. "Jack Lands Dead." *Brenham Daily Banner*, January 14, 1890.
9. *The Daily Banner*, August 12, 1877; "The Owl Brotherhood." Brenham Daily Banner, August 5, 1886.
10. "Owlisms." *The Daily Banner*, August 2, 1878.

11. "Radical Precinct Meeting." *The Daily Banner*, August 9, 1878.
12. *The Daily Banner*, November 25, 1879. (Headline obliterated.)
13. "Negro Fatally Shot." *The Daily Banner*, April 1, 1879.
14. "Killing of Gibson." *Brenham Weekly Banner*, April 4, 1879.
15. *The Galveston Daily News*, April 15, 1879.
16. Federal Census, 1880, 1900.
17. "Terrible Fuss." *Brenham Weekly Banner*, November 1, 1878.
18. "Mob Law" *The Daily Banner*, August 20, 1880.
19. "The Recent Lynching." *The Daily Banner*, September 9, 1880.
20. "The Recent Lynching." *Brenham Weekly Banner*, August 26, 1880.
21. "Mob Law." *The Daily Banner*, August 20, 1880.
22. "The Lynching Business." *The Galveston Daily News*, August 20, 1880.
23. *The Daily Banner,* August 26, 1880.
24. *Brenham Daily Banner*, December 13, 1883.
25. *Brenham Daily Banner*, September 7, 1884.
26. "KuKluxed." *Brenham Daily Banner*, August 17, 1885.
27. *Brenham Daily Banner*, December 19, 1888.
28. *Brenham Daily Banner*, August 17, 1886.
29. "The Races." *Brenham Daily Banner*, June 9, 1883.
30. "Races" *Brenham Daily Banner*, June 6, 1884.
31. "Jack Lands Dead." *Brenham Daily Banner*, January 8, 1890.
32. "Jack Lands Dead." *Brenham Daily Banner*, January 14, 1890 .
33. "An Appointment." *The Daily Banner*, October 4, 1877.
34. *Brenham Daily Banner*, Sunday, June 18, 1882.
35. "Mad Dog Killed." *The Daily Banner*, November 28, 1877; "An Ox Thief." *Brenham Weekly Banner*, August 22, 1879; *The Daily Banner*, July 17, 1880.
36. *The Galveston Daily News,* December 27, 1878.
37. "District Court." *Brenham Weekly Banner,* June 23, 1881.
38. "Notable Darkey Dead." *Brenham Daily Banner,* April 19, 1889.

39. "Killed in Brenham." *Weekly Democratic Statesman,* July 27, 1876.
40. "Special to the Herald." *The Dallas Daily Herald,* July 25, 1876.
41. "Captured." *Brenham Weekly Banner,* November 29, 1878.
42. "Armed." *The Daily Banner,* July 19, 1878.
43. "Colored Policeman," "Jail Fight," and "District Court." *The Daily Banner,* August 9, 1878.
44. *Brenham Daily Banner*, November 30, 1894.
45. *Brenham Daily Banner,* July, 12, 1898.
46. "Negro Killed at Chappell Hill." *Brenham Weekly Banner,* January 6, 1881.
47. *Brenham Daily Banner*, January 4, 1881.
48. "John Traylor Killed." *Brenham Daily Banner*, November 25, 1886.
49. "City Council Proceedings." *The Daily Banner,* April 17, 1878; "Council Proceedings." *The Daily Banner,* April 10, 1879.
50. "Commissioner's Court." *Brenham Weekly Banner,* January 9, 1880; "Mayor's Court." *The Daily Banner,* June 24, 1880; "The Inquest." *Brenham Weekly Banner,* January 6, 1881; "Killed on the Track." *Brenham Daily Banner,* November 16, 1881.
51. "Council Proceedings." *Brenham Daily Banner,* April 14, 1881.
52. "Death of Harry Key." *Brenham Banner,* April 23, 1908.
53. "Council Proceedings." *Daily Banner*, March 3, 1896.
54. "City Council Proceedings." *Brenham Daily Banner,* April 8, 1902; "Council Proceedings." *Brenham Daily Banner,* January 21, 1896.
55. *Brenham Daily Banner*, August 14, 1900.
56. *Brenham Daily Banner,* November 17, 1900.
57. *Brenham Daily Banner*, August 31, 1900; "Cotton Pickers Wanted." *Brenham Daily Banner,* August 31, 1902; "After Laborers." *Brenham Daily Banner,* November 4, 1902; "Negroes Shipped Out." *Houston Post*, October 29, 1903.

58. "The End of the Tragedy." *The Houston Daily Post*, October 12, 1897.
59. "Bloody Sunday Night." *Brenham Daily Banner*, October 12, 1897.
60. Ibid.
61. "Contempt of Court." *Brenham Daily Banner*, March 31, 1898.
62. "Negro a Poor Shot." *Houston Post*, July 13, 1907.
63. "Texas News." *Tri-Weekly State Gazette*, January 29, 1872.
64. "City Council Proceedings." *The Daily Banner*, June 19, 1878; "Two Discharges." *The Daily Banner*, July 5, 1878.
65. "Council Proceedings." *The Daily Banner*, April 26, 1879.
66. "Council Proceedings." *The Daily Banner*, January 7, 1880; "Council Proceedings." *The Daily Banner*, May 4, 1880; "Council Proceedings." *Brenham Daily Banner,* May 19, 1880.
67. "In Uniform." *Brenham Weekly Banner*, June 9, 1881.
68. "Three Negroes Shot." *Brenham Daily Banner*, September 20, 1881.
69. "Mysterious Owner." *Brenham Daily Banner*, February 2, 1887.
70. Ibid.
71. Ibid.
72. "A Pistol Shot." *The Daily Banner*, July 25, 1880.
73. "A Shindy." *Brenham Daily Banner*, May 6, 1882.
74. Ibid.
75. "Council Proceedings." *Brenham Daily Banner*, May 9, 1882.
76. Ibid.
77. Ibid.
78. Ibid.
79. *Brenham Daily Banner*, May 10, 1882.
80. *Brenham Daily Banner*, May 19, 1882; October 9, 1883.
81. "Mayor's Court." *Brenham Daily Banner*, August 10, 1882.
82. "Suspended." *Brenham Daily Banner*, August 15, 1882.
83. "Ed Inge, Again." *Brenham Daily Banner*, August 17, 1882.

84. "Mayor's Court." *Brenham Daily Banner*, August 19, 1882.
85. "The Owl Meeting." *Brenham Daily Banner*, March 6, 1883.
86. "Special Police." *Brenham Daily Banner*, May 13, 1883.
87. *Brenham Daily Banner*, October 30, 1884.
88. *Brenham Daily Banner*, November 2, 1884; this was likely a paid insertion, followed by a notation "Oct. 30$^{th}$, 1485" similar to those used for ads.
89. *Brenham Daily Banner,* November 6, 1888.
90. *Brenham Daily Banner*, November 22, 1890.
91. *Brenham Daily Banner*, November 23, 1890.
92. "Attempt to Break Jail." *Brenham Daily Banner,* April 21, 1893.
93. *Brenham Daily Banner,* September 2, 1892.
94. *Brenham Daily Banner,* January 29, 1897.
95. *Brenham Daily Banner,* May 24, 1893; June 1, 1893, "Brenham Budget." *The Galveston Daily News*, June 1, 1893.
96. "A Church Row." *Brenham Daily Banner*, December 11, 1896.
97. "Forcibly Entered." *Brenham Daily Banner*, December 15, 1896.
98. "Fun at the Depot." *Brenham Daily Banner*, July 11, 1896.
99. *Brenham Weekly Banner*, August 5, 1897.
100. A Foot Race" *Brenham Daily Banner,* June 25, 1898.
101. "The City Council." *Brenham Daily Banner,* June 5, 1900.
102. "Meeting of City Fathers." *Brenham Daily Banner*, July 3, 1900.
103. Ibid. ; June 19, 1900.
104. "The Mayor Took a Fall." *Brenham Daily Banner,* June 19, 1900.
105. "City Council Proceedings." *Brenham Daily Banner*, April 8, 1902.
106. *Brenham Daily Banner,* August 2, 1902.
107. "The Fire." *Brenham Daily Banner*, September 11, 1902.
108. "Ed Inge Dead." *Brenham Daily Banner*, September 27, 1902.
109. Ibid.

**Chapter 14**
1. "Emancipation Day." *Brenham Daily Banner,* June 20, 1884.
2. "2 - Emancipation Celebration." *Brenham Daily Banner,* June 20, 1894.
3. "2 - Days, Emancipation Celebration 2-Days." *Brenham Daily Banner-Press*, June 8, 1922.
4. "Emancipation Celebration by Colored Persons." *Flakes Daily Bulletin*, December 31, 1865.
5. Records of the Assistant Commissioner for the State of Texas, Bureau of Refugees, Freedmen, and Abandoned Lands, National Archives Microfilm Publication M821, Roll 4, Letters Received (Entered in Register 1), A-C, 1866-67, Image 533.
6. Ibid..
7. Ibid.
8. *Brenham Daily Banner,* October 1, 1896.
9. "June 19 Celebration in Brenham." *Brenham Evening Press,* June 19, 1908.
10. *The Daily Banner,* May 28, 1878.
11. "Emancipation Day." *The Daily Banner,* June 20, 1878.
12. "2 – Days Emancipation Celebration 2 – Days." *Brenham Daily Banner-Press*, June 8, 1922.
13. "Emancipation Celebration." *Brenham Weekly Banner,* June 1, 1905.
14. "Emancipation Celebration." *Brenham Weekly Banner,* June 22, 1905.
15. "Goddess of Liberty." *Brenham Daily Banner,* June 12, 1889.
16. "Emancipation Day." *The Daily Banner,* June 20, 1880.
17. "Emancipation Day." *Brenham Evening Press*, June 19, 1908.
18. "Emancipation Celebration." *Brenham Daily Banner,* June 20, 1894.
19. "Emancipation Day." *Brenham Daily Banner,* June 18, 1897.
20. "Negro Educator Sways Multitude in Outbursts of Fiery

Eloquence." *Brenham Daily Banner-Press*, April 16, 1917.
21. "Emancipation Celebration." *Brenham Daily Banner*, June 19, 1902.
22. Ibid.
23. M.W. Stearns, "George Washington Smith Rocks Cradle of Jazz, Two years Older Than Jelly-Roll He Carves Regulation Cats in Texas," *Down Beat* 5, no. 4 (April 1938): 13. Accessed at http://www.doctorjazz.co.uk/page10bc.html.
24. "Emancipation Day." *Brenham Evening Press*, June 19, 1908.
25. *Brenham Weekly Banner*, June 18, 1891.
26. *Brenham Daily Banner*, May 26, 1891.
27. Ibid.

## Chapter 15

1. *Dallas Herald*, March 9, 1867, reporting on the *Banner*'s contemporaneous account of the fire.
2. "How Brenham War Claims originated. *Brenham Daily Banner*, December 28, 1915."
3. National Archives Microfilm Publication M821, Records of the Assistant Commissioner for the State of Texas, Bureau of Refugees, Freedmen, and Abandoned Lands, 1865-1869, Roll 5, Image442.
4. "Firemen Will Celebrate Fiftieth Anniversary on Monday, May 26." *Brenham Daily Banner*, May 23, 1917.
5. *Brenham Weekly Banner*, June 6, 1886.
6. "Organized." *Brenham Weekly Banner*, June 17, 1886; *Brenham Daily Banner*, June 30, 1886; "Council Proceedings." *Brenham Daily Banner*, July 21, 1886.
7. "A Camp Fire." *Brenham Daily Banner*, September 6, 1893.
8. "Burned." *Brenham Daily Banner*, October 17, 1889.
9. "The City Council." *Brenham Daily Banner*, June 5, 1900.
10. *Brenham Daily Banner*, June 5, 1900, June 21, 1900, p1; "Colored

Fire Department." June 23, 1900.
11. "Brenham Fire Department." *Brenham Daily Banner*, May 22, 1901.
12. "City Council in Session." *Brenham Daily Banner*, June 4, 1901.
13. "The Juneteenth." *Brenham Daily Banner*, May 12, 1900; June 12, 1900; "Emancipation Celebration." *Brenham Daily Banner*, June 10, 1901
14. "Neat Work." *Brenham Daily Banner*, June 13, 1901.
15. *Brenham Daily Banner*, June 16, 1901.
16. "Emancipation Celebration." *Brenham Daily Banner*, June 20, 1901.
17. *Brenham Daily Banner*, November 9, 1901.
18. *Brenham Daily Banner*, June 28, 1901; July 31, 1901; November 17, 1901.
19. "The Juneteenth." *Brenham Dailly Banner*, April 18, 1902; May 14, 1902; "The Goddess Chosen." June 12, 1902.
20. *Brenham Daily Banner*, August 7, 1902; "Prominent Negro Dies." *Brenham Daily Banner*, January 15, 1903; "Laid to Rest." *Brenham Daily Banner*, April 28, 1903.
21. Washington County Records, Deed Book 50, pages 418-420; Washington County Records, Deed Book 53, pages 494-497.
22. "Emancipation Celebration." *Brenham Weekly Banner*, June 15, 1905.
23. *Brenham Weekly Banner*, June 22, 1905.
24. Ibid.; *Brenham Weekly Banner*, June 29, 1905.
25. "Brenham Budget." *Houston Post*, June 13, 1906; "Emancipation Celebration." *Brenham Express Press*, May 6, 1910; "Colored People Are Holding Two Large Celebrations Today." *Brenham Daily Banner*, June 19, 1913.
26. Washington County Records, Deed Book 65, pages 602-605; Washington County Records, Deed Book 67, pages 613-614.

**Chapter 16**
1. "A New Park." *Brenham Daily Banner*, July 17, 1893.
2. "Park Association Organized." *Brenham Daily Banner*, July 19, 1893; "About Those Unjust Charges." *Brenham Daily Banner*, July 29, 1893; "*Brenham Daily Banner,* August 1, 1893, p. 5: August 6, 1893.
3. Washington County Records, Deed Book 50, pages 418-420
4. *Brenham Weekly Banner*, August 10, 1905.
5. "His Leg Cut Off." *The Galveston Daily News*, October 17, 1896; *Brenham Daily Banner*, October 18, 1896.
6. *Brenham Daily News*, December 5, 1895.
7. Washington County Records, Deed Book 67, pages 83-84; Washington County Records, Deed Book 67, pages 614-615.
8. Washington County Records, Deed Book 67, pages 614-615.
9. "Colored People Hold Celebration." *Brenham Daily Banner-Press,* April 13, 1917; "Good Scores Made by Crack Shots." *Brenham Daily Banner-Press,* April 16, 1917.
10. "Big Celebration!" *Brenham Daily Banner-Press*, June 10, 1918; the same ad ran for several days preceding the event.
11. "2-Days Emancipation Celebration 2-Days." *Brenham Daily Banner-Press,* June 8, 1922; "2 Celebrations of Emancipation Day Occur Here.", *Brenham Daily Express-Press*, June 19, 1922.
12. "2 Celebrations of Emancipation Day Occur Here." *Brenham Daily Banner-Press*, June 19, 1922.
13. Two Emancipation Daily Celebrations Held in Brenham." *Brenham Daily Banner-Press*, June 19, 1923.
14. Fortunately, through a series of serendipitous synchronicities this researcher was able to locate the original location of the property sold to the Hook and Ladder Co. No.2, reconveyed to M. W. Becker and then later sold to Chauncey Williamson, utilizing the description on the deed to match it up with the 1940 Census Enumeration Map for Brenham. I recognized

this general location, having driven by it on multiple times on visits to Brenham and recalling that Eddie Harrison had indicated it to me years before as now the site of Hattie Mae Flowers Park.

**Chapter 17**
1. 1880 U.S. Census.
2. This and some other interesting background material come from a video of a Juneteenth Celebration oral presentation on the Henderson family given on June 21, 2021, at the Washington-on-the Brazos Historical site, and found at https://www.facebook.com/WashingtonOnTheBrazosSHS/videos/328223752126059/.
3. The affidavit is found in the Washington County Clerk records, Vol. 164, page 146.
4. The marriage record is from the Washington County Clerk Records. The deed is found there in Vol. 197, page 1.
5. "Ed Henderson on Trial for Running a Gambling House." *Brenham Daily Banner-Press*, September 21, 1925.
6. "Neu's Column." *Brenham Daily Banner-Press*, September 23, 1925.
7. "Ed Henderson Paroled." *Brenham Daily Banner-Press*, November 2, 1925.
8. "County Judge Gets 37 Petitions for Beer Sale Permits." *Brenham Banner-Press*, September 2, 1933.
9. "Negro Youth is Held on Charge of Throwing Bomb." *Brenham Banner-Press*, February 7, 1936; "Ten Negroes Face Charges in Dice Game." *Brenham Daily Banner-Press*, September 9, 1937; "Negro Dies of Wounds After Café Shooting." *Brenham Banner-Press*, January 19, 1940.
10. Charles Swenson, "An Introduction to Brenham's Emancipation Celebrations, 1878 to 1923," unpublished paper

presented by Charles Swenson at the Juneteenth Celebration, Washington on the Brazos, June 21, 2016.
11. "No Co-operation Hurst Nineteenth Observance Here." *Brenham Daily Banner-Press*, June 19, 1924.
12. "Notice of Thanks." *Brenham Daily Banner-Press*, June 23, 1925.
13. "Notice." *Brenham Banner-Press*, May 4, 1926.
14. "Trouble Between Whites and Negroes Smoothed Out by Chamber of Commerce." *Brenham Daily Banner-Press*, March 25, 1925.
15. "Notice." *Brenham Daily Banner-Press*, July 6, 1925.
16. Henderson was adept at using newspapers to publicize his park, including paid advertisements. There are too many references in the Brenham papers to cite here regarding the various events held at North End Park, but they can readily be found at the Portal to Texas History website database.
17. "Southern Pacific Colored Employees Enjoy Picnic Here." *Brenham Banner-Press*, August 13, 1932.
18. Ibid.; "Dock Workers of Houston Picnic at North End Park." *Brenham Banner-Press*, July 30, 1935.
19. "Juneteenth Celebration Opens Here." *Brenham Banner-Press*, June 19, 1939.
20. "Look! Fun! Music!" *Brenham Banner Daily Press*, September 27, 1930.
21. "Colored County Fair Big Success; Banners Awarded." *Brenham Banner-Press*, October 10, 1934.
22. Ads for these and many more can be accessed at The Portal to Texas History digital newspaper archive by using North End Park as a search term.
23. *Brenham Banner-Press*, June 20, 1939.
24. "Negro Woman Dies of Knife Wound Inflicted at Dance and Another Negress Held in Jail." *Brenham Banner-Press,* August 29, 1933.

25. "Ten Injured When Grand Stand Falls at North End Park." *Brenham Banner-Press*, July 22, 1936.
26. "Henderson Club House at North End Park Burns." *Brenham Banner-Press*, December 5, 1936.
27. "Colored Red Cross Group Meeting Due." *Brenham Banner-Press*, February 29, 1944.
28. "The Spectator." *Brenham Banner-Press*, February 2, 1944.
29. "Over $4,000 War Bonds Are Sold By Colored Division." *Brenham Banner-Press*, July 11, 1944.
30. "Committees Meet at 9:30 at City Hall." *Brenham Banner-Press*, October 24, 1945.
31. *Brenham Banner-Press*, October 9, 1946.
32. "Victory Medals to be Given Negro Veterans, June 20." *Brenham Banner-Press,* June 18, 1948.
33. "Present City Officials Ask Re-election." *Brenham Banner-Press*, February 24, 1950.
34. "City Obtains East End Park for Negroes." *Brenham Banner-Press*, August 22, 1950. Henderson was paid $4,250 for the park.
35. Ibid.
36. The warranty deed was filed on August 16, 1950, in the Washington County Clerk's office, in Vol. 167.
37. Ibid.
38. Ibid.

www.ingramcontent.com/pod-product-compliance
Lightning Source LLC
LaVergne TN
LVHW070728030725
814910LV00024B/162